DATE DUE

GAYLORD   PRINTED IN U.S.A.

The Virtues of Our Vices

The Virtues of Our Vices

A Modest Defense of Gossip, Rudeness, and Other Bad Habits

Emrys Westacott

PRINCETON UNIVERSITY PRESS

Princeton and Oxford

Copyright © 2012 by Princeton University Press

Published by Princeton University Press, 41 William Street,
Princeton, New Jersey 08540

In the United Kingdom: Princeton University Press, 6 Oxford Street,
Woodstock, Oxfordshire OX20 1TW

press.princeton.edu

Library of Congress Cataloging-in-Publication Data
Westacott, Emrys.
    The virtues of our vices : a modest defense of gossip, rudeness, and other bad habits /
Emrys Westacott.
          p.   cm.
    Includes bibliographical references and index.
    ISBN 978-0-691-14199-2 (hardcover : alk. paper)   1. Vices.   2. Conduct of life.
I. Title.
    BJ1534.W47 2012
    179'.8—dc22   2011006595

British Library Cataloging-in-Publication Data is available

This book has been composed in Garamond Premier Pro and Raleigh Gothic
Printed on acid-free paper. ∞
Printed in the United States of America

10 9 8 7 6 5 4 3 2 1

To Vicky

Contents

The Virtues of Our Vices

Introduction

Should you tell a friend something you've heard about a mutual acquaintance? Would it be rude to address someone by his first name rather than using his title? What does it say about me if I laugh when someone tells a sick joke? Is it snobbish to assume that *New York Times* readers are likely to be better informed than people who prefer the *National Enquirer*? Can I think your beliefs ridiculous while still respecting you as a person?

Questions like these may seem small, but they are the very stuff of everyday ethical life. Books on applied ethics, especially college textbooks, typically discuss the Big Issues—abortion, capital punishment, euthanasia, affirmative action, nuclear deterrence, immigration, world poverty, and so on. Such topics are undeniably important. They are the focus of national debates, and the stakes are high; consequently, they have attracted more attention from professional philosophers. But it is the smaller questions, the microethical issues, that take up the bulk of whatever time most of us spend in moral reflection and decision making. After all, few people are in a position to sign or commute death sentences, but nearly all of us have to deal regularly with questions such as those mentioned above.

This book contains five studies on topics in everyday ethics: specifically, rudeness. gossip, snobbery, humor, and respect. Each essay is self-contained, but the collection is unified by recurring interlocking themes and a common philosophical approach. Clearly, the number of topics covered could be greater. I chose to write on these particular issues because I find them inherently interesting, and because I hope that what I have to say will be of interest to others.

Some might consider topics such as gossip, rudeness, or snobbery rather trivial, unworthy subjects for philosophical reflection. Aren't philosophers supposed to be engaged in nobler enterprises, like defining the essence of Being or formulating fundamental principles of justice? But this criticism rests on a narrow conception of philosophy as well as a rather unimaginative view of ethics. There are plenty of reasons why the topics discussed here deserve the attention of philosophers.

First, and most obviously, they concern matters that often figure very importantly in our day-to-day lives. Feeling that a colleague has been rude to you, for instance—or even worse, that you have been rude to her—can have a major impact on your mood, on your relationship, and on the way you view your workplace. The dark mood may well persist for some time, coloring all your experiences, incapable of being lifted even by the news that at UCLA they have finally discovered the essence of Being!

Second, our everyday thinking and conduct regarding commonplace matters are the most important indicators, both to ourselves and to others, of our true moral values and character. Certainly, they count for more than purely hypothetical scenarios in which we imagine how we would handle terrible dilemmas involving lifeboats, terrorists, deathbed promises, or runaway trains. Thought experiments involving extraordinary situations are a standard device used by ethicists to clarify some issues, and they can undoubtedly be useful. But their distance from everyday life is a drawback. They place abstract moral principles in sharp relief but lose the grainy complexity of real-life decision making. One of the points that regularly emerges from the following inquiries is just how complex everyday moral life can be, how many factors, how many variables we have to take into account at times. Given this complexity, our ability much of the time to negotiate more or less satisfactorily the moral problems we encounter is really quite remarkable.

Third, reflecting on quotidian ethical issues often yields insights into the character of our society, the trends we are part of, the assumptions we take for granted, the ideals we cherish, and the contradictory commitments we may harbor. Applying philosophy to everyday life offers an unusual but valuable window on cultural phenomena. It is one of the ways that philosophy can perform its Hegelian function of grasping its own time in thought, one of the ways in which, as a culture, we can try to become more self-aware.

One thing linking all five essays is that to a greater or lesser extent each of them challenges common sense. In my view, some of what passes for common sense on everyday ethical issues is confused, simplistic, or unthinkingly narrow and conventional. We all tend to wish that things were simpler and more clear-cut than they really are, so we often favor universal principles, unconditional rules, and blanket judgments. We repeat these thoughtlessly, no matter how absurd. "If you can't say something nice about someone, don't say anything at all." (So don't report that arsonist to the police.) "Don't do anything you'd be ashamed to tell your mother." (Even though the shame you feel may be a neurotic effect of your mother's Puritanism.) "Do to others what you would have them do to you." (So if you would enjoy being groped by others, it's fine for you to grope them.)

Especially popular are blanket condemnations: Never talk about someone behind his back. Never laugh at another person's misfortune. Never speak ill of the dead. Never tell lies. Following such principles rigidly would certainly make moral life simpler in some ways, but that is a weak argument in their favor since circumstances often call for sensitive and discriminating responses rather than slavish obedience to universal rules. Practical moral wisdom means recognizing complexities, not spray painting over them with crude precepts. Most people recognize this in practice, even if they still pay lip service to the rules in an abstract way.

That being said, I concede that in these studies I, too, will sometimes take a conventional, widely accepted moral principle for granted. In the essay on gossip, for instance, I assume without argument that telling malicious lies about other people is wrong. But this approach is defensible, I believe, for two main reasons. First, the moral tenets being assumed are, in my view, fairly easy to defend as conducive to individual and social well-being; and second, in inquiries of the sort attempted here, some kind of stable framework is necessary. I would not claim that every normative assumption made is beyond challenge. But my purpose is not to rethink our morality from the ground up. It is, rather, to look at places where some of our moral conclusions do not sit well with each other or with other values we uphold, and to suggest ways in which loosening our moral corsets might enable us to breathe more freely.

Language itself sometimes stands in the way of a more nuanced approach, and this is one place where philosophical analysis can be helpful. Words are like labels: they are useful, a helpful shorthand; but often we slap them on things carelessly and then assume no further analysis is needed. We call someone a "snob" or we describe a joke as "sick," and the act of labeling encourages us to think we have advanced our understanding. It also settles whether the thing in question is naughty or nice. In their ordinary usage words like "gossiping" or "snobbery" are inherently pejorative: when we apply them to an action or an attitude, we unavoidably convey disapproval. This can make it harder to achieve both a more precise, analytical understanding of the concepts in question and a more open-minded appraisal of the sort of behavior they describe. In some cases the critical character of the word can blind us to the positive qualities of the behavior.

Philosophical analysis at times involves trying to remove the label in order to examine the thing in question closely without letting the label dictate one's findings in advance. Afterwards, we may favor a more discriminating labeling system, one that, say, distinguishes between different kinds of disrespect, or between acceptable and unacceptable forms of rudeness. Philosophical analysis also attends to the labels themselves, and in some of the essays I try to construct more precise definitions of the key concepts. This enterprise can be valuable, I believe, even when a fully satisfactory definition turns out to be elusive. Philosophical definitions are very different from those found in a dictionary. The dictionary tells us how a word is generally used; but a philosophical definition tries to draw the boundaries of a concept, showing what falls under it and what does not. Of course, the boundaries of moral concepts are not sharp the way those of mathematical concepts are. And, as Aristotle says, we should not look for a degree of precision beyond what is appropriate to our subject matter. All the same, striving for as much precision as we can manage is a fruitful methodology. The sort of intense scrutiny it requires can yield a whole world of unexpected insights into our language, values, history, culture, and ideals.

The analyses I offer are primarily philosophical. Their chief goal is to clarify the nature and meaning of key concepts, to articulate arguments, evaluate ethical standpoints, and support specific conclusions. They are not intended to be value-free or value-neutral. They are normative in the sense that they can be used to appraise what people think, say, and do. But they are intended to take us beyond the rather crude assumptions underlying everyday moral discourse and make room for the possibility that what are commonly deemed moral failings may sometimes be acceptable or even praiseworthy.

Much of the existing scholarship on the topics covered here has been undertaken by historians, anthropologists, psychologists, and other social scientists or culture critics. This research is tremendously interesting, and my own thinking is certainly informed by it. However, a philosophical perspective that demands close attention to the meaning of terms and the logic of arguments while articulating and defending explicit value judgments can, I hope, offer a valuable supplement to these more empirical approaches.

Normative ethics offers moral judgments on people and their behavior; it is willing to assert that things are good, bad, right, wrong, acceptable, unjustified, and so on. Some readers may be automatically dubious about this kind of enterprise, and to explain why I do not share their misgivings, some account of my general philosophical outlook may be helpful here.

Philosophy, including normative ethics, is not science, not even social science; but its claims can still be judged according to criteria of reasonableness. They will usually fall short of certainty, but to be dissatisfied with the less-than-certain is unreasonable, a hangover from the idea that philosophy should deal only with a priori knowledge, with propositions that are necessarily and universally true. Conclusions that are probable, plausible, useful, or insightful are worth seeking and are often the best we can hope for.

Reasonableness, in ethics as in science, is primarily a matter of coherence. How well does a particular claim fit in with all of our other beliefs, practices, and commitments? From this point of view, the difference between descriptive claims and normative claims—the so-called fact-value gap—while useful and important in some contexts, should not be viewed as absolute. We call scientific claims "true" when they cohere with our other beliefs about nature—in other words, when they are reasonable in light of all our other beliefs. We judge moral claims in essentially the same way. Contemporary flat-earthists and contemporary advocates of slavery are refuted by similar means: their views are shown to be glaringly at odds with a framework of other beliefs that have become (or that we think should become) widely accepted.

Morality, in my view, is not some special nonnatural domain. It is a human invention, although as a number of recent studies in evolutionary ethics have suggested, it probably has its roots in our evolutionary heritage. For the most part, moral systems were not consciously designed with particular ends in mind; they emerged naturally, and those that helped their societies to thrive tended to be selected in. Within recorded history, moral revolutionaries like Moses, the Buddha, Socrates, Jesus, and Muhammad sought more or less consciously to construct new ethical systems. They did so with certain goals in mind, and in most cases viewed the moral rules they proposed as reflecting a divine will. This divine sanction justified viewing the rules as objectively correct; it also provided people with a motive to abide by them.

The Enlightenment secularized our view of morality but sought to uphold the objective status and binding force of moral principles by seeing them as dictates of Reason rather than divine commandments. Since the eighteenth century the secularization of our culture has proceeded apace, and this has made possible a more relativistic view of reason and a more flexible conception of morality. Of course, there are plenty of religious believers who still think that the moral precepts they favor express God's will. The more traditional among them even hold that we have a duty to make our society mirror some divinely ordained ideal. But a thoroughly secular approach sees things differently. Morality is a tool. It is a set of values, beliefs, principles, practices, and ideals that we use to help promote certain personal and social goals. Naturally, people can and do sometimes disagree over what these goals should be. Fascists will sacrifice individual rights to achieve a certain kind of political state; liberals see the state as serving to guarantee basic individual rights. Some people posit ideals of nonviolence and brotherly love; others value rugged individualism and the frontier spirit. But wherever there is common ground, there is room for reasoned discussion, and we can entertain some hope that, in the long term, people's fundamental values will tend to converge.

We cannot demonstrate the correctness of our basic values or ultimate ideals to those who do not share our assumptions. All we can do is articulate them as clearly as possible, offer attractive pictures of what we consider an admirable society and an enviable lifestyle, and compare these to others that are available. But the situation is not really different in the domain of scientific knowledge. Darwinians cannot *prove* the theory of evolution to dyed-in-the-wool creationists who insist that only what conforms to a literal interpretation of the Bible can be true. All they can do is point to what they see as the desirable consequences of adopting an evolutionist perspective: for instance, satisfying explanations of diverse phenomena, better predictions about future observations, and beneficial spin-offs in agriculture, medicine, and environmental science. We can, if we wish, call those who reject science "irrational" and those who reject modern liberal values "immoral." But these labels are not arguments; they merely mark the place where debate on the basis of shared assumptions gives out.

The normative standpoint underlying these essays is unexceptional and broadly utilitarian. I believe our ultimate goal should be a world in which unnecessary suffering is minimized and where most people live interesting, fulfilling lives, enjoying the security of basic rights, opportunities for pursuing their chosen goals, plenty of leisure, diverse pleasures, and the well-being that comes from participating in a vibrant culture and belonging to a supportive community. For anyone who shares something like this ideal, moral issues generally boil down to the question of whether pursuing a course of action, adopting a public policy, being a certain kind of person, cultivating certain attitudes, and so on, will help or hinder its realization.

From this utilitarian perspective, I offer analyses that bring out some of the unrecognized merits and benefits of what are often viewed as moral failings. Some benefits may be immediate and concern only the agents involved: gossiping, for instance, can be therapeutic; rudeness can be an effective educational strategy. Other benefits come indirectly and concern society at large. Sick humor can be viewed as the sharp edge of an important instrument of social criticism; withholding respect from certain beliefs may be a necessary move in the ongoing struggle to build a more rational society. Quite often, as Adam Smith pointed out, what is commonly viewed as a private vice may be a public virtue.

The perspectives I offer can hardly be considered a "revaluation of all values." Part of my purpose, though, certainly is to shake up some of our default opinions and conventional wisdom on the issues discussed. And in doing so I hope that we can become not just more self-critical but also, paradoxically, more forgiving, both of ourselves and of others. For we live in interesting times, and this makes everyday moral life more complicated than it is in societies where the rules and the social roles are relatively fixed and not subject to critical questioning.

One can imagine a society's moral beliefs and values as represented by three concentric rings. Inside the inner circle lies whatever is almost universally accepted or praised; within the outer band lies whatever is generally condemned. In contemporary America, for instance, freedom of worship, universal education, and virtues like generosity or courage would fall within the inner circle; slavery and bullying would be plotted in the outer zone. In ancient Israel, the inner circle would contain, among other things, monotheism, capital punishment for murderers, and virtues like generosity or courage; the outer circle would contain such things as homosexuality, the eating of pork, and bullying.

The middle band is the domain of moral controversy. Here the beliefs are in motion, some moving outwards from acceptability to unacceptability, others moving in the opposite direction. Since the Second World War, for instance, interracial relationships have become increasingly accepted while corporal punishment has come to be increasingly condemned. In stable,

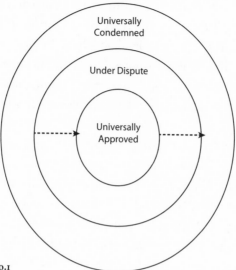

Figure Intro.1

tradition-based societies, this middle band is relatively narrow and any movement across it tends to be slow. There is less that is morally controversial, and changes in attitudes can take generations. In dynamic modern societies, by contrast, owing to the influence of forces such as technological innovation and cultural pluralism, the middle band is much wider and the movement across it can be surprisingly fast. Witness the changes in attitude within Western society over the past one hundred years on issues relating to such matters as sex, the workplace, relations between spouses, or relations between children and adults.

The practice of philosophical reflection and criticism is one of the forces that can broaden this middle band. Such reflection is, in turn, prompted by and feeds on issues that have become controversial, questions to which traditional answers no longer seem adequate. The process is not painless. The wider the domain and the faster the changes in attitudes, the more uncertainty and anxiety people are likely to feel regarding moral issues. But this anxiety, while uncomfortable, should be welcomed rather than lamented. It inevitably accompanies the critique of traditional authorities and conventional wisdom, and the movement toward a more self-aware, self-critical culture that this critique makes possible.

A common response to our ethically interesting times and the anxieties they induce is to play it safe. One way of doing this is simply to abide by traditional conventions. Another way is to opt for doing nothing over doing something. Another way is to follow some general principle rigidly, almost blindly. Yet playing it safe is not always the most admirable or fruitful course of action. To be sure, a fuller, freer engagement with a world in which categories, terminologies, expectations, and norms are in constant flux inevitably means that one will make mistakes. Lines will be crossed, traditions challenged, conventions violated, sensibilities offended. But those who never risk sinning are not entitled to cast stones. When we make a mistake, we should not assume that this reveals a morally tainted soul. It could just be that we are understandably confused at times because moral navigation in a complex and rapidly changing world is difficult. So we should combine a commitment to rigorous thinking with a willingness to be forgiving when we slip up. And we should remember, thinking holistically, to be grateful that we live at a time when this sort of confusion is possible.

1 The Rights and Wrongs of Rudeness

Rudeness is widely perceived to be a common moral failing; moreover, it is generally thought to be on the rise. In a 2002 opinion poll conducted in the United States, nearly 80 percent of respondents said that lack of respect and courtesy should be regarded as a serious national problem, and 61 percent believed that people treated each other with more respect in the past.[1] Of course, these perceptions are nothing new. Pollsters in ancient Athens, Elizabethan England, or nineteenth-century America would probably have reported similar findings. Regret (especially among older people) over the decline in moral standards (especially among younger people) is a cultural commonplace.[2] For this reason alone we should view such opinions skeptically.

It is also possible that a decline in the social importance of formal etiquette—wearing exactly the right clothes, using exactly the right mode of address, and so forth—is taken by some as evidence of a decline in civility. Yet this trend might equally well be viewed as a shift in our culture's conception of what constitutes politeness. Moreover, as historian John Kasson argues, there are many respects in which manners could be said to have improved over the last two hundred years.[3] Indeed, when one considers the obvious progress that has taken place over the past century in the struggle to guarantee equal rights, opportunities, and respect for minorities, women, gays and lesbians, people with disabilities, and other groups that have long suffered from prejudice and discrimination, the poll results cited above are really quite surprising.

The idea that standards of civility are in decline thus deserves to be questioned. But so, too, do the underlying normative assumptions that rudeness is always bad and that any increase in rudeness must therefore also be bad. Instead of unthinkingly joining the general jeremiad, therefore, I believe we should first try to understand better both the concept of rudeness and the social situations in which it is employed. In this chapter I will construct a philosophical definition of rudeness and use it to develop a schema that can help us both classify the main forms of rudeness and assess the extent to which rude behavior is or is not excusable. The proposed analysis brings to light some of the presuppositions underlying our common normative judgments about rudeness and indicates how these judgments might be challenged. In particular, it reveals when and why intentional rudeness might be morally acceptable, and it suggests that an increase in rudeness—whether real or merely perceived—may sometimes be viewed as a sign of cultural health rather than of moral decline.

Examples of rudeness

Let us begin by calling to mind some clear examples of rudeness. These can serve both as data to work from and as a concrete touchstone against which to check any generalities we may be tempted to venture.

- failing to return a greeting
- refusing to shake hands
- swearing at someone
- calling someone names
- pushing someone out of the way
- interrupting a speaker
- talking when you should be listening
- not listening when you should be listening
- using demeaning terms ("ladies," "boy")
- being overfamiliar
- making crude sexual advances or allusions
- dressing inappropriately on formal occasions
- phoning someone and then putting her on hold
- putting your finger in your nose in public
- not removing your shoes where this is normal practice
- clipping your fingernails during an interview
- eating spaghetti with your hands
- arriving late for an appointment and not apologizing
- abruptly hanging up on someone
- transferring an item from someone else's shopping cart to your own
- showing up to a potluck without a pot
- entering someone's office without knocking

- texting in class
- sleeping in class (apparently this used to be quite common before the advent of texting)

Since there are unlimited ways of being rude, the list is no doubt rather arbitrary, but it is intended to be wide-ranging. A few points emerge straightaway. Rudeness, unlike some unethical acts such as murder or kidnapping, is very common. Most of us manage to get through life without committing murder; it is sometimes hard to get through the day without being rude to someone. But although we are all guilty of rude behavior at times, that does not make us all rude people. A murderer is one who has committed murder, and a single violation of the sixth commandment makes you a murderer for life. Rudeness is not like that; occasional lapses are to be expected, and we all make them. So most people cannot be classified as either rude or polite *simpliciter*. Some are rude often, others infrequently; some in small ways, others in ways that really matter. And while most of us think of ourselves as polite, we can all have blind spots (e.g., lapses in table manners, unpunctuality, garrulousness).

Precisely because rudeness is quite common, it is not a trivial issue. Indeed, in our day-to-day lives it is possibly responsible for more pain than any other moral failing. We while away countless hours mentally replaying slights we have—or believe we have—suffered, inventing wittier, sharper, more dignified, or more hurtful ripostes. Or, if we are prone to moral anxiety, we worry about whether something we did or said was rude or was perceived to be so by others. Moreover, rudeness often causes more distress than do other injurious acts. Most of us probably think of theft, for instance, as a more serious moral offense than discourtesy. But I believe I would be less upset if someone stole my camera than if a colleague walked into my classroom, strode between me and the class, spoke briefly to a student, and then left without speaking to me or even bothering to close the door. Being robbed is a misfortune; being treated rudely threatens one's self-respect. In the first case we lament; in the second case, we seethe.[4]

A familiar and venerable kind of philosophical project is to ask what all the listed examples of rudeness have in common in order to identify some element that we can then claim is the essence of rudeness. The description of this essence will state the necessary and sufficient conditions for an act's being rude, and this description can serve as our working definition of the concept. This is the kind of inquiry pioneered by Socrates, but most philosophers nowadays are skeptical about the possibility of always finding a common core shared by every instantiation of a concept. As Wittgenstein persuasively argues, a concept can be perfectly intelligible even if the instances merely overlap with one another in various ways.[5] Nor must a concept have sharp boundaries in order to be useful. Many concepts do not. For example, there is no minimum number of centimeters of rain that must fall in a day for that day to be classified as "rainy," but this does not mean the concept of raininess is incoherent or incomprehensible. We use it all the time without creating confusion. Like raininess, rudeness is a concept with blurred edges, but this does not make it suspect or detract from its usefulness. It just means that whether or not an action is rude is sometimes a matter about which we can have legitimate doubts and disagreements.

This becomes even more obvious if we try to distinguish between rudeness and other closely related concepts such as impoliteness, discourteousness, vulgarity, irreverence, disrespect, impertinence, insolence, uncouthness, or inconsiderateness.[6] Clearly, these do not all mean the same thing. Each carries its own particular emphasis, connotations, and implications. Insolence implies a scornful attitude toward someone or something thought worthy of respect. To be uncouth is to offend the sensibilities of others by a display of crudeness or vulgarity. To be impertinent is to assume some sort of entitlement beyond what one may legitimately claim. Nevertheless, the terms listed do form a dense cluster of interrelated and overlapping meanings.

I do not intend to define rudeness as distinct from, say, irreverence or impertinence, or vulgarity. Rather, I propose to use the term in a general sense as a rubric under which many of these other forms of behavior fall. I do believe, however, that it is possible to construct a general definition of rudeness. Because the concept has blurred edges, this definition cannot hope to capture all and only instances of rudeness with the rigor and precision of a definition in mathematics. But it will, I believe, suffice for our purposes, and the process of developing and testing this definition can help us to think more clearly about what the concept means, how we actually apply it, and how we should apply it.

A definition of rudeness

I propose the following definition.

An act is rude if it meets two conditions:

a. it violates a social convention; and
b. if the violation were deliberate, this would indicate a lack of concern for another person's feelings (or, in other words, a willingness to cause someone pain).

Before we look at how this definition applies to various cases, a few preliminary points are worth noting.

First, the term "social convention" (hereafter, just "convention") is intended very broadly. A convention is a rule stipulating how one should behave in certain situations. Examples would include these: You should not push in front of people in a line. You should take your shoes off before entering a mosque. You should not make faces at people. Often the rules are unwritten, but they do not have to be. The Princeton College handbook of 1756 lays down the following rule: "Inferiors, when they come into the company of a superior or speak to him, shall show their respect by pulling their hats."

It is hard to imagine calling an act rude that does not involve the violation of some norm or convention. Mere indifference to another's feelings would certainly not suffice. Boxers fighting are doing their best to beat each other up, but they do so within and according to the rules of the ring.[7]

However, the *mere* violation of a convention does not constitute rudeness. For example, wearing odd socks, eating dessert before the entrée, or referring to oneself in the third person all violate conventions but are not necessarily rude. What could make these violations rude is the possibility that they cause someone pain or discomfort. Wearing red and yellow socks at a funeral, or ordering dessert as an appetizer at a formal dinner might well do this, and that is why in such situations we might criticize these violations.

It would be too simple, though, to say that an act is rude if it violates a convention and causes offense. After all, the reaction of the offended party might be completely unpredictable and unreasonable. A student whose failure to wear matching socks around the house unaccountably upset a roommate could hardly be accused of rudeness. This problem is avoided by the somewhat convoluted form of part (b) of the definition.

The first thing to notice about (b) is its conditional form ("*if* the violation were deliberate . . ."). The reason for this is that the definition must capture the fact that rudeness need not be intentional.[8] If, in the cinema, I become so engrossed in the film that I start dipping into a stranger's popcorn bucket, forgetting that my partner is sitting on my left rather than my right, I am clearly doing something rude. This is indicated by my profuse apologies should I ever discover my mistake, even though I violated the relevant convention unintentionally. (How to respond if a stranger starts dipping into your popcorn is an interesting question. Most people would probably just move their popcorn to the other hand, but a more creative response might be to start taking sips from the stranger's soda.)

The other point to notice about (b) is that it assumes that in most cases reasonable people will agree about whether certain actions are likely to hurt another's feelings. Obviously, there will be controversial cases. But I do not think it is a weakness in the definition that its application involves making reasonable inferences about the states of mind that would normally be produced by deliberate violations of social conventions.

The definition also allows for the fact that rudeness need not be recognized as such by the "victim." You may tell me I have "a mind like a steel trap," implying that it lets nothing in and nothing comes out. But I may be too obtuse to grasp your meaning, perhaps thinking that you are complimenting me on the way I tenaciously hold on to the truth once I've discovered it. In this case, you have not failed to be rude; your rudeness has just failed to register with me.

One final point to note is that according to the proposed definition, rudeness is not necessarily wrong. Now for some, this will constitute an objection to the definition. Anne Lloyd Thomas argues that the term is irreducibly pejorative. According to Thomas, "'Rude' is a value word: when we say 'X is rude' we criticize or condemn a person or action or type of action for a particular kind of behavior."[9] The problem with this approach, however, is that it implies we could never coherently describe an action as rude yet justified. Surely, though, we do sometimes want to say this. Suppose you refuse to shake hands with a person you consider morally repugnant—a war criminal, a traitor, or a person who callously destroyed the life of someone you love. Most people would say that your refusal in such a case is not just understandable but justifiable. Assuming this is so, how should we describe your behavior? As both rude and right? Or as right and *therefore* not rude?

Thomas's analysis implies that we should prefer the second option. To the objection that there are situations where we believe rudeness is warranted, she argues that our descriptions of these situations will serve as excuses for behavior that, if it is identified as rude, is presumed to be wrong. In my view, this puts a little too much weight on the conceptual analysis of terms as opposed to the cultural mores that underlie the way we use them. We feel the need to excuse rudeness when we think it justified not because the *concept* of rudeness is inherently pejorative but because the default attitude in our culture is that it is wrong to be indifferent to another person's feelings. The expression "punch on the nose" is not intrinsically pejorative; but we would similarly feel the need, if reporting that we had punched someone on the nose, to explain why we thought we were justified in doing so.

In fact, as we shall see, there are various circumstances in which rudeness is morally acceptable. When analyzing these cases, one could conceivably argue that the context makes the action not an instance of rudeness at all. But I believe it is usually more illuminating to see the context as determining not whether the action is rude but whether it is justifiable. This is especially the case when we consider instances of intentional rudeness.

Classifying and appraising forms of rudeness

The above definition of rudeness makes possible a certain classification of the main types of rudeness and suggests general guidelines for judging how excusable or blameworthy a person's conduct is in any particular case. Both are indicated by figure 1.1.

The diagram indicates the sort of questions we should ask, and the order in which we should ask them, in order to determine both whether or not people have acted rudely and, in the event that they have been rude, their degree of culpability. The lines of the tree culminate in boxes that are gradated from black to white—an admittedly whimsical but nonetheless effective way of figuratively representing the moral condition of the agent's soul—darkest black representing maximal blameworthiness, pure white signifying complete excusability.

The first two questions determine whether a given action falls under the general definition of rudeness. The questions that follow concern the agent's knowledge, intentions, and level of awareness. They identify eight possible "polar" situations that could obtain—these being extreme instances of inexcusability or justifiability—and help determine to which of these the action in question is closest. The eight polar situations can be summarily described as follows:

1. You don't know the convention but ought to.

    E.g., After living in Japan for a year, foreigners should know that they are expected to take off their shoes when

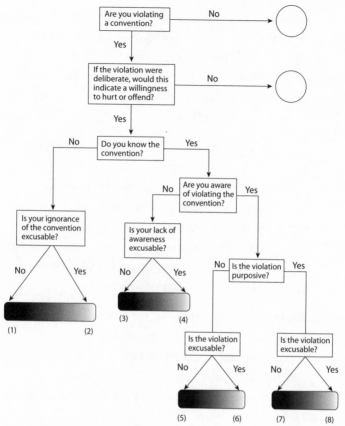

Figure 1.1. Classifying and appraising rudeness

entering a house. Visitors to North America should know, after a few months, that they are expected to tip in restaurants.

2. You don't know the convention and cannot reasonably be expected to know it.

E.g., A three-year-old in a restaurant who blows hard through a straw into her drink to make bubbles and noise will not be judged morally deficient. She may, of course, be quickly introduced to the convention that one is not supposed to do this ("Don't do that!" "Why not?" "It's rude."), although it will be many more years before she attains the maturity and wisdom to understand exactly why this kind of fun is prohibited.

3. You know the convention, are not aware of violating it, but ought to be.

   This is probably the most common form of rudeness. Examples are legion: talking when the convention requires silence; constantly interrupting other speakers; failing to give subordinates sufficient attention or respect; staying at a party longer than the host would like; treating old people as if they were simpleminded.

4. You know the convention, are not aware of violating it, but your lack of awareness is excusable.

   E.g., Someone who, because he is emotionally distraught, fails to ask a visitor to sit down; someone who falls asleep in a lecture after being up all night working as a volunteer firefighter.

5. You know the convention, are aware you are violating it, but are not purposely being rude (i.e., being rude is not part of your intention); however, the violation is inexcusable.

   E.g., Inappropriate sexual groping; queue jumping.

6. You know the convention, are aware you are violating it, but are not purposely being rude; and the violation is excusable.

   E.g., Slapping a hysteric; opening someone else's mail to prevent a crime.

(We might note here that one especially common moral dilemma concerning rudeness arises when one has to decide whether or not to say or do something that might be criticized as an instance of failing to "mind your own business": for example, telling parents that they are being overindulgent or excessively strict with their children. Most such cases fall between (5) and (6). Deciding when intervention is justified can be very difficult. Many of the ethical queries addressed to "Dear Abby" or discussed by Randy Cohen in his *New York Times Magazine* column "The Ethicist" are of this sort.)[10]

7. You know the convention, are aware of violating it, and are purposely but inexcusably being rude.

    E.g., Insulting someone using racist epithets; spitting at someone because she didn't vote the way you did.

8. You know the convention, are aware of violating it, and are purposely but justifiably being rude.

    E.g., Refusing to shake hands with someone who has betrayed you; walking out of a lecture in which the speaker uses racially offensive terms to identify ethnic groups; refusing to participate in a ceremony you find morally objectionable.

Application of this analysis

The analysis schematized by the diagram is admittedly abstract. But it can nevertheless help to clarify (a) the circumstances in which we judge actions to be rude; (b) whether or not our judgment is justified; (c) precisely what it is we are finding fault with when a person acts rudely; (d) when and why we are sometimes willing to excuse rudeness; and (e) the way in which blameworthiness and excusability in this area are matters of degree. Let us see how it applies in a couple of specific cases.

Example A: In a departmental meeting a man keeps reading a professional journal. He doesn't read it all the time, but he delves into it whenever the discussion starts to bore him, and he clearly devotes a significant portion of his attention to it. Accused of being rude, he denies it, arguing that he is able to pay sufficient attention to the meeting while looking at the journal. He says he is simply trying to use his time efficiently.

Is there a convention that one does not read material unconnected to a meeting during a meeting? This is not a black-and-white issue. In a very large meeting, where hundreds of people are gathered in an auditorium, one could perhaps do this without risk of offending anyone. But if the meeting is of a kind and size where everyone can see what everyone else is doing, most would agree that some such convention exists.

So we ask the second question: if the violation of the convention were deliberate, would this indicate a lack of concern for someone else's feeling? I would say the answer is pretty clearly yes. Most people will feel at least somewhat aggrieved, annoyed, insulted, or upset if they notice that while they are speaking, one of their colleagues is reading something quite unrelated to the topic under discussion. We are not, of course, assuming at this point that the violation of the convention *is* deliberate; we are just using the hypothetical question to ascertain that the behavior in question is indeed rude.

Given that we have here an instance of rudeness, we can next ascertain to what extent and in what respect the person is at fault. Does he know about the convention? While one can imagine some scenario in which a recent arrival from a different culture might be ignorant of the relevant convention, in almost all cases one encounters, the individual can be assumed to know the convention simply in virtue of being a long-standing and participating member of our culture. So we proceed to the next question: is the person aware that he is violating a convention?[11] Here again, in the situation we are imagining, the answer will usually be yes. Self-awareness is, of course, a matter of degree. At one end of the spectrum is someone who deliberately, perhaps even ostentatiously, reads while a colleague speaks. This person is being *purposely* rude—to be rude is part of his purpose, perhaps as a way of gaining revenge or showing disrespect. At the other end of the spectrum is the case of someone who first started perusing the journal at a point when the meeting was bogged down in a technical discussion that didn't concern her, and who then chooses to keep reading while tuning out the rest of the meeting. It is possible, of course, to imagine a meeting so boring, a journal article so captivating, and a reader so interested in the topic of the article that the violation would be almost completely unconscious. But such cases would be unusual.

The chances are, then, that the person we have described is basically aware that he is violating a convention, and even though he may not actually be doing it purposely, he is nevertheless aware of what he is doing and is willing to risk offending or hurting the feelings of other people. The final question to ask is whether such a violation is morally justifiable. Again, it is not difficult to dream up circumstances in which we would forgive the violator entirely: something in the article could have triggered an original idea that will eventually benefit millions of people. But in the case of normal people in normal meetings reading a normal journal article, this sort of excuse will not normally be available. It is most likely that they are simply willing to risk causing offense because their preference for reading outweighs their sense of obligation to respect the convention that one listens to one's colleagues during meetings.

Example B: A male high school principal addresses a group of parents, all of whom happen to be female, as "ladies." Fifty years ago this would have been unremarkable. Today, there are still places where it is normal practice, but many people now view the term "ladies" as somewhat demeaning. It connotes delicacy and distance from the world of work, action, and decision making. It sounds condescending, and insofar as it helps to sustain outmoded ideas about femininity, it belongs to a way of thinking and speaking that continues to limit women's freedom.

Is the high school principal being rude? That depends entirely on the historical and geographical circumstances. In some places he would be conforming to rather than violating a convention. But elsewhere his use of "ladies" would be resented in the same way, although perhaps not to the same extent, as would his use of terms like "Red Indian," "colored," "half-breed," "coolie," or "lunatic." In these latter places, the conventions have changed, and if the principal were deliberately violating them, this would indicate a willingness to risk offending his audience. So in these situations, he is being rude. The issue now becomes *why* he is being rude and to what extent his rudeness is blameworthy or excusable.

One possibility, of course, is that he is being jocular and using the term tongue in cheek. In that case, the violation of convention is conscious and purposive.[12] Whether or not the humor is acceptable depends on all sorts of subtle variables such as the principal's reputation, his relationship to his audience, the character of his audience, the topic under discussion, and so on. Another possibility is that he is unfamiliar with the feminist critique of terms like "ladies" and not attuned to the cultural changes that have rendered it suspect: in other words, he is ignorant of the relevant convention. In that case, the question becomes to what extent this ignorance is excusable or blameworthy. A Southerner in his sixties, raised to respect traditional notions of chivalry, or someone whose first language is not English, will probably be cut more slack than a Yankee yuppie. Irony and ignorance are the two most probable explanations. It is, of course, conceivable that the principal knows that the term offends some women and is being momentarily thoughtless and insensitive; it is also possible that he is willfully trying to cause offense; but neither scenario is very likely. More likely is the possibility that his use of the term "ladies" is an unconscious going on semiconscious move designed to give him the upper hand in the conversation—a subtle power play that establishes him as the professional authority to whom the "ladies" should defer. In this case, it seems fair to assume that he must be at least somewhat aware of both the convention and the fact that he is violating it.[13]

The cases discussed are deliberately somewhat messy. It is not part of my project to provide some algorithm that can be applied mechanically to any situation to yield a definitive moral judgment. On the contrary, one obvious conclusion to emerge is that any reasonable judgment about the rudeness of an action is relative to the specific context in which the behavior being judged occurs. I take it to be a virtue of the approach I have outlined that it highlights rather than hides this situational relativity.

Objections

One objection to the proposed definition of rudeness that will probably occur to many readers is that it covers too much. Suppose I break into a man's house, steal some valuables, start a fire in the basement, and then shoot him when he tries to escape. We would not normally describe such behavior as rude. Yet it seems to satisfy the conditions laid down by my definition. Clearly, I am violating conventions—in this case the laws against burglary, arson, and murder. My actions are deliberate violations of these laws and obviously indicate a willingness, even an intention, to cause someone harm. So according to my definition, I have acted rudely. But do we really want to say that theft, arson, and murder are instances of rudeness?[14]

A simple and, I believe, adequate response to this objection is to accept that actions like theft, arson, assault, kidnapping, and murder are indeed rude. But they are not *only* rude; they invite criticism on other grounds as well; and our intense disapprobation has to do mainly with the other, more serious negative aspects of these actions. An analogy might help here. Suppose a gang of crooks commits an armed robbery in the course of which they park next to a fire hydrant and, when making their getaway, exceed the speed limit. These relatively minor infractions will not motivate the police to go after the gang; nor, if the crooks are caught, will they be given parking and speeding tickets. The police will naturally focus on the more serious offenses. Although the traffic violations are still illegal actions, the enormity of the crime renders them insignificant. To be sure, it sounds a little odd to say that murder is rude, but that is just because it would normally be perverse of someone to pay attention to the fact that a killer has acted impolitely when the other moral, criminal, and tragic aspects of murder are so much more important. It sounds odd to say that the stars shine in the daytime, but they do. We just don't notice them because their light is overwhelmed by that of the sun.

An alternative response would be to accept the criticism and to limit the sort of convention that rudeness violates to what we might call a convention of manners. This would enable us to avoid what linguists call "pragmatic infelicities" such as "murder is rude" and other odd-sounding implications of our initial definition. It would do this by tying the philosophical definition of rudeness more closely to ordinary linguistic usage, where "rudeness" is an antonym for "politeness." Narrowing the definition in this way would also enable us to make sense of statements like "The bank robbers weren't rude to anyone during the robbery." On the definition as initially proposed, this is oxymoronic. Yet we all understand what it describes: the robbers said "please" and "thank you" and observed most of the normal social niceties. On the other hand, just as there is something odd about the statement "murder is rude," there is also something odd or "pragmatically infelicitous" about statements such as "The rapist had very good manners and was at no point rude to his victim." So the appeal to linguistic oddness is hardly a slam-dunk argument.

In my view, neither the broader nor the narrower definition is objectively right or wrong. Questions like these have to be settled on pragmatic grounds. And I believe that defining rudeness by reference to the broader notion of a convention raises fewer difficulties and yields more insights than narrowing the definition by specifying that the conventions violated are conventions of manners. Advocates of the narrower definition may argue that we should be able to distinguish between actions that are *merely* rude and actions that go beyond mere rudeness, and that the narrower definition helps us do this. But it is not clear how it can help us draw this distinction unless there is a way of identifying "conventions of manners" that doesn't make reference to notions like "politeness" or "rudeness." Moreover, although the demand that we distinguish between what is merely rude and what goes beyond rude seems reasonable at first sight, I consider it dubious for two reasons.

First, the expression "go beyond rudeness" is liable to mislead us. It contains the implication that rudeness is at the trivial end of the spectrum of morally reprehensible behavior. But it ain't necessarily so, both because not all rudeness is reprehensible, and because rudeness can sometimes be very serious in terms of the immediate suffering caused or the long-term consequences that ensue. Moreover, the general level and type of civility in a society are also important determinants of that society's cultural quality. Edmund Burke even maintained that "manners are of more importance than laws."[15] The temptation to trivialize rudeness is perhaps reinforced by the fact that most forms of rudeness are not prohibited by law. The exemplars of rude behavior that we most readily call to mind also tend to be relatively unimportant actions—such things as people pushing in line or being overfamiliar. But rudeness can be devastating. Imagine the emotional impact of having someone you love spit in your face. And as a character trait, a propensity to be rude is hardly a superficial or incidental quality. It can bespeak a lack of respect or a lack of concern for others—moral failings that most of us would consider quite serious.[16] Thus the very notion of the "merely rude" is suspect.

Second, even if we accept that acts can be ranged on a spectrum of moral seriousness, and that mere rudeness tends to occupy the slighter end, it is still difficult to draw a sharp line between the merely rude and the rude-plus. Consider the following series of convention violations that might occur in a letter:

a. I make a grammatical mistake. This violates a convention, but it falls short of rudeness since it fails to meet the second condition of my definition.

b. I use an incorrect form of address (e.g., I write "Dear Miss Smith" instead of "Dear Dr. Smith"). This is rude according to my definition; if it were done deliberately it would indicate a willingness to offend. How one judges the violation depends, of course, on whether it is accidental, deliberate, justified, and so on.[17]

c. I write in an open letter to a newspaper, "Dear Miss Smith, You are an ignorant idiot." This is obviously rude and obviously intentional. It does not seem to be anything more.

d. I write, "Dear Miss Smith, You are a child-abusing alcoholic, and unless you send me $500 I will post the video clips that prove it on YouTube." This is rude, and it also constitutes blackmail, which deepens its moral reprehensibility and makes it illegal to boot.

Most of us would agree that in normal circumstances (d) is worse than (c). But it is hard to identify any further condition satisfied by (d) but not by (c) that makes (d) necessarily worse. The motive may be baser, but it does not have to be. The harm done to Dr. Smith is likely to be more serious; but it may not be. And the fact that blackmail is illegal seems irrelevant, since this could easily not be the case. Thus, to those who think they can define rudeness in a way that makes possible a principled separation between rudeness and other acts that offend or harm others, I would issue this challenge: identify the condition that *mere* rudeness fails to meet but which is met by these other harmful acts. Perhaps it is possible to tighten the definition of rudeness in this way; but in the absence of plausible suggestions, it is reasonable to be skeptical.

Acceptable intentional rudeness

John Henry Newman wrote, "[I]t is almost a definition of a gentleman to say he is one who never inflicts pain"[18] (to which some wit wickedly added—"unintentionally"). If we interpret this definition of a gentleman more broadly as a characterization of a perfectly well-mannered person, it is rather appealing. It chimes with the definition of rudeness offered above, and also with the familiar but still valuable notion that good manners and social grace are largely a matter of doing what makes other people feel comfortable and not doing what causes discomfort.

There is an often-told parable of an aristocratic lady (in some versions it is Elizabeth I) who perfectly exemplifies this ideal of considerateness. One day she invited a loyal but lowly servant to have lunch with her and some courtly friends. Before the meal was served, a bowl of water was passed around for the diners to rinse their fingers in. When the bowl was passed to the servant, she misunderstood its purpose and, putting it to her lips, drank out of it. As the other guests started to snigger at this faux pas, the hostess took the bowl and put it to her own lips, thereby saving her servant from embarrassment.

However, the definition of rudeness given earlier, and the analysis it supports, implies that there are times when good manners may legitimately be suspended or overridden. Of the eight "polar" situations identified in figure 1.1, two (numbered 6 and 8) involve actions that are known by the agent to be rude but which are nevertheless morally acceptable.[19] The difference between them is that in one case (6) being rude is not part of the agent's purpose, whereas in the other case (8) it is.

I believe that these situations, where we may justifiably risk offending or hurting the feelings of another person, can usually be placed under one of five headings: emergencies; promoting long-term benefits; making a statement; humor; and pedagogy. Let us consider these in turn.

Emergencies

The general principle here is uncontroversial. Everyone would agree that the normal niceties of social intercourse should be suspended or ignored if a crisis suddenly arises. If I am talking to you and you see a child about to chase a ball into the street or grab hold of a freshly painted railing, you should interrupt and shout a warning without any preliminary apology. The normal convention is that you keep listening until I've said what I have to say, or at least until I say something you feel the need to comment on. Where the need to stop listening and turn your attention elsewhere is not too pressing, you would normally indicate that you have to suspend that convention using a formula such as "Excuse me" or "Pardon me." In effect we have here a convention for suspending a convention. Literally, you ask my indulgence or even my forgiveness for an action that would otherwise be rude. But if there is no time for that, you simply act. Interestingly, even though the acceptability of suspending the convention in an emergency is generally understood, you will still probably ask to be excused retroactively, saying, once the crisis is over, something like "Sorry about that . . ."

Of course, people can disagree over whether a situation constitutes the sort of emergency that justifies violating a convention. Suppose we are talking on the phone and I suddenly say, "Gotta go!" and hang up. If I tell you later that I saw someone stealing clothes from my clothesline, you will probably accept this as a reasonable excuse. If I tell you that I noticed it was beginning to drizzle, and needed to take the clothes in, you will probably feel that a fuller explanation could and should have been given at the time. But there is no clear line between emergencies and nonemergencies, in part because different people have different crisis-point thresholds. The best rule of thumb to employ here is probably the Golden Rule: we should ask whether we would be offended or hurt if in a similar situation we were on the receiving end of the convention violation.

Promoting long-term benefits

Sometimes, slavishly abiding by a convention may result in serious long-term harm to oneself or others, while violating it is likely to produce beneficial consequences. Of course, this is true in the case of emergencies as well, but some situations would not normally be described as emergencies since there is ample opportunity for reflection prior to action. For example, there are topics that many people consider unsuitable or inappropriate for discussion with anyone other than a few privileged family members and friends—matters such as salaries, personal hygiene, marital intimacies, or a person's self-destructive habits. Talking about such issues invites the charge of failing to "mind your own business." Yet occasions can arise where the best course of action is to risk being thought rude in order to help iron out a problem (for instance, when two people are estranged owing to a misunderstanding) or to confront a person with a truth he is unable or unwilling to recognize (for instance, that he is becoming an alcoholic, showing favoritism to one of his children, spending himself into misery, treating his partner badly, or getting married to the wrong person).[20] Often, the primary beneficiary of such interventions is intended to be those who are also most likely to be hurt or offended. This will not, of course, necessarily lessen the affront they feel; on the contrary, it can even seem to compound impertinence with condescension. But ideally, at least, the rudeness will be forgiven in virtue of the good intentions behind it or the positive consequences that flow from it.

Making a statement

In the sort of situations considered so far, the rudeness is incidental rather than integral to the purpose of the action. It just so happens in these cases that the best means to bring about a certain end involves violating a convention. More interesting, though, are those situations where the rudeness, although morally acceptable, is much more willful, and where violating a convention is itself part of the action's purpose. I would suggest that the two most common reasons for this sort of deliberate rudeness are to make some sort of statement and to be humorous. We will consider these in turn.

Here are some examples of people making statements through actions that satisfy the definition of rudeness:

- giving someone the finger
- calling someone a "bloody idiot"
- refusing to shake hands with someone
- not conforming to a dress code

- not singing the national anthem (where doing so is clearly expected)
- pointedly not using a person's title
- same-sex couples kissing in public
- African Americans in the 1950s ignoring segregationist restrictions on where they may sit, eat, drink, etc.

Typically, the statements made by convention-violating actions such as these will be about either (a) the agent; (b) the person or persons at whom the action is directed; or (c) the convention that is being violated. These categories are not exclusive.

The simplest cases that fall into this category involve someone speaking abusively to someone else, perhaps calling him a jerk, or telling him in salty language to go away. In such cases, the statement is usually about the person being addressed, but sometimes the speaker's primary purpose is to communicate her own state of mind. Whether or not one considers the rudeness justified depends on one's general position regarding explicit rudeness and the specific circumstances surrounding the incident. Some people operate on the principle that explicit incivility should always be eschewed: they choose always to comport themselves in a certain way, perhaps in accordance with the teachings of an apostle of nonviolence. Most people, though, have what we can call a "warranted incivility threshold." By this I mean not the point at which they, as a matter of psychological fact, lapse into incivility, but the point at which they believe themselves justified in doing so.

In most cases the justification will refer to some previous action by the person being addressed, which the speaker believes calls for an especially forceful response. The response could serve more than one purpose. If I abuse you for cutting me off in traffic, for instance, I could be trying to educate you, letting you know that you've broken a rule. I could also be trying to tell you a home truth about yourself—that you are a lousy driver. Or I might be using rudeness as a way of impressing upon you just how upset I am. In each case, rudeness serves to communicate something.

Of course, sometimes we may justify our being rude to people simply on the grounds that they deserve it. In effect, this amounts to saying that the purpose of the incivility is to make them suffer: my being rude to them is a punishment inflicted on them for their wrongdoing. This may, in fact, be how many people would justify some of their decisions to cross the incivility threshold. We should note, though, that this is a different kind of justification altogether, since the rudeness is not now understood to be primarily concerned with making a statement. We might also observe that if the purpose of the punishment is to deter other transgressions, then it is ultimately being justified as a form of pedagogy or as a means to secure long-term benefits.[21]

As mentioned above, statement-making rudeness most often says something about either the agent or the "victim." If I offer you my hand and you refuse to shake it, this will normally be understood, first of all, as a statement expressing your opinion of me. There are, of course, situations where this assumption would be mistaken. You could be unfamiliar with the custom; you could be trying to avoid giving me your cold; you could believe that it is wrong for unrelated men and women to touch one another (an interesting example of social conventions conflicting). But we are concerned here with rude behavior that is assertional, and understood in this way, your action probably means that you despise me, perhaps because I am guilty of some terrible crime, or perhaps because I betrayed your trust. In these situations, it may also indicate that you do not forgive me. Your refusal might, in addition, affirm a belief you hold about yourself: perhaps that you are superior to me or in some sense "cleaner," and that you should preserve this condition.

It often happens that an individual will find herself in the middle of a group where everyone else is following a convention that she does not wish to follow. In these situations she can feel considerable pressure to conform to the convention—for instance, to pledge allegiance to the flag, to sing the national anthem, or to bow her head when everyone else is praying. By not conforming, she can make a statement about her own position or beliefs: "I don't really belong to this group"; "I do not share your beliefs"; "I am not the kind of person who makes gestures of submission"; "I am a Christian and follow to the letter Jesus' command to eschew oaths"; "I disapprove of the war currently being fought by the government of the country symbolized by the flag." Her actions may also express her view of the convention itself: "I disapprove of the way flags and anthems are reinforcing forms of nationalism that I consider morally unhealthy and politically dangerous"; "I disapprove of this moment of prayer since I believe it violates the principle that the state should not promote any form of religious worship."

Challenging the conventions is an interesting and sometimes valuable function of rude behavior. People who refuse to go along with some widely accepted convention are often viewed from the vantage point of the mainstream as difficult, self-important, attention-seeking boat-rockers. They may be, of course. But in many cases they are people who have reflected seriously on the significance of a convention and have decided that it expresses or is associated with beliefs and values they do not wish to support. Their situation is analogous to that of writers who know full well that the time-honored conventions of good writing forbid the

splitting of infinitives or the ending of sentences with prepositions, but who choose to pointedly split them anyway, hoping
thereby to strike a blow against prescriptive conventions they
disagree with.

Unfortunately, it is often hard to avoid the stark choice of
either conforming to or violating a convention. When the national anthem is played, you must either stand or remain seated:
ploys such as pretending to look for something on the floor are
awkward and demeaning. If the pope and the queen of England
come to your backyard cookout, you have to decide whether or
not to bow when introduced and use phrases like "Your Holi-
ness" and "Your Majesty." In such situations, thoughtful people
can be genuinely torn between not wanting to embarrass or offend anyone and wishing to comport themselves in accordance
with their beliefs. When the latter motive prevails, it is important to recognize that their rudeness may be a sign of both intellectual autonomy and integrity.

A well-known, probably false, but still wonderful anecdote
about Beethoven illustrates several of the points just made. The
composer was walking through a park with Goethe, twenty years
his senior and the most celebrated German author of his time.
Noticing that a small group of nobles accompanied by their en-
tourage were coming toward them along the same path, Goethe
followed the custom of the day and stepped aside, bowing to his
social superiors as they passed. Beethoven, however, kept to his
course, plowing straight through the middle of the group, hands
behind his back, head high, eyes forward. Catching up with his
companion, a shocked Goethe asked how he could be so disrespectful toward the nobility, to which the great composer re-
plied, "There are thousands of them, but only two of us."

Humor

One of the most common forms of humor that many of us engage in is mock rudeness. Here are a few examples:

- I address a friend in derogatory terms ("Mornin', meathead!").
- I address a friend inappropriately ("Hey, sexpot!").
- I transfer items from a friend's shopping cart to my own.
- I ostentatiously check that the cash a friend has handed to me is legal currency, biting the coins and holding the notes up to the light.
- I snap my fingers at my host to indicate that I want another beer.

Now one could object here that joking and teasing of this sort does not really constitute rudeness, at least not always. In the examples just given, conventions are clearly being deliberately violated, but does this indicate a willingness to offend? The answer seems to be that sometimes it does and sometimes it does not. Teasing can be quite aggressive. If I introduce a distinguished speaker from an elite university by thanking her for "condescending to come down from her lofty perch," the hostility is fairly apparent and the risk of offending great. If I make a face at a close friend, the risk of offending her is virtually nil.

The question of whether or not mock rudeness should be counted as a form of rudeness in fact introduces an additional complication. There are conventions relating to the violation of conventions. Harmless teasing involves violating a convention in ways that are socially acceptable—acceptability being determined by further conventions (metaconventions). The rather hostile introduction just described would be "offside" in a formal setting, but at a more intimate, relaxed gathering it could be a pleasantry enjoyed by all. However, metaconventions are no more clear-cut than first-order conventions. Although in many cases it is clear enough whether someone is out of line, the boundary markers are broad and fuzzy, allowing plenty of scope for reasonable people to disagree.

On the question of whether or not mock rudeness should be counted as a form of intentional rudeness, we have two options. One option is to distinguish between teasing that remains "on-side" and teasing that strays "offside," and count only the latter as rude. In that case, the conventions being violated are the offside laws, so to speak—the metaconventions that determine whether or not someone has shown poor taste or "gone too far." The other option is to classify all mock rudeness as purposive rudeness and to see the metaconventions as marking the admittedly often blurred line between the acceptable and the reprehensible. In my view, this second option is preferable since it makes for a some-what simpler analysis. This is, of course, a pragmatic justification, but that is in order. Not a lot hangs on the choice made, and the phenomena we are examining do not, by themselves, necessitate one particular theoretical scheme. Critics who prefer a different tack should feel free to chart an alternative course.

Mock rudeness is so ubiquitous in our culture that it is worth asking what purposes it serves. Take an example mentioned ear-lier: I attract the attention of a friend by shouting, "Mornin', meathead!" I do this to be funny but, as is well known, what people do to be funny and what they find amusing are often very revealing, So what does this sort of joking achieve? Two func-tions seem to be especially important. First, teasing is one way that we establish, affirm, and strengthen bonds of friendship and intimacy. This is not true of every relationship, of course; intimacy is presumably possible where teasing never occurs. But in our increasingly informal culture such relationships are probably quite rare. Indeed, how much license you have to transgress normal rules of polite behavior is often a fair indicator of how close you are to someone. The door-knock test—would you enter a person's house or office without knocking, or after knocking but before he answers, or only after he has opened the door to you?—is one useful boundary marker. The french-fry test—would you take a french fry from another person's plate without asking?—is another.

Of course, casualness and informality, while they typically characterize close relationships, are not guarantors of genuine intimacy; nor should the quality and value of a relationship be viewed as a function of them. While the absence of teasing often indicates coldness or even fear, banter can easily become a substitute for, or even an obstacle to, genuine conversation. Furthermore, as we noted earlier, even when the setting is thoroughly informal and the relationship close and strong—say, between boisterous bantering siblings who share bedroom, bathroom, and confidences—there are still conventions in play. Even here, hanging up without saying goodbye, failing to keep an appointment for a trivial reason, using terms of abuse stronger than those generally accepted within the group—these behaviors may cross a line, causing offense and inviting criticism. And close relationships commonly introduce additional conventions that one is expected to observe, such as demonstrating affection with hugs and kisses, or helping one's host to clean up after a meal.

The other main function of mock rudeness is to provide a way for us to engage in power struggles within safe parameters. One does not have to be a dyed-in-the-wool Nietzschean to recognize that bantering is commonly agonistic. Even the most good-humored teasing contains the threat of something stronger, like the pat on the cheek from the Godfather signifying the possibility of something less gentle. In most relationships and in most groups, power is not distributed symmetrically; teasing is one important way in which asymmetries and pecking orders are established, sustained, and challenged.[22] To be able to come up with spontaneous and original jests, insults, or witticisms at someone else's expense raises one's standing relative to one's victims. Those who realize that they are less adept at this sort of jousting must either accept their situation or deploy cruder tactics such as clichéd insults or a louder voice. Here, too, mock rudeness can sometimes become genuinely offensive and harmful, just as the rule-governed violence in an ice hockey game occasionally slides into a genuine brawl.

Pedagogy

A rather different kind of intentional rudeness that is morally acceptable occurs in certain pedagogical contexts. The sergeant major who tells a recruit that he's a "piece of rat crap not fit to be flushed down the toilet, let alone wear military uniform" is obviously being deliberately rude. He may, of course, just be a bully who enjoys abusing his position, knowing that he is protected from any riposte by strict military rules. But it is generally accepted that the sergeant major's task of turning raw recruits into toughened soldiers and the group into a disciplined cohesive unit requires the suspension of social niceties observed outside the barracks. In effect, this is another case of intentional rudeness being justified by its long-term benefits. But it is also, like teasing, a case where metaconventions permit transgressions of rules that operate elsewhere. This is the point of the hackneyed line "You're in the army now, soldier!" The sergeant is, among other things, a teacher; and teachers sometimes use rudeness as a pedagogical tool, speaking to or about students in a manner that would be unacceptable outside the classroom. In the past such treatment was commonplace and generally approved: in traditional British schools it was considered essential! Increasingly, though, it has come to be viewed as pedagogically unsound and morally suspect. The reasons for this bring us back to an issue raised at the outset—the perceived decline in civility.

The perceived decline in civility

Rudeness, I have argued, always involves the violation of a convention. Civility, politeness, and good manners rest on the observance of conventions. In communities where the form of life is overwhelmingly shaped by long-standing traditions, the social conventions that stipulate how people should behave in various situations are well defined and universally known. Modernity, however, is Heracleitean. We live in a world of continual change where "all that is solid melts into air." Ever since Marx identified this as the defining characteristic of modern society, it has been a commonplace that knowledge, technology, economic organization, lifestyles, beliefs, and values are constantly evolving. And so, too, are our social conventions. The complex consequences of this social dynamism include, among other things, technological and political progress, artistic innovation, greater social mobility, excitement, anxiety, and confusion.

Consider a few examples of how conventions have changed over the past hundred years:

- Men no longer lift their hats to women.
- Women no longer have to keep their arms and legs covered in public.
- Swearing has become more socially acceptable both in private and in public.
- The occasions when men are expected to wear ties are far fewer.
- People have more freedom to grow their hair long, shave their heads, dye their hair green, display tattoos, ornament themselves with nose rings or lip studs, and so on, without making themselves social outcasts.
- Booing, hissing, and catcalling at theatrical performances is no longer acceptable.
- Dropping round at someone's house without phoning beforehand is now frowned on in many communities.

Confusion over what the rules are, when they apply, and to whom, are inevitable in a period of rapid cultural change. And with the coming of e-mail, cell phones, BlackBerrys, iPods, the Internet, Google, Facebook, and so on, the rate of change in the ways we interact has become positively bewildering at times. Such confusion naturally leads to more instances of people violating, or being perceived to violate, social conventions. This creates the impression that civility is on the decline, but the impression may be misleading, more an effect of living in a dynamic modern society than a result of the continually deepening moral turpitude of the rising generations.

Take, for example, the way in which we address each other in writing. It is common for people raised when letter writing was still normal to be affronted by the terse, hasty, informal, and slapdash character of many e-mail messages they receive. This is especially true when the message comes from someone occupying a lower rung on the social hierarchy: a student to a teacher, for instance, or a child to a grandparent. Where the recipient is expecting a formally composed letter that moves from "Dear So-and-so" to "Yours sincerely," they receive a jumble of unpunctuated abbreviations and elisions ("Yo prof, cant make class, CU2mro"). Apart from any aesthetic objections they may have to this form of writing, it is also hard for them not to feel slighted by it. Yet the sender probably intended no disrespect at all. She was simply operating with a different set of epistolary conventions, communicating in a way that is perfectly acceptable within her own peer group.

A similar confusion often arises over titles and forms of address in ordinary conversation. I have heard college professors complain when some undergraduate has addressed them by their first names rather than more formally as "Dr." or "Professor" So-and-So. "What gives with today's students?" they ask. "Who do they think they are? When I was a student, I would never have dreamed of calling my professors by their first names."

The complainer is correct. In the past students were expected to address their professors more formally, and they understood this expectation. But since the Second World War, the domain in which our culture insists on formal proprieties has clearly shrunk; casualness and informality have become the norm in many spheres, including the academy. For a long time now, most professors have addressed students by their first names, and quite a few have invited students to reciprocate.[23] In this situation uncertainty is understandable. And if a student happens to have spent a lot of time with professors who operate on a first-name basis, is it unreasonable for them to assume that other professors will find this acceptable also?[24]

This example in fact illustrates more than just the difficulty of knowing what is appropriate when the conventions are in flux. It also exemplifies an ongoing conflict between two general principles governing social relations. On the one hand, we have a *hierarchical principle*, which supports asymmetrical expectations in relationships. This principle underlies the idea that children should be seen and not heard, should respect their elders and obey their parents. It is still evident at times in the way doctors and nurses interact with each other and with their patients. And it obviously informs most teacher-student relationships. The Confucian code, which lays down strict rules to ensure that children, parents, siblings, spouses, friends, and so on offer and receive appropriate degrees of deference, is one of the best-known and most thorough realizations of this principle. Quite often, these strict codes of etiquette are one of the means used by the privileged to express and reinforce their dominant social position.[25]

On the other hand, an *egalitarian* principle, according to which all individuals are entitled to equal opportunities, rights, and respect, has become fundamental to modern moral and political thinking. And egalitarianism seeks to level hierarchies. In recent times notable progress has been made in this direction, most obviously in the way that various kinds of discrimination have become unacceptable in many social spheres. But egalitarianism has also found expression in, and altered, the warp and woof of everyday life in homes, at school, in the workplace, and on the street. Families are less authoritarian, more democratic. Fewer jobs require uniforms that make immediately apparent differences in rank. According to some reports even college professors are less pompous than in the past.

These two principles—the hierarchical and the egalitarian—are constantly jostling for predominance.[26] Most of us endorse egalitarianism in a general way but still go along with traditional hierarchical practices on many occasions (for example, using or insisting on titles, pulling rank, accepting or expecting status-based privileges, deferring to seniority). This is neither surprising nor necessarily objectionable. Both principles have cogent rationales. Equality fosters friendship, self-respect, and, sometimes, better decision making. But hierarchy, too, can serve valuable purposes. A well-defined structure of authority is more efficient in some situations (for example, in the army, or on board the USS *Enterprise*), and it also helps to maintain a useful distance between, say, teacher and pupil, or doctor and patient.

Hierarchies are deeply entrenched in most cultures since they are typically bound up with child-rearing practices, educational organization, and the division of labor, all central to the well-being of a society. For this reason, what may look like a shift toward more egalitarian relationships will often mask continuing differences in real power. Even where first names are used, teachers still grade students, and bosses can still fire workers.

But although the new egalitarianism and informality may sometimes create misleading impressions about the true nature of relationships, this is not a reason for preferring something like the transparency of military protocol. Social conventions, rules of etiquette, modes of address, and so forth are not mere shells that contain forms of life, without affecting them, the way glass bottles hold wine without affecting its taste. Changes in protocol both reflect and promote changes in the way people interact and relate to one another. The fact that nowadays fewer sons call their

father "Sir" indicates a real shift in the character of father-son relationships, part of a gradual democratization of the family. The
formality with which Jane Austen's characters treat each other
compared to how people interact today is linked to the fact that
the sexual inhibitions and taboos operating among the English
upper middle classes at the end of the eighteenth century were
much tighter than those prevailing today.

The perennial complaint that civility is declining while rudeness is on the rise is thus probably misplaced. The problem is not
that people today are trampling underfoot the time-honored
rules of polite behavior. The problem is, rather, that these rules
are in flux, and there is consequently some confusion about what
they are and what abiding by them signifies. Inevitably, in these
circumstances, it will often happen that one person's confusion
leads to another person's taking offense. But confusion and anxiety are part of the price we pay for living in a dynamic culture.
Offense, too, is an unavoidable by-product of moral progress.
The struggle to claim equal rights for ethnic minorities, women,
and gays would never have got off the ground if people had eschewed any action likely to cause offense.

This is not to suggest that we should cheerfully countenance
uncivil behavior. The rituals and requirements of civility make
possible so much that we cherish in our social world. But we
should be cautious and, as a culture, self-conscious, before we
jump on the bandwagon of tongue-clickers and head-shakers,
all remembering a golden age of good manners. The imagined
alternative to our present fluid situation is a rooted stability in
which everyone knows and does what is expected of him at all
times. This Confucian ideal stimulates nostalgic longings, but,
like all ideals and most rememberings, it is *idealized*. Moreover,
even if it were historically true, it is not a real option today. Our

culture and our social conventions seem likely to keep changing for a long time to come. Our task is thus not to return to some golden age of civility but, rather, to self-consciously establish social conventions that adequately express our values (for instance, a judicious egalitarianism), foster sound moral attitudes (for instance, respect for persons, tolerance of different lifestyles), and facilitate understanding. We should also, where possible, establish conventions that contribute to making our culture more beautiful.

2 The Ethics of Gossiping

According to legend, King Midas witnessed a musical contest between Apollo and Pan and let it be known that he considered Pan the finer musician. Angered at this, Apollo gave Midas the ears of a donkey to symbolize his foolishness. From that time on, Midas always wore a special hat to cover his ass's ears and keep his shameful secret hidden. Only the king's barber knew about the ass's ears, and he was told that if he ever breathed a word to anyone, he would be put to death. For many years the barber managed to keep mum, but the desire to tell what he knew built up inside him until it became overwhelming. Unable to hold in the secret any longer, he ran to the woods, dug a hole, and shouted into it, "The king has ass's ears! The king has ass's ears!" He then filled the hole in and returned to the palace, somewhat relieved of his burden. Unfortunately for him, the next spring some green reeds grew on the spot where he had dug, and when the wind blew through them, they began to whisper, "The king has ass's ears! The king has ass's ears!" Soon the message was picked up by the trees and birds, and before long the truth was known throughout the kingdom.

One aspect of this story that we can all sympathize with is the barber's intense desire to let out what he knows about the king. It is a very human urge, to tell each other what we know about each other. So in some ways it is surprising that gossiping should historically be viewed with such suspicion when it is something we do so naturally. Then again, perhaps that is precisely why moralists have felt the need to erect taboos here—to keep a natural but potentially harmful impulse in check. Either way, the legend of Midas's barber testifies to the fact that the urge to gossip runs deep in human nature.

Gossiping is not a subject that has ever attracted much attention from moral philosophers. One reason for this might be that it is generally viewed as not important enough to merit serious philosophical attention. Another reason might be that it is automatically viewed by many with disfavor; indeed, the term itself carries so many negative implications and connotations as to make a neutral appraisal of the practice virtually impossible. But the ethical issues surrounding the practice of gossiping are well worth discussing. For while a question of the form "Should I tell A something I know about B?" may not sound all that momentous, it is, nevertheless, a moral dilemma most of us confront on a regular basis. And while the concept of gossip may indeed be pejoratively loaded, that fact does not help us resolve such dilemmas.

The few contemporary thinkers who have discussed some of the moral issues surrounding gossip usually proceed either by accepting a standard definition of gossip or by trying to construct a more sophisticated definition. Both approaches involve working from something like the accepted conception of gossip, with its various and mainly negative associations—for example, of its being idle, trivial, invasive, malicious, and potentially harmful. One then asks questions such as these: Are such features necessary? What positive functions might gossip serve? To what extent are the negative aspects outweighed by the positive?

Although I, too, will take up some of these questions, my approach will be rather different in that it is, to begin with, more abstract. The kind of moral dilemma I am interested in has this general form: Should I tell one person (call him Adam) something about another person (call him Jake)? Clearly, a reflective response to this problem raises a higher-level question: what moral considerations should govern what I say to Adam about Jake? But to answer these questions, we do not need to have in hand a definition of gossip. Rather, what we need are general normative principles that can be applied to circumstances where we are talking about other people just as they can be applied to other morally problematic situations.

I do not believe there is a single general principle that by itself enables us to distinguish between permissible and impermissible talk about others. Yet any attempt to rationally justify the decisions we make has to involve some appeal to principles, even if these do not by themselves completely vindicate our action. Intuitions may count for something in ethical reasoning, but the simple fact that different people have different, even conflicting, intuitive responses to particular moral dilemmas vitiates any simple appeal to intuition. I propose, therefore, to proceed, at least initially, by constructing a sort of sieve formed from generally accepted moral principles, which can serve to filter out talk about others that is either clearly objectionable or clearly acceptable.

We can then focus our attention more precisely on the sort of talk that, being neither, raises the most controversial and interesting questions.

Throughout, my primary concern is with the normative issue: when is talk about others morally acceptable and when is it not? Here, as with many other ethical questions, I do not believe there is a single correct answer, binding on all human beings. But within a particular culture there will usually be a determinate set of generally accepted tenets, shared values, acknowledged interests, and respected ideals. These inform, in different ways, the alternative positions open to the participants in that culture and establish parameters of credibility within which any ethical view should fall. It would be dogmatic to assume there is *only* one coherent position available to us, or, for that matter, that there necessarily is *even* one view that satisfies these requirements while remaining internally consistent. This caution has been underlined in recent times by the emergence of the Internet and, with it, new and conflicting ideas about the norms that should govern what people publish online. But it is reasonable to assume that reflection on how our judgments might be justified can clarify the nature of our disagreements and thereby help to extend consensus and promote tolerance.

Narrowing down the domain

Our domain is talk about other people.[1] You cannot gossip about animals, computers, or anything nonhuman. Nor can you gossip about yourself or about the person to whom you are talking, although you can, of course, disclose information regarding someone else while talking about yourself. There can certainly be moral constraints on what one may say about oneself or one's interlocutor, but these are, for the most part, of a different sort. To keep things simple, we will assume throughout that the talk in question is about just one other person, since it makes no difference in principle whether the subject of the gossip is one or many. Our first task is to narrow down this domain, setting aside what is uncontroversially wrong or right, in order to clarify exactly what kind of talk about others might occasion moral disagreement. The underlying moral principles I invoke in doing this are assumed to be widely accepted on account of their general usefulness.

Malicious or self-serving lies

Deliberate, ill-intentioned lies about another person can be excluded straightaway since they violate commonly accepted ethical rules. Lying is not, of course, the same thing as simply spreading false reports about someone. Although such talk might be slanderous, if I believe what I say to be true I am not necessarily at fault. Whether or not I am at fault, and to what extent, depends on two considerations:

i. How reasonable is it for me to believe in the truth of what I say?
ii. How damaging is what I say to the reputation of the person I am talking about?

The more damaging the talk, the greater my obligation to be sure that it is correct. Not everyone will agree with this, but it does accord with our common moral beliefs and practices. I will surely—and rightly—have fewer epistemological scruples about telling Adam that Jake sometimes puts his shirt on inside out than about passing on a report that Jake has been accused of sexual harassment.

This first exclusion is limited to *malicious* or *self-serving* lies because there are so many circumstances that crop up in which most people consider well-intentioned lies to be morally acceptable. Nearly all of us regularly utter untruths to spare someone's feelings, to boost a person's confidence, to protect a reputation, to avoid dangerous complexities, and so on. It would be at odds with common sense to classify all such actions as unethical. This is not to suggest that well-intentioned lying is never wrong. But most of us would only *automatically* condemn a person for lying when the motive is to injure another person or to satisfy some personal desire.

Regarding this first exclusion, someone might offer the following casuistry. Gossip often takes the form of a mediated report, as when I say, "*Eve told me* that Jake has been accused of sexual harassment." In this case, I can be virtually certain that what I say is true, since, strictly speaking, I am merely reporting something I experienced myself: viz., part of my conversation with Eve. Therefore I need not concern myself with the *truth* of what Eve said.

This is a clever move, and it in fact reinforces the point just made. One can, so to speak, gossip responsibly or irresponsibly. There is a difference between my telling Adam what Eve told me about Jake, and my telling him (on the basis of something I heard) that Jake has been accused of sexual harassment as if this were an established fact. But in most situations I cannot use this sort of argument to escape responsibility for my decision to pass on gossip about someone. My statement may have the *form* of a report about what Eve said, but its *matter* clearly concerns Jake.[2]

Talk that violates someone's rights

Like malicious lies, talk that rests on or involves a violation of someone's generally acknowledged rights can be presumptively condemned. This would include, for example, passing on information obtained by illegal means such as phone tapping. It would also include breaches of confidence where the right to confidentiality is institutionalized as in legal or psychiatric consultations. The concept of rights invoked here does not require any sophisticated metaethical justification. What is important for our purposes is simply that it be *generally acknowledged* within our culture that a person enjoys the right in question. Most, but not all, such rights are protected by law.

Talk that disregards someone's claims

The term "claim" here means an expectation that is generally acknowledged to be normatively justified but which lacks the institutionalized weight of a right. An example will clarify the distinction. If I am a doctor and I tell Adam about Jake's consultation with me concerning his impotence, I violate Jake's rights. The same is true if I obtained the information by secretly rifling through another doctor's confidential files. But suppose I learn about Jake's impotence through some accidental circumstance such as receiving a misdirected letter? In that case, my passing on the confidential information would not be viewed by most people as technically violating Jake's rights. Nevertheless, we all recognize that in this situation Jake has a legitimate claim on me to remain silent. By contrast, if, from browsing through old newspapers, I discover that Jake has spent time in prison, I have no prima facie obligation to keep this information to myself.

Since a claim is rather less than a right, it seems appropriate to speak of "disregarding" a claim rather than of "violating" it. But for our purposes the distinction between rights and claims does not need to be sharp since talk that fails to respect either is equally excluded from consideration. It should also be evident that the distinction, like the scope of the concepts themselves, is culturally relative. But I do not see this as a problem. I have defined both rights and claims by reference to what is "generally acknowledged" within our culture. The reason for doing this is to avoid begging any questions by introducing explicitly normative concepts before it is necessary to do so.

However, it might be objected that by appealing to received opinion in this way I am, in fact, assuming too much from the outset. Some gossip may disregard someone's generally acknowledged claims yet be morally acceptable. And, of course, academic ethicists will have no difficulty conjuring up scenarios involving the usual suspects—terrorists, war criminals, racist mobs, or knife-wielding rapists—in which lies or breaches of confidence would appear justified. Such examples do indeed prove that the moral proscriptions invoked so far are not absolute. But they need not block the course of our argument if we specify that we are concerned with the legitimacy of gossip in normal circumstances. Exceptions to the principles invoked can be allowed, but only in *exceptional* circumstances, to prevent some great harm, promote some great good, or right a serious wrong. Here and in what follows, then, I assume that we are operating in normal circumstances where we feel no great pressure to suspend these principles.[3]

Before we narrow our domain further, some additional points about breaches of confidence are worth making. By excluding talk that violates rights or disregards claims, we have, ipso facto, excluded all breaches of confidence. These include situations where I myself would not be directly breaking a confidence but am aware that my knowing what I know is the result of someone else's doing so. Thus if Jake tells Adam in confidence that he is looking for another job, and Adam tells me—while sheepishly admitting that Jake asked him not to tell anyone—then I would feel obliged to not extend the chain. Were I to do so, I would incriminate myself in the initial breach of confidence. Admittedly, this rule seems to be relaxed when, because the person being discussed is a public figure, the information quickly becomes public knowledge. For example, we cheerfully pass along media reports about the private affairs of a Michael Jackson or a Bill Clinton, as revealed by people who have worked for them, even though we know that the initial leak involved a breach of confidence. In such cases it seems that we do willingly extend the breach of confidence and feel little compunction about doing so. Exactly why this is so is an interesting question. Perhaps shared guilt is borne more lightly. Or perhaps, and more justifiably, we think that in these circumstances it is unlikely that our words will add to whatever harm the initial breach of confidence may have produced; so we are in the happy situation of being able to gossip without guilt, which is perhaps one reason why celebrity gossip is so popular.[4]

Talk that directly promotes more good than harm

Now that we have ruled out lies and any talk that violates a person's rights or disregards her claims, it is appropriate to introduce utilitarian considerations. The next question to ask ourselves, given that the above provisos are met, should be this: will what we say directly promote more good than harm? If we think it will, then it is morally justifiable. If not, then further questions need to be asked.

The criterion introduced here needs to be clarified in several ways. First, the "good" in question includes the avoidance of harm. Thus if by telling Adam that Jake's marriage is on the rocks, I prevent Adam from making an acutely embarrassing faux pas, that would count as a significant good. Second, the good in question here should not include the pleasure experienced by the people gossiping. This is not because such pleasure counts for nothing, but because to count it here would mean assuming in advance that those who regard gossiping as a "guilty pleasure" that can never be good are wrong. The immediate pleasure taken in gossip will therefore be considered only later. Third, the term "directly" indicates that the connection between the communication and the good in question is fairly simple and clear, one that does not involve many further causal links. For example, if I tell Adam that the babysitter he is thinking of using has a serious drug abuse problem, this will lead him to use a different babysitter and thus lessen the likelihood of his children's being put at risk. The connection between my giving him this information and his avoidance of risk is direct. Later, I will discuss some of the indirect goods that gossip promotes, but these are not being considered at this point.

Talk that directly promotes more harm than good

If I think that passing on some information about another person is likely to directly produce more harm than good, I should not pass it on. For example, spreading the word in an intolerant community that Jake served a prison term for tax evasion many years ago, knowing that a likely consequence is that he and his entire family will be cold-shouldered by their neighbors, would be wrong for this reason.

This criterion and the one discussed in the previous section obviously hang together. Indeed, there is no principled reason for considering one before the other. This is apparent from the fact that some talk could directly produce both significant goods and significant harms.

In introducing the idea of making utilitarian calculations, one can expect to encounter certain familiar objections to utilitarianism. It will be pointed out, for instance, that the consequences of one's actions are often difficult to predict accurately (as the story of Midas's barber memorably illustrates); also that some positive and negative consequences are incommensurable. But such objections are out of place here. All we are doing at this stage is narrowing the field of our inquiry by declaring certain kinds of talk to be fair or foul in a rough-and-ready way. Of course we cannot predict with perfect accuracy the effects of what we say; but we can (and should) make informed and reasonable judgments about probable consequences. Certainly, there will be cases where the likely goods and harms we have to consider cannot easily be weighed against one another, or where we may reasonably disagree over whether a certain total outcome justifies an action. But these problems for utilitarian theory need not detain us. The utilitarian considerations invoked here are intended to be quite crude. If the probable total outcome of talking about someone is obviously good, then talk. If it is obviously bad, desist. If it is neither or unclear, then further reflection is required.[5]

The course of the argument so far is represented by the upper half of figure 2.1. With each question we put aside the obviously bad and the obviously good in order to home in on talk about other people that is neither. Two more questions allow us to narrow the domain still further.

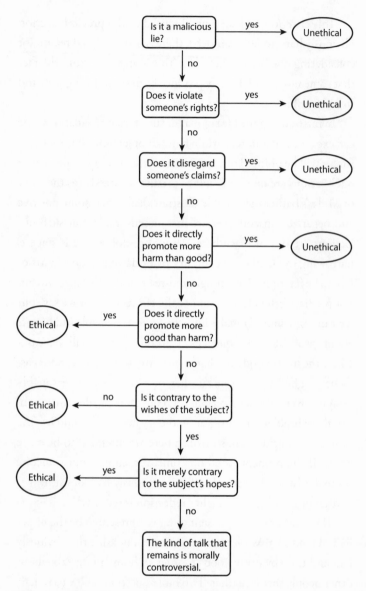

Figure 2.1. Eliminating talk that is morally uncontroversial

Talk not contrary to the wishes
of the person being talked about

Most actions we deem wrong are clearly contrary to someone's wishes.[6] If what I say is not judged wrong according to norms already considered, and if I may reasonably assume it doesn't go against the wishes of the person being talked about, then it is hard to see what objection there could be to it. Such talk can therefore be declared morally acceptable. This declaration of innocence in fact covers the bulk of our conversation about other people. Which restaurant Jake went to last night; which college he attended; what kind of car he drives: we talk without qualms about such matters because we assume that Jake would have no objection. Before we move on to consider talk that does not pass this test, however, two qualifications are in order.

First, at this point in our deliberations we should allow the wishes of the dead to have as much weight as the wishes of the living. A person's death often lessens our concern for her wishes (although in some cases it can intensify this concern). But few of us would defend the extreme position that once a person is dead, her wishes count for nothing; most of us acknowledge some obligation to respect the wishes of the dead—or at least some of the dead. Later on we can take into account the way our sense of obligation seems to diminish with the passage of time.

Second, it might be objected that there are situations in which, although the person being discussed is comfortable with what is said, some third party may not be. For example, Jake may not mind in the least my telling Adam that he is gay, or that he has converted to Catholicism, or that he has served time for knifing someone; but his father might be deeply ashamed of him on these counts. Such talk might thus be held objectionable, even though it does not contradict Jake's wishes, since it is contrary to the wishes of some other person.

This objection raises some complicated issues. Possibly we might want to make exceptions to the general rule when, because we are especially close to the person whose wishes are contradicted, the claims of loyalty command our silence. Putting aside the possibility of such exceptions, however, we can deal with the problem in the following way. If the connection between Jake and the third party is very close (for example, if he is Jake's father), and if Adam knows Jake's father, then in some sense the gossip about Jake is also about the father. This would be more apparent in a less individualistic culture than our own: for example, a culture where the reputation individuals enjoy is closely tied to the reputation of those around them. In these circumstances the gossip would be contrary to the wishes of one of its subjects and so cannot at this point be deemed acceptable. If, however, the person whose wishes are contradicted is not closely associated with Jake, or if Adam does not know that person—which is to say he does not really perceive Jake as connected to that person—then the wishes of the person in question may be ignored. To rule otherwise would be to put our conversations about people under excessive constraints. For instance, we would be obliged to worry about the wishes of all the admirers—and detractors, for that matter—of any public figure whom we wished to discuss, and that would be absurd. The fact that *you* hate the idea of anyone's saying anything that damages the reputation of Lady Gaga is hardly a reason for two other people to put fetters on their conversation.

Talk merely contrary to the hopes
of the person talked about

We have declared talk not contrary to another person's wishes to be unobjectionable. However, actions that *are* contrary to someone's wishes form a spectrum ranging from the highly objectionable to the perfectly acceptable. At the highly objectionable end are acts that violate a person's rights. Next to these come acts that disregard someone's legitimate claims. Talk falling into either of these categories has already been ruled out. At the other end of the spectrum are acts that, while contravening a person's wishes, would be acknowledged by that person to be warranted according to generally accepted conventions. For example, hitting a home run, asking a high price for one's house, or voting for a certain candidate in an election: these actions contravene respectively the wishes of the pitcher, the buyer, and the rival candidate. The conventions in question are rarely explicitly articulated, but their presence in many situations is apparent. Since the expression "contrary to a person's wishes but acknowledged by that person to be justifiable according to generally accepted conventions" is a rather unmemorable mouthful, I will refer to acts that meet this description as being contrary to a person's "hopes."

Grasping social conventions of this sort is an important part of growing up. It is because young children have not grasped them that they do not distinguish between acts that are merely contrary to their "hopes" and acts that contravene their wishes in such a way as to give them legitimate grounds for complaint. Thus small children are likely to be equally outraged whether you beat them at cards or steal their ice cream. Both actions will be immediately denounced as "not fair!" Furthermore, we tend to recognize these conventions from some perspectives but not others. Parents regularly talk to one another about their teenage children. The teenagers may well object strenuously to having their affairs discussed, but most of the time their wishes will be blithely ignored. Indeed, this is one of the things the teenagers continually complain about to their friends—quite unconcerned about whether their parents wish to be discussed critically by a group of teens.

We can now narrow our domain one more time by asking whether the talk in question, although contrary to someone's wishes, merely goes against her hopes. Examples of such talk would be expressing a low opinion of work that a person has presented to the public, criticizing the position of a rival candidate in an election, or writing a negative annual review of a subordinate's job performance.[7] If what we say falls into this category, then it is morally acceptable. If not, then its moral acceptability remains undetermined by any of the criteria we have applied so far and is therefore likely to be a matter of controversy.

Our focus from this point on is confined to the kind of talk that is not filtered out by any of the preceding considerations: that is, talk about another person that contains no malicious or self-serving lies, does not violate anyone's rights, does not disregard anyone's legitimate claims, cannot be either justified or condemned on straightforward utilitarian grounds, is contrary to the person's wishes but not merely contrary to their hopes. For simplicity's sake, unless a different meaning is indicated I will henceforth use the term "gossip" to refer solely to talk that meets this description. The process of elimination that has allowed us to define the term "gossip" in this restricted sense is illustrated by the decision tree in figure 2.1.

This is an appropriate juncture to take note of the fact that the advent of the Internet and, with it, the blogosphere, social network Web sites, and a range of technologies that allow instantaneous dissemination of information to the world, is forcing us to think hard about the norms that should govern how we talk about others.[8] For the Internet changes some of the variables. A comment on a blog intended for a few can suddenly be read by millions. A statement once made may be impossible to remove from the blogosphere or even effectively retract (although we might note that almost three thousand years ago Hesiod complained that "talk is mischievous, light, and easily raised, but hard to bear and difficult to be rid of. Talk never wholly dies away when many people voice her").[9] Given the speed with which digital information can be spread and the potential size of the audience, the consequences for both the sources and the subjects of whatever is published can be huge. Without question, the Internet has lowered the privacy threshold: those who have grown up with it tend to be much more comfortable than their elders about making public the intimate details of their lives.

Yet the sort of principles we have been invoking still seem reasonable and applicable, even when the "talk" in question is a blog posting rather than a coffeehouse conversation. For example, there are countless tales of individuals who have suffered because someone has posted false information about them on a Web site. In these cases, if the falsehood was willful almost everyone will condemn it as a lie, just as they would if it was told in a face-to-face conversation. If it was an honest mistake, then the perpetrator will be condemned less severely, but essentially the same considerations that we invoked earlier will come into play. How reasonable is the belief that was broadcast? How damaging is it to the subject's reputation? Clearly, the nature of the Internet means that the potential harm is very great. Overnight a person can become a laughingstock or a target of vitriolic attacks from strangers. And as Daniel Solove observes, "the internet lacks the village's corrective of familiarity."[10] So it is incumbent upon us, before we post anything on the Web about anyone, to be especially sure that what we are saying is true, and to consider carefully the possible consequences of our action, regardless of whether what we say is true or false. The point here is that the moral precepts we consult are not so different. We just need to be aware that writing something on a blog is not the same as whispering in someone's ear, for the global village is very different from a real village.

Although we have managed to whittle down the field of our inquiry quite considerably, the domain that remains is still large. In fact, it contains a good deal of what we ordinarily describe as gossip. Moreover, what remains cannot be examined in the manner employed up to now. So far, we have been able to proceed more or less systematically, taking various moral considerations in an appropriate order. In doing this, we have also been able to stay close to—and perhaps to some extent vindicate—received opinion. But we can no longer proceed in this way for two reasons. First, our moral judgments about what I am now calling gossip are irreducibly complex, requiring us to weigh up many diverse considerations that defy any attempt to arrange them in order of logical priority. Second, it is no longer possible to appeal to "generally acknowledged" principles or values; for there is no general consensus in our society about whether or not such gossip is morally acceptable.

What I propose to do, therefore, is to consider in turn two possible attitudes toward what I am now calling gossip, both of which are fairly widespread. These are (a) the view that all gossip is morally objectionable; and (b) the view that all gossip is morally acceptable. I will argue that none of the arguments that might be given in support of (a) are very convincing. The case for (b) is much stronger, but this view must ultimately be judged too simplistic also. I therefore endorse a third position, (c) the view that some gossip is morally objectionable and some is morally acceptable, but with the rider that *most* gossip should be considered unobjectionable. This position is indirectly supported by the critical examination of the arguments in defense of (a) and (b), which brings to light many of the considerations that inform our judgments in particular cases and thereby reveals just how complex these judgments often have to be.

Reasons for condemning all gossip

Condemnation of badmouthing others goes back a long way.[11] Moses told the children of Israel, "Do not go up and down as a talebearer among your people,"[12] although, as Joseph Telushkin remarks, this is probably the least observed of all the Torah's 613 commandments.[13] Nevertheless, it is still quite common to encounter the view that all, or almost all, gossiping (using the term in its unanalyzed sense) is objectionable. People who take this line might accept the qualifications introduced above that specify when talk about others is permissible (for instance, when it is contrary to no one's wishes). But in the absence of these they issue a blanket condemnation that takes in all of what we are now referring to as gossip. This attitude is by no means perverse. There are several arguments that can be given in support of it, most of which appeal to tenets and values embedded in our moral culture. But neither by themselves nor collectively are these sufficient to justify the position in question. Here, I will examine what I take to be the strongest of these arguments.

When I gossip, I cannot sincerely
universalize the rule I am following

This, of course, is the sort of thinking advocated by Kant. Whenever I act, according to Kant, I am following a maxim or rule. For instance, if I buy nonorganic rather than organic apples because they are cheaper, I am acting on the maxim that financial considerations may decide which food I buy. To universalize a maxim is to imagine it as a rule that everyone unfailingly follows. Kant argues that if I act on a maxim I cannot universalize, a kind of contradiction is generated. If, for instance, I steal rather than work for a living, then I am doing something that would be impossible were everyone to follow suit. The contradiction thus generated reveals that my behavior is irrational.[14]

It is hard to see, though, how this kind of argument rules out gossiping. When I gossip to you about Eve, I follow the maxim that it is morally acceptable to talk about other people (provided that I am not telling willful lies, violating rights, disregarding legitimate claims or clearly causing harm—these having already been excluded from the sense of "gossip" being used here). Could I universalize this maxim without inconsistency? It is hard to see a problem here. One can imagine quite easily how it would be were everyone to gossip; indeed, large numbers of people do gossip pretty freely and the world still turns. A world full of gossips is thus possible; nor is there any obvious reason why I could not sincerely wish to inhabit such a world.

When I gossip, I do to others what
I would not want them to do to me

The strict Kantian argument may not be appropriate or persuasive in this case; nevertheless, underlying it is the objection to gossip that immediately springs to many minds: I would not want others to gossip about me; therefore I should not gossip about them. For if I gossip about them, I contravene the Golden Rule: Do as you would be done by.

There are several reasons for not accepting this as a conclusive argument against gossiping in general.

First, it is not obvious how the Golden Rule should be applied since the rule itself does not tell us *whose* wishes should take priority. If I decide not to tell Adam something detrimental to Jake's reputation, then I am perhaps acting toward Jake as I would wish him to act toward me. But since Adam is just dying to hear what I know about Jake, in refusing to spill the beans I am going against Adam's wishes. Thus with respect to Adam I am breaking the Golden Rule, for if I were in his shoes, I would want to be told. Clearly, some principle other than the Golden Rule has to be introduced here to justify upholding the rule in relation to one person rather than another.

Second, we cannot apply the Golden Rule without further specifying *which* wishes should be taken into account. The distinction introduced earlier between acting against another's wishes and merely going against his hopes makes this very point. If I dash someone's hopes—as when I score a winning goal, or reject an article—I am violating the Golden Rule, taken literally and without qualification; but that does not mean I am necessarily doing anything wrong. The same general point can also be made on slightly different grounds. Let us suppose I am the type of person who likes to be challenged aggressively in a discussion. I therefore challenge my interlocutors aggressively, reducing them to tears in the process. In this case I may be at fault, yet in the most obvious sense I am doing to others as I would have them do to me. Similarly, although many people do not like to be talked about in a way that damages their public reputation, some may not mind, agreeing with Oscar Wilde that "there is only one thing in the world worse than being talked about, and that is not being talked about."

The natural response to this line of reasoning by defenders of the Golden Rule is to describe the action in more general terms so that it becomes something the agent clearly would not like. Thus I may enjoy being aggressively challenged, but I do not like being made to feel weak, anxious, and fearful; therefore I should refrain from acts that produce such feelings in others. But this response effectively defends the Golden Rule by appealing to a simpler principle: Don't do to others what they don't like—or, in other words, Don't act contrary to people's wishes. This principle, as we have already seen, cannot be accepted unconditionally. Moreover, appealing to it to condemn gossip is not much of an argument. After all, according to our definition, gossip is *always* contrary to someone's assumed wishes. To assume that it must therefore be always wrong is thus a dogmatic move unless further arguments for affirming the principle are forthcoming.

So a simple invocation of the Golden Rule does not justify declaring all gossip to be objectionable. The Golden Rule is certainly embedded in our ethical culture—so much so that it is one of the first principles we consult when confronted with a moral dilemma. But it can be applied only in conjunction with other moral principles. Furthermore, we often consult it merely as a pragmatic rule of thumb rather than as an imperative that carries its own authority. Since human beings are similar in so many ways, considering our own preferences is often a reasonable way of deciding what other people's wishes are likely to be. But if we did not already think there was something wrong with going against a person's wishes in certain situations, the Golden Rule would be otiose.

To this the critics of gossip might respond that even if the Golden Rule is not so fundamental a tenet as is often thought, the general principle underlying it is nonetheless sound. And that principle is, simply, Don't act contrary to people's wishes without good reason. Now, the analysis undertaken so far has indicated several kinds of valid reasons for acting against someone's wishes: for instance, where doing so would be contrary only to what I called their hopes, or where doing so would probably promote some significant good. But in the case of morally controversial talk about others—gossip as defined above—these justifications are lacking. Therefore, the imperative not to contradict people's wishes without good reason holds sway here. And as for justifying this principle further, what does one need to say except that the reason for not going against people's wishes is that they don't like it!

There are three reasons for not accepting this argument as conclusive. First, it does nothing to overcome the problem of determining whose wishes and which wishes are more deserving of consideration. Second, as I shall argue later, most gossip can be justified on utilitarian grounds that we have not yet considered: that is, by reference to the pleasure experienced by those who gossip, or by the many goods promoted in subtle and indirect ways by the social practice of gossiping. In other words, we have not yet exhausted the "good reasons" that can justify acting contrary to another's wishes.

Third, there is a case for viewing much of what we are calling gossip as falling under the rubric of being merely contrary to the "hopes" of the person being talked about. What this means, it will be recalled, is that although contrary to that person's wishes, the action would be acknowledged by her to be justifiable according to generally accepted conventions, as when a reviewer criticizes an author's book. Now I would argue that in our culture a good deal of gossip can be legitimized in this way. Few of us want to be gossiped about. But we accept that this is going to happen, and this knowledge influences both our conduct and our willingness to gossip about others. Sometimes these forms of communication even enjoy a semi-institutionalized status. For example, how do my colleagues find out whether or not I am a good teacher? Primarily, perhaps, by institutionalized methods: sitting in on classes, reading student and peer evaluations, reviewing my syllabi, and so on. But what they hear off the record, from colleagues, students, former students, friends of students, parents of students, and the like, also influences their opinion— and rightly so. If these people pass along critical opinions about my teaching, they certainly act against my wishes. But I cannot honestly say that in doing so they are behaving unethically. As I do my work, I am fully aware—indeed I expect—that people will talk about how good a job I am doing. And when I, in turn, discuss the quality of another person's work, I participate in the same social practice. Earlier, we situated gossip between disregarding someone's legitimate claims and merely going against his hopes. What I am now suggesting is that the latter category may extend further than at first appeared. Thus a good deal of what we have called gossip should be seen as more similar to the act of writing a negative book review than to the act of betraying a secret.

Our acknowledgment of these unwritten conventions that render gossip permissible is perhaps most apparent when we feel that the person we are discussing *deserves* to be the subject of critical opinions. If a professor repeatedly makes passes at or has affairs with his teaching assistants, he can expect to be gossiped about. We usually feel less compunction about communicating this sort of information to others than we would about passing along news of some other aspect of his life for which he is not considered responsible: for example, the fact that his father was a criminal. Our relative lack of compunction is due, at least in part, to the thought that being gossiped about is part of the price one pays—and deserves to pay—for acting unethically. It is thus a penalty that we would expect to pay ourselves—and so might ruefully accept—if we acted in the same way.

The above considerations are all intended to reinforce the point that appealing to the Golden Rule is not sufficient to exclude as unethical all, or even most, of what we are calling gossip.

When I gossip, I treat another person
purely as a means to my own ends

This argument rests on the widely accepted Kantian principle that we have an obligation to respect the autonomy of all human beings; we should therefore never treat them merely as means to our own ends. Gossiping, it might be said, violates this principle because when I talk about someone in a way that ignores her wishes, often with no other goal than to enjoy the immediate pleasure gossiping brings, I am using that person for my own purposes. To that extent I am failing to treat her with respect.

Engaging in gossip (as we have defined it) certainly involves acting contrary to another person's wishes. But that is not quite the same thing as "ignoring" his wishes. It would be more accurate, I believe, to say in most cases that his wishes are *overridden* by other considerations. Proof of this is the fact that in different circumstances we can feel more or less compunction about going against his wishes. For example, where we are close to the person and know him to have a particularly intense distaste for having a certain matter—one for which he is in no way responsible—discussed by others, we might well choose to refrain from gossiping. This indicates that we are not usually oblivious to the wishes of those we talk about; we keep their wishes in mind but may not give them much weight.

That is one reason for rejecting the argument from the "ends principle." There is a stronger objection to it, though, which is simply that it involves a strange, misguided description of what is going on in most instances of gossip. Just because I act contrary to someone's wishes does not mean that I am undermining her autonomy or failing to respect her rationality. This is an appropriate way to describe actions where I manipulate another person by force, threats, or deception. If I borrow money from you and don't pay you back, I am using you. Had you known you wouldn't be repaid, you might have decided not to lend me anything. My deception thus undermined your rational decision-making process. This is the sense in which it fails to respect your autonomy. But gossip need have no effect on its subject. Your behavior may be the occasion for a conversation about you; but the people having that conversation are not doing anything that impinges on your rationality. So to call it a violation of the ends principle is credible only if we stretch that principle beyond the point where it can maintain its prima facie plausibility. Possibly some gossip should be condemned from the standpoint of the ends principle; but it is hard to see how all, or even most, of it could be.

When I gossip, I damage someone's reputation,
which constitutes a tangible harm

This argument rests on a certain view of reputation, a view endorsed by the Duke of Norfolk in Shakespeare's *Richard II*:

The purest treasure mortal times afford
Is spotless reputation; that away,
Men are but gilded loam or painted clay.[15]

Now there is no doubt that damage to a person's reputation can be accompanied by other harms such as loss of job, loss of privileges, loss of friends, disrespectful treatment by others, and so on. These are tangible harms that are *experienced* as such by an individual; they should therefore figure in any utilitarian calculation regarding the rightness of saying something detrimental to someone's reputation. As consequences of gossip, however, such harms may be offset by other good consequences. For example, my revelation to Adam that Jake is cheating on his spouse may lead him to be cold-shouldered by some; but this may, in turn, act as a deterrent to other would-be adulterers, thereby producing more good than harm overall.

More fundamentally, though, I would deny that Jake's loss of reputation in Adam's eyes, *abstracted from any sufferings that this leads to on Jake's part*, should be considered a tangible harm. The reason is simple: it is not something that is experienced; it is not *suffered*.[16] Of course, it is quite possible that Jake will come to suffer from the knowledge that Adam has a lower opinion of him. But that will be the result of some further action: a change in Adam's demeanor toward him, or his being told (by Adam or someone else) that Adam now knows the truth about him. In itself, another person's opinion of one is neither good nor bad.[17]

Of course, not everyone will agree that only what is experienced by someone should count as tangibly good or bad. But leaving aside the problem of *why* we should accord a value to something independent of anyone's experiences, such critics must still concede that in that case there can be other nonexperienced tangible goods, such as knowing the truth. It is easy to see the instrumental value of truth; correct beliefs help us cope with the world more effectively. Just why we should regard the holding of true beliefs as *intrinsically* valuable is no clearer than why we should regard loss of reputation in someone else's eyes as intrinsically bad. But anyone who insists that Adam's lower opinion of Jake constitutes, in itself, a real harm, should also recognize that Adam's coming to have a truer opinion about Jake can be viewed, in itself, as a tangible good.

Gossiping is spiritually unhealthy

The term "spiritually unhealthy" is not entirely satisfactory since it carries religious or metaphysical connotations that are not intended. But the basic idea is simply that certain habits and practices are bad for one's psychic and moral health in the same way that smoking or eating too much junk food are bad for one's physical health. Gossip, on this view, is not unethical in the sense of violating some principle that ought to govern one's dealings with other people. Rather, it is criticized as an activity that does not belong to an ideally good or beautiful life, and which, if indulged in, can become a habit that pulls one away from that ideal.

Why, exactly, would gossiping not be part of the good life? Two reasons might be given to support this claim. A weak reason would be that gossiping is a waste of time, like watching too much television. People who stand around talking about others all day long leave little time for more valuable occupations. This is a weak argument because it is not really an objection to gossiping as such (and certainly not to gossip as more narrowly defined above). The fact that some people watch too much television hardly proves that no one should watch any. And the fact that some people spend more time than is good for them gossiping is no ground for condemning all gossip. Really, what is being criticized here is shallow living—something we are continually discovering new ways to achieve. But there is no reason to suppose that engaging in gossip is at odds with the attempt to live less superficially. On the contrary, since one of the benefits gossip can bring is a deeper understanding of human nature and social institutions (see below), it is more plausible to think that a willingness to talk about people—which at times will involve gossiping—may be an integral part of the "examined life." This is why we find Socrates, in Platonic dialogues like the *Meno* and the *Gorgias*, freely discussing the failings of others in the course of his philosophical inquiries.

A deeper reason we might have for viewing gossip as a spiritually unhealthy practice is that we conceive of the ideally good or beautiful life as one free from any trace of maliciousness, schadenfreude, or pleasure taken in someone else's failings. Moral purity of this kind is one of the hallmarks of the saint. In addition, the saintly ideal is characterized by utter selflessness: a preference for suffering harm rather than inflicting it, and a willingness to sacrifice one's own pleasures and interests rather than oppose those of another. Since gossip is quite often accompanied by a feeling of pleasure in another's misfortune, and since, by definition, it involves acting against that person's wishes, to engage in gossip is to fall short of this ideal.

The image of saintliness sketched here is undeniably one of the ideals that has shaped our present moral outlook. But, as has often been pointed out, the ideal is in some ways paradoxical, and it does not compel unqualified admiration. It is paradoxical because, although the life of the saint exhibits extreme selflessness in one sense, it can also be viewed as thoroughly self-centered. The quest for personal purity, while it directs us toward selfless conduct, is not necessarily a selfless enterprise. And the ideal is not compelling because the saint, even when devoted to the welfare of others, is something of a social misfit. Dostoyevsky's "idiot," Prince Myshkin, illustrates this point perfectly. He has the personality of a saint; but for that very reason he struggles to fit into the social world; and his interventions, although intended to help others, often have unfortunate consequences.

The saint is an otherworldly figure, drawn toward the cloister or the cave. Part of us respects the saintly ideal of inner purity; but part of us scorns it—and rightly so. For we are social beings, and perhaps more than anything else in the world we like to think and talk about ourselves and each other. An ethic that places impossible constraints on one of our favorite activities is misguided because it cuts too much against the grain of human nature as this finds expression in our own culture and in most others. The saint represents one ideal of the good life. But it is only one such ideal; there are many others. And while simplicity, innocence, and purity certainly have a strong nostalgic appeal, the saintly life achieves these at the risk of being less rich, complex, active, adventurous, challenging—one might say less human—than alternative ideals.[18]

Gossiping is wrong because other people's
private affairs are none of my business

This is perhaps the most common argument put forward by
those who feel an instinctive distaste for all gossip. But it is not
the sort of argument that can withstand much critical scrutiny.
Why aren't other people's so-called private affairs my business?
The assertion that they are not could, of course, be made true
by definition: "private" means my business, not yours! But this
settles nothing. Defenders of gossip can simply deny that what is
being called "private" should be classified as such.

On the other hand, if it is not a mere truism, the claim that
a person's private affairs are no one else's business can be challenged. Exactly where, and on what grounds, do we draw the line
between what is and what is not my business? Why doesn't the
simple fact that I am interested in something make it my business? Still more fundamentally, what makes it wrong for me
to talk about something that is, for whatever reason, "not my
business"? Such questions raise doubts about the possibility of
elucidating in a useful way the notion of something's being "my
business." And they also lead one to suspect that the elucida-
tion would quickly boil down to one of the objections already
discussed: for instance, that gossiping involves acting contrary
to another's wishes (which we already know), or that discussing
people in a manner that is contrary to their wishes is spiritually
unhealthy.

Still, those sympathetic to the "none-of-your-business" objection might try to support it by claiming that to gossip about others is to violate their right to privacy. And since we ruled out early
on all actions that violate a person's rights, we should therefore

declare unethical all of what we are now calling gossip. The problem with this argument, of course, is that the key claim—gossip violates a person's right to privacy—is highly controversial. What we ruled out of court earlier was any action that violates a person's *generally acknowledged* rights. It may be conceded that some sort of right to privacy is generally recognized in our culture; it is certainly recognized in law. But there is no consensus over what constitutes a violation of that right. And the claim that to gossip about someone (in the sense defined earlier) infringes on her right to privacy is a very difficult claim to support. Such a claim, in essence, asserts that we have a right to not have certain aspects of our lives discussed by others. But it is hard to see what the basis for this supposed right could be.

We have considered six reasons for issuing a blanket condemnation of the kind of morally controversial talk that falls into the category we designated "gossip." Some of these objections to gossip deserve to be taken more seriously than others, and do, to be sure, raise legitimate concerns. But none are powerful enough—taken singly or in combination—to justify a taboo against all such talk. In fact, as we will see, the arguments for bringing gossip out from under its traditional cloud of moral suspicion, taken together, carry considerably more weight.

Reasons for countenancing all gossip

Given that there is no single reason or set of reasons for condemning all gossip, it is worth asking whether there are grounds for declaring it all morally acceptable. Here, too, we will find that the arguments are not sufficient to support such a sweeping conclusion. So much is perhaps predictable. What is less predictable, though, is that once one starts to consider the utilitarian arguments for countenancing gossip, it becomes apparent that, by and large, there is far more to be said for it than against it.

One nonutilitarian argument for sanctioning gossip is simply that it does not, given our definition, violate anyone's rights. The argument obviously rests on the general premise that whatever does not violate a person's rights is morally acceptable. This kind of thinking, often associated with libertarianism, has its advocates. But it surely rests on an impoverished conception of morality. The concept of rights, even if it is extended to include what we earlier called "claims," simply is not rich enough to serve as the sole marker dividing permissible from impermissible behavior. It is possible publicly to humiliate a person for no particularly good reason without violating that person's rights. An ethical theory that saw nothing wrong in this would be suspiciously at odds with some of our fundamental values.

A much more plausible defense of gossip can be mounted on utilitarian grounds. Earlier, when setting aside what we judged to be morally uncontroversial talk about others, we applied, among other criteria, crude utilitarian considerations. Talk expected to produce more harm than good was declared unethical; talk thought likely to produce more good than harm was deemed morally acceptable (provided certain basic principles were not violated). At that stage of the argument, however, we were considering only consequences of a certain kind—namely, specific events, situations, or experiences (not counting any immediate pleasure experienced by the speakers) that the talk in question has played a major and fairly obvious causal role in bringing about. We excluded from consideration the immediate pleasure felt by those engaging in gossip. This was to avoid assuming from the outset that critics of gossip who believe that such pleasures should carry no weight whatsoever are wrong. And we ignored, also, the possible indirect social benefits promoted by gossip because these, too, are controversial and therefore could not be appropriately introduced at a stage where we were merely trying to eliminate the uncontroversial. It is now time to take these further goods into account.

Immediate pleasures experienced
by those engaging in gossip

Gossiping can give rise to various kinds of pleasure. Here I will briefly identify what I take to be the most important. Obviously, many of these overlap and are interrelated.

Schadenfreude: We often experience a degree of malicious pleasure in someone else's failings or misfortunes.

Smugness: Discussing another person's failings or misfortunes can produce a smug sense of self-satisfaction at one's own comparative virtue, abilities, or wisdom.

A feeling of power: To know something detrimental to the reputation[19] of another person gives one a sense of power, both over the person concerned and in relation to those who are not yet in the know. Releasing this knowledge momentarily heightens this feeling. This is why many of us enjoy being the one able to relate the information, why we sometimes hold back from discharging it as soon as possible, and why the pleasure of disseminating the news is in proportion to the size of our audience.

Titillation: Gossiping can be titillating because of the subject matter, which often relates to such inherently interesting topics as sex, money, or power. But in many cases its power to titillate stems more from the fact that we are discussing aspects of a person's life that, by convention, are kept secret. The gossiper may, in this respect, be plausibly compared to the voyeur. Knowing what one is not supposed to know, and talking about things one is not supposed to talk about, are, in themselves, strangely exciting. Of course, if we were less puritanical, less concerned with personal privacy, and less suspicious of gossip in the first place, this aspect of gossip's pleasurableness would largely evaporate. As with sex, it would perhaps be better if we did not have so many neurotic hang-ups about it, but the fact that we do have these hang-ups gives rise to kinds of pleasure we would not otherwise experience.

Catharsis: Gossip undoubtedly can have a cathartic function, providing a release for negative feelings such as anger, frustration, bitterness, envy, or resentment. This in itself can ease the painful tension characteristic of such states, a tension that, if not reduced in some way, might well have a corrosive effect on our own spiritual health and happiness.[20] This is an additional point to be made against the argument considered above that engaging in gossip is a spiritually unhealthy practice. It is important to bear in mind, here, that we are not just talking about simply "bad-mouthing" people—that is, expressing strongly critical opinions of their character, work, or behavior. We are also talking about passing on information about them. In some situations, of course, to do this may well have devastating consequences for the person concerned or for others. But let it be recalled that talk likely to produce significantly more pain than pleasure has already been excluded from our purview. Given these qualifications, the cathartic function of gossip can be given its due weight. This may not be all that great (although it can be, as the story of Midas's barber makes clear). But alternative ways of working out one's negative feelings toward others are, on the whole, less appealing.

Chapter 2

People are an especially interesting topic of conversation: For most people the world over, conversation is one of the most enjoyable and rewarding recreational activities. This is true even when the subject matter is something other than people. But of all the things we like to talk about, human beings—their character, conduct, and relationships—surely rank as the most interesting to us. This is proved by the fact that we spend more time discussing people than anything else.

Of course, we've all heard it said that "bright people talk about ideas, mediocre people talk about things, and small people talk about people." But there is no particular reason to think this adage true. On the contrary, to not be curious about one's fellow human beings could more reasonably be viewed as a species of dullness, akin to having no interest in science or the arts. As to why people interest us so much, the reasons are many: they can have a massive effect on our lives; they are uniquely complex; they are neither completely predictable nor completely unpredictable; they are to some degree mysterious; and probably, most important of all, they are like ourselves, which means that whenever we talk about other people, we are, in some sense and to some extent, talking about ourselves.[21]

Solving mysteries: As was just noted, one reason people are interesting is that they present us with something mysterious. This is true even of so-called simple souls. All we can observe is their behavior, including their linguistic behavior. What we desire is an explanation of this behavior in terms of beliefs, feelings, motives, and intentions. Being able to explain it is both satisfying in itself and useful in helping us to better anticipate their future actions, an ability we value for obvious reasons.

Most of the time, of course, we feel that we do have an adequate explanation in hand. If a friend starts test-driving new cars, and we happen to know that her present car is old, unreliable, and in need of expensive repairs, an obvious and satisfactory explanation of her behavior presents itself. But if she begins to dress differently, or make regular trips to another town, or turn down all social invitations, or spend money with unaccustomed extravagance, or behave with uncharacteristic coldness toward us, then we naturally look for an explanation. Some will say this desire for an explanation is sheer nosiness, but even they must confess that it is entirely natural. What makes the new behavior pattern mysterious is the fact that it cannot be explained on the basis of our present knowledge. We therefore need further information; and the most likely way of obtaining this information, if the horse's mouth is unforthcoming, is usually through conversation with other people. Exchanging such information need not, of course, be morally controversial. But sometimes it can be, particularly if it concerns an aspect of a person's behavior about which the person is secretive. In such cases gossip can render the opaque more clear and thereby afford us a particular and uniquely human kind of pleasure.

Learning is enjoyable: As Aristotle remarks, the desire to know is part of human nature. Satisfying this desire is therefore an important source of pleasure. Obviously, we are not equally interested in all kinds of knowledge, and a mass of trivial information about other people, even private information about our acquaintances, would bore most of us. But achieving a better understanding of the character, motives, actions, and relationships of someone we know—whether it be an acquaintance or a public figure—is something most of us desire, as is a deeper understanding of human beings in general. And gossip is indispensable to our achieving such insight. When we learn that an apparently happy marriage is on the rocks, that a respected figure is abusive to his family, that a moral evangelist is a spendthrift, or that a sober citizen goes on periodic benders, we are conscious of attaining a shrewder insight into human character. A better understanding of people is arguably one of the benefits and one of the pleasures brought by advancing years. But it is hard to see how it would be possible without a willingness to discuss people in a way that goes behind the appearances and, in many cases, against their wishes.

Now it has to be admitted up front that the nature of some of the pleasures just described is ethically dubious according to conventional norms. We are generally critical of schadenfreude, smugness, or taking delight in one's power over others, and it is easy to see why. We view individuals for whom these are major sources of pleasure as excessively egoistic. They cannot be trusted to have the spontaneous concern for the welfare of others, especially those close to them, that makes for good friends and loving relationships. It could be argued, therefore, that these "guilty" pleasures are offset by the disutility promoted by the personalities of those who enjoy them to excess. But there is no obvious reason to view the other pleasures mentioned in an unfavorable light. On the contrary, since people who enjoy these pleasures are likely to understand themselves and others better, they are also more likely to be sympathetic and valuable companions. A healthy interest in our fellow human beings is thus, to use one of Hume's categories, a quality that is useful to both ourselves and others.[22] Besides, all things being equal, we should be grateful for the opportunities for pleasure that life offers us, not have a bad conscience about them. Talking to people about people is one of these. To refrain from it for fear of moral corruption is a form of moral neurosis.

An extreme expression of this neurotic attitude is the Talmudic precept "Don't speak well of your friend, for although you will start with his good traits, the discussion might turn to his bad traits."[23] It is hard to imagine how anyone could think the world would be a better place if we all eschewed even favorable comments about one another. But perhaps the precept was offered tongue in cheek. After all, elsewhere the Talmud tells us that one day "we will be held accountable for all the permitted pleasures we failed to enjoy."

Goods promoted indirectly by gossip

In addition to the immediate pleasure experienced by those engaging in gossip, there are a number of other important goods, generally of a social rather than personal nature, that the practice of gossiping helps to promote.[24] These include the following.

Gossip improves our understanding of social reality

As noted above, most of us are to some extent engaged in the ongoing project of trying to better our understanding of the world we live in. A particularly important and interesting part of that world involves other people, interpersonal relationships, and the social institutions within which these relationships are embedded. False impressions about individuals, their character, motivations, interests, actions, and relationships are like false data to a researcher. One important function that gossip can and often does serve is to correct false impressions, thereby making people and social phenomena in general more comprehensible. It is through gossiping that we test our own interpretation of people's behavior, finding out whether others see things as we do or differently. A better understanding of these things is valuable both in itself and for the further benefits it brings.[25]

But paradoxically, given its reputation, gossip also facilitates moral reflection. Most people naturally think in concrete rather than abstract terms. They are less likely to ask whether the maxim of an action can be universalized, and more likely to ask whether Jake's behavior yesterday is comparable to Melissa's last week. This is why the most effective moral teaching has often been presented through parables and fables where issues are given specificity. So granting ourselves some license to talk about others, including their virtues and vices, carries this benefit also.

Gossip facilitates the operation of social institutions

This is probably the most important good resulting from the insights into our social reality that gossip provides. Indeed, it is no exaggeration to say that many complex social institutions could scarcely function without gossip. Consider, for instance, a university. For the university to function, faculty and administrators must work reasonably well with each other. Inevitably, though, situations arise in which the faculty would like to understand more fully than they do administrative decisions that affect them. Why did this person resign? Why was that person fired? Is the dean looking for another job? What does the provost think of the dean? Is the president respected by the board of trustees? Simply reading the official memos put out by administrators is not always going to yield adequate insight into what is going on. Yet this is not necessarily because the administrative bureaucracy is pathologically secretive. Sometimes—quite often in fact—it is just inappropriate to broadcast certain information. The fact that two deans have an unreasonable antipathy toward one another would not be openly stated in an official memo. If someone expressed this view at a meeting it would be unlikely to appear in the minutes. But this fact perhaps needs to be known and taken into account by faculty and administrators who have to make decisions affecting academic programs, curricula, intercollegiate relations, or individual careers. It is important to stress that what is at stake here is not simply whether or not a person's desire to know is satisfied. People *need* to know certain things if they are to make rational, informed decisions. And if the official channels do not provide the information they need, then they must obtain it through unofficial channels, by far the most important of which is gossip.

Gossip counteracts secrecy

King Midas understandably did not want his subjects to learn about his ass's ears: they signified that he was a fool. But the people have a legitimate interest in knowing whether their rulers are foolish or wise. From their point of view, the barber performed a public service when he let out the king's secret. This conflict of interests between the many and the few can be found in every hierarchical society.

The ideal of a world without secrecy, in which everyone's circumstances, relationships, actions, and motives are open to the scrutiny of all, is neither realizable nor desirable. But in the world as it is, secrecy, particularly on the part of those in power, is often excessive and objectionable. The instinctive self-interest of the rich and powerful warns them that it is often against their interests for the exact extent, nature, origin, and uses of their wealth to be public knowledge. And in so many of our social institutions, both public and private, there is a widespread and often reprehensible tendency for management to withhold information from those working under them—a strategy that helps to exclude the latter group from participation in decision making and puts them at a disadvantage when they are allowed to participate. Insofar as gossip helps to counteract this sort of secrecy, it can be a useful, even essential instrument for resisting entrenched systems of power and domination. Of course, those who wield power will also make use of gossip; the files of J. Edgar Hoover offer a spectacular illustration of this. But in general, the dissemination of information about such things as salary discrepancies, bonuses, executive perks, kickbacks, nepotism, vested interests, conflicts of interest, and so forth, benefits the powerless more than the powerful for the obvious reason that the former have less to hide.[26]

Gossip helps enforce social mores

People who transgress a community's norms and conventions are likely to be the subject of much critical conversation. Knowledge of this fact deters many would-be transgressors. Of course, the threat of legally enforced penalties, or socially imposed penalties such as ostracism, is often more powerful. But shame, or the prospect of shame, can exert considerable pressure on most people, as can the simple desire to be spoken of well rather than ill. If gossip were rare or unknown in our community, these fears and desires would naturally have less motivating force.

Obviously, though, enforcing a society's mores is not always a good thing. It all depends on the mores in question. Knowing that one's behavior will be critically discussed by others may have deterred some would-be adulterers or wife-beaters. But it has also been a source of fear and anxiety for gays, partners in miscegenetic relationships, and others who act contrary to an oppressive moral orthodoxy. For this reason, we have to acknowledge that the role gossip plays in encouraging people to conform to the existing mores does not always redound to its credit, and the good that it sometimes promotes has to be weighed against the harm it can undoubtedly do.

Gossiping can foster intimacy between people

This is certainly not the most obvious of the indirect goods promoted by gossip. But given that intimacy, when desired and enjoyed by those concerned, is a good thing, it should not be overlooked. There is a kind of closeness that might result simply from sharing secrets about a third party or from common participation in a session of unrestrained criticism directed at other people. And there is, in addition, a more subtle link between gossip and intimacy. For the avoidance of gossip would place significant constraints on what one may say in conversation; and in many situations we must transgress those constraints if we are to confide in another, or have so-called heart-to-heart talks with them about things that concern us nearly. The quality of our closest and most valued friendships can thus rest upon, or at least be enhanced by, our willingness to engage in gossip.

Earlier, we argued that where talking about others does not violate anyone's rights or disregard his legitimate claims, a crude utilitarian calculation may be sufficient to justify (or condemn) such talk. To avoid assuming too much, we excluded from this initial reckoning the goods we have just considered, namely, the immediate pleasures involved in and the indirect benefits promoted by the practice of gossiping. As we have seen, these additional goods are many, varied, and significant. Taken individually, no one of them is weighty enough to constitute a sufficient reason for countenancing all gossip. But one could argue that, taken together, they tip the balance in favor of this view.

In my opinion, this is a powerful argument, but it cannot support the sweeping conclusion that all gossip is acceptable. A simple example is sufficient to illustrate the problem. Suppose I tell the audience at a conference a gratuitous piece of information about a colleague that I am sure she would prefer others not to know: for example, that she is a close relative of a notorious terrorist. The information is publicly available, so no rights or claims are being violated. The immediate and long-term consequences of my act are not such as to decide the issue: some members of the audience experience a slight thrill; my colleague experiences some discomfort. My action, being contrary to her wishes but not merely contrary to her "hopes," falls under the rubric of what we have termed gossip, and nothing we have said so far clearly rules it out as unethical. Yet most of us would unhesitatingly judge it to be morally wrong.

We need not undertake a detailed analysis of just why we would condemn such an action. Suffice it to say that there are further considerations that inform our moral judgments and complicate the process by which we arrive at them. In this case, for instance, we would presumably take into account such factors as the *degree* to which my action was contrary to my colleague's wishes, the nature of my relationship to her, whether and to what extent I owe her my loyalty, and to what extent she bears responsibility for the facts concerning her that I am relating to others. Moreover, we *ought* to take such things into account. Issues such as loyalty or desert are neither empty nor irrelevant. They are, however, "messy" and thus present difficulties for any attempt to reach neat conclusions through an oversimplified account of our moral deliberations.

The complexity of ethical judgment

The example introduced at the end of the preceding section is intended to support the view that blanket moral judgments are not possible regarding gossip as we have defined it. Sound judgment will often be complex, taking into account many considerations. We can get a better idea of just how complex and finely balanced our judgments have to be by briefly identifying some of the main considerations that guide us when we try to determine whether, in any particular instance, it is morally acceptable to gossip. The list is not exhaustive; but I believe it covers the most important variables to which we need to be sensitive in our deliberations.

- *Justice*: To what extent are the people we are speaking of responsible for the facts about them that we are discussing?
- *Seriousness*: How contrary to their wishes is our talk?
- *Motive*: What are our motives in engaging in gossip? To what extent are we motivated by a desire to inform, a need to discuss, a wish to gloat, etc.
- *Source of information*: How did we come by our information? Is it publicly available? How reliable is it?
- *Our relationship to those about whom we are talking*: How close are we to them? To what extent do they have a claim on us not to act contrary to their wishes? Interestingly, though not unnaturally, our sense of obligation toward another person is often affected by that person's death. Thus unless we are constrained by a strong sense of loyalty—the kind usually felt only toward close friends and relatives—most of us gossip cheerfully about the dead; and the longer they have been dead, the less compunc-

tion we feel, presumably because we believe it less likely that anyone (including ourselves) will suffer as a result of what we say. Certainly, contemporary scholars writing about famous individuals now deceased rarely appear to recognize any constraints at all; nor are they usually criticized for disseminating sordid, reputation-damaging details about the character and conduct of these individuals.[27] Most writers and readers appear to agree with Lytton Strachey that "discretion is not the better part of biography."

- *Our relationship to those we are talking to*: How close are we to our confabulator? How sure can we be about what this person will do with the information we impart? It is noteworthy that most of us talk much more freely about others to our partners or spouses than to anybody else. This is true even of those who are generally very critical of gossiping. In effect, we seem to allow the fact that we are talking to our partner or spouse to render us exempt from constraints we would respect were we talking to anyone else. The most plausible explanation (and partial justification) for our making this exception is that in the case of someone we know so well and whose interests are so close to our own we feel reasonably certain that our talking to them will not have unforeseen or undesirable consequences.

- *The relationship between the recipient and the subject of the gossip*: Are they acquainted? If so, what is the nature of their relationship? If not, are they ever likely to meet?

An intelligent moral judgment about whether, in a specific instance, one should gossip will have to be alert to the possible relevance of all these questions and, no doubt, many others besides.

Conclusion

Three general conclusions emerge from our inquiry. First, there is nothing *necessarily* wrong with gossip (as the term is commonly understood). Talk about others may be wrong for all kinds of reasons, as we have seen; but it may also be perfectly acceptable. Second, if the talk in question is an instance of gossip as more narrowly defined above, then it cannot ipso facto be declared either right or wrong. An irreducibly complex judgment will be required that weighs diverse claims and considerations against one another. Third, notwithstanding this last point, we should be suspicious of the censorious attitude that moralists have traditionally taken toward gossip. As we have seen, there is more to be said in its favor than is commonly appreciated, and very often more to be said for it than against it. In relation to both the individual and society it has many positive aspects that tend to be overlooked. A proper appreciation of these should make us less ready to condemn it and feel less guilty about doing it.

3 On Snobbery: Is It Sinful to Feel Superior?

Snobbery is an important topic. In the American elections of 2004 and 2008, John Kerry and Barack Obama were regularly accused of elitism by Republicans who claimed to be on the side of "Joe Six-Pack." Indeed, during the 2008 election the *Weekly Standard* ran an "Obama Snobbery Watch" to document the candidate's alleged elitist lapses. Nor was this merely a specious charge trumped up for tactical reasons by right-wingers. Serious political analysts such as CNN's John Roberts claimed that the Democrats' failure to win the White House in 2000 and 2004 was due to their being "perceived as a party of secular snobs."[1]

In everyday life also, snobbery matters. It can make a real difference, opening and closing doors, advancing or frustrating careers, breeding resentments, starting fights, and souring relationships. We are all familiar with the feeling that someone is looking down on us, and most of us respond the same way: we don't like it. But the reason we are all acquainted with this feeling is that examples of snobbery can be found just about everywhere: at the concert hall, in art galleries, and on the highway; at conventions, trade fairs, weddings, and funerals; in shops, restaurants, offices, hotels, high schools, and hospitals. There have even been rumors—unsubstantiated but persistent—of an occasional sighting in the groves of academia.

There are plenty of interesting questions to be addressed concerning snobbery. How should it be defined? What distinguishes it from other forms of prejudice or arrogance? What, exactly, is objectionable about it? Does it carry any benefits? Can we distinguish between snobbery and elitism? Are all forms of snobbery and elitism morally objectionable? Attempting to answer such questions throws light not just on snobbery itself but also on intriguing aspects of contemporary culture and the sort of changes we are currently experiencing.

Some examples of snobbery

As always, it is best to begin with the concrete, calling to mind diverse examples of the sort of thing we are taking about. Immediately it becomes obvious that there are an unlimited number of things we can use as an excuse for looking down on some of our fellow human beings. Here are a few:

- family
- education
- erudition
- occupation
- religion

- geographical origin
- nationality
- ethnicity
- sexual orientation
- property

- wealth
- fame
- influence
- social connections
- institutional associations
- age
- experience
- mode of speech
- physical appearance
- dress
- cultural attainments
- aesthetic taste
- home decor
- recreational pursuits
- vacations
- reading habits
- eating habits
- car ownership
- pets
- offspring

Just what evolutionary advantage was conferred by a tendency to one-upmanship it is hard to say; but the trait certainly seems to be widespread and deeply ingrained. It is a fair bet that if we ever do encounter aliens from outer space, it won't be long before we find ourselves casually remarking that our sun appears to be bigger, or hotter, or older than theirs.

Expressions of snobbish attitudes can be quite explicit:

"At Harvard we admit only the best and the brightest."

"Compared to Christianity, Hinduism is a rather primitive religion."

"I find it hard to take seriously the views of someone who does not know the difference between 'affect' and 'effect.'"

"Only the French palette can be trusted to identify that *je ne sais quoi* that distinguishes the truly superior wines."

"Any adult who enjoys reading comic books must suffer from arrested intellectual development."

But snobbery also manifests itself in subtler ways through the condescending assumption, the arrogant smirk, the wrinkled nose, or the supercilious inflection. The underlying thoughts may not be made explicit, but they can be inferred on the basis of a person's actions, words, or demeanor. From your detached responses and wandering eyes it becomes obvious that the instant you learned I was not a partner in the firm but merely an intern, you decided I was not worth talking to. When I describe a job candidate as "impressive, considering she graduated from a state school," I betray a certain way of thinking about educational institutions.

Of course, snobbish assumptions do not have to be downward-looking or derogatory. "She went to a private school, so she must be academically well-prepared." "He's a doctor, so I think we can trust him." Here the inferences are positive. But the compliment invariably has a complement, so to speak—in these cases, an unspoken negative implication about the products of state schools or the probable integrity of nonprofessionals.[2]

Toward a definition of snobbery

According to the *Oxford English Dictionary*, the etymology of the word "snob" is obscure. One theory takes it to be derived from the abbreviation *s. nob*. This stood for *sine nobilitate* (which, as any educated person knows, is Latin for "without nobility"). Registrars at Oxford and Cambridge, when compiling lists of students, used to write *s. nob.* next to the names of students who were not from aristocratic families. So on this account, "snob" originally denoted a person who lacked nobility, and by a rather odd inversion it eventually came to mean one who looked down on such people.

An alternative view, somewhat supported by the *OED*, is that the word originally meant a cobbler or cobbler's apprentice, and came to be used, perhaps by the "gownsmen" in Cambridge, as a slang term for any "townsman," especially one who belonged to the menial classes and lacked gentility. It then came to denote, in turn, a person whose lack of breeding and good taste is very obvious, a person who tries to boost her social standing by imitating or associating with her superiors, and, finally, one who looks down on people she views as her social or cultural inferiors.

This last meaning has become the dominant one and roughly corresponds to what we find in any contemporary dictionary. But dictionary definitions are not especially revealing; they tell us little more than how a word is used. A philosophical analysis, by contrast, seeks to unpack the concept much more thoroughly, identifying its central core and plotting its limits. And the task of constructing it can bring to light all sorts of assumptions, values, and distinctions that the concept harbors and which tell us interesting things about ourselves and our culture. This is the sort of definition aimed at here.

We typically think of snobbery as a sort of attitude. As already noted, it can be expressed explicitly, or it can be something we infer on the basis of either what people say and how they say it, or what they do and how they do it. Now attitudes are generally rather fuzzy things, hard to catch and put into a definitional bottle. But contained within, or underlying, or informing every attitude is a belief; and beliefs can be described more precisely. They can be articulated through language; they have a meaning; and they can be true or false. I therefore propose to define snobbery in terms of beliefs. Approaching things this way will, I hope, make it easier to pin down more precisely what sort of thought processes are involved, what it is people find objectionable about snobbery, and whether their objections to alleged instances of snobbery are reasonable or unreasonable.

Ascribing a belief to someone is usually unproblematic when he cheerfully affirms that belief. It is trickier if he denies holding the belief in question.[3] The problem, of course, is that beliefs are in themselves invisible. So a person accused of holding a certain belief that he doesn't actually affirm can always deny it. ("I know you think I believe philosophers are smarter than historians, but honestly, I don't, I really don't!") Since we cannot open up a person's head and point our accusing finger at the belief in question, we can never prove directly that anyone holds any particular belief. But we can reasonably infer what people believe from the things they say and the way they behave. Where these conflict, we usually give priority to deeds over words. If you say you believe the Red Sox will win but bet five hundred dollars on the Yankees, it is reasonable to infer that deep down you think the Sox will blow it once again.[4]

To ascribe a belief to a person does not mean that this belief is continuously or consciously present in her mind. It means either that she would affirm it if asked, or that it is clearly implied by other things she says, or that ascribing it to her helps make sense of certain behavior that would otherwise be hard to understand. If, for instance, I always hide the silverware before my brother-in-law comes to stay, it would be reasonable to attribute to me the belief that he might try to steal my spoons, even though I might never utter the suspicion out loud.[5]

In trying to define snobbery I propose to start out with a very general characterization and gradually refine it. Ideally, a definition would capture every instance of snobbery and nothing that was not snobbery—in technical terms, the necessary and sufficient conditions for an action or belief's being correctly classified as snobbish. But this ideal is a guiding star we steer toward rather than something we can expect to realize perfectly. An exact fit between definition and the thing being defined may be obtainable in the hard sciences or where the connection is made analytic. But in the philosophical study of everyday morality and cultural norms, we are not likely to achieve this. We should be content if we can construct a definition that captures the phenomenon fairly well.

We can begin with a general idea:

Def. 1. Snobbery: believing that you are superior to another person.

This points us in the right direction. Insofar as snobbery involves some sense of superiority, it surely is always superiority over other human beings that we are talking about. We can be snobbish *about* our dogs, or our computers, but we are not snobbish *toward* them. Of course, most of us do consider ourselves superior to rocks, plants, and the so-called dumb animals. And philosophers through the ages have industriously—even anxiously—provided all sorts of justifications for this attitude: divine decree, language, reason, free will, self-awareness, moral conscience, aesthetic sensibility, and so on. Yet this sense of superiority over the rest of nature is not snobbery; it is more a kind of simpleminded smugness that we can all fall back on, no matter how low down our particular social totem pole we might be, whenever our self-respect needs a boost.

Still, this first definition is obviously too simple since a person can feel superior to others in several ways. There is, for instance, the sense of *total superiority*, involving the belief that one is simply better than others in all ways and at all things. But this is not so much snobbery as a kind of insanity—the sort of hubris we associate with tyrants like Caligula who surround themselves with sycophants to applaud their eminence as soldier, statesman, scholar, athlete, and musician.

Much more common is a sense of *specific superiority*: I believe myself superior to others not in all respects but in certain ways that I consider especially important. I recognize that you are a better mechanic than me, but I look down on you because I'm a creative artist, or because I've read more books, or because I make more money.

There is also what one might call a sense of *general superiority*. This does not embrace the absurdity of thinking that one excels in all fields. It is more a kind of complacency, an assumption that in some vague way one is better than others in the things that matter. Those who enjoy this quality recognize easily in others: "He's sound," they say. "He's got it." "He's reliable." "He's one of us." This attitude is nicely captured by Thackeray when he compares British to Continental snobbery: "About the British snob . . . there is commonly no noise, no bluster, but the calmness of profound conviction. We are better than all the world; we don't question it; it's an axiom."[6]

Typically, belief in one's general superiority is not free-floating but rests on a belief in some specific superiority. I compare myself favorably with others on the grounds that I am more street-smart, more erudite, more professionally successful, physically stronger, richer, better looking, or more experienced; and imperceptibly I drift toward enjoying a vaguer but more overarching sense of betterness. Since the sense of specific superiority seems to be more basic, we will write this into our definition, returning later to elaborate further on what the idea of a general superiority involves.

Let us consider, then,

Def. 2. Snobbery: believing you are superior to another person in certain respects.

This is an improvement, but it is clearly still too general. We can hone it further by making an important distinction between

a. believing you are superior by virtue of your individual qualities; and
b. believing you are superior by virtue of belonging to or being associated with some group.

In my view, snobbery always involves beliefs of type (b). To see why, let us consider more closely beliefs of type (a).

There is nothing extraordinary or necessarily objectionable about my believing that I am superior to someone else in certain respects because of particular qualities I possess or experiences I have had. Imagine a team working on some project. One says, "I'll cut up the wood since I'm pretty experienced with chain saws." Another says, " I used to be a graphic designer, so I should probably handle the publicity." A third says, "I'm licensed to drive trucks, so I'll do the driving." Here each individual implicitly claims that he is probably better than the others at performing some task; and each supports that claim with some information about himself that seems relevant. Nothing objectionable has occurred.

Suppose, though, the first had said, "Chainsawing is man's work, so I'll cut the wood." Here, the assumption of a specific superiority is likely to raise hackles since it rests on an appeal to group membership that in itself seems irrelevant.

If a person claims some sort of specific individual superiority, our reaction depends on

a. the sort of superiority claimed;
b. the extent to which the claim seems justified; and
c. the manner in which the claim is made.

When Usain Bolt won the gold medal for the men's 100 meters at the 2008 Olympics, he told interviewers that he had set out to be the world's best sprinter and could now proudly claim to be just that. I imagine that few, if any, were shocked at such a brazen claim to superiority. In part this is perhaps because the claim is indisputable. There are precise criteria for determining who is the world's fastest runner over 100 meters, and Bolt had evidently satisfied these criteria. If, by contrast, someone claimed to be the world's best poet, or the world's best plumber, we would find her assertions ridiculous. We have no clear-cut criteria of superiority in poetry or plumbing, so we are immediately skeptical about such claims and find them inappropriate.

Yet the issue is not just whether or not we have precise criteria. In 2007 Bill Gates was the world's richest man, and this, too, is a measurable kind of superiority. But for him to boast about it, or even call attention to it, would appear unseemly. Context is all-important. In sports we sometimes make allowances for the fact that success requires tremendous levels of competitiveness and self-confidence, so we may excuse an athlete who occasionally breaches the normal conventions of modesty.[7] In most fields, though, we demand that these be observed. A musician who trumpeted how many Grammys she had won or a chef who ranked himself above his rivals would be widely criticized as conceited.[8]

Of course, claims are different from beliefs. Claims are beliefs that are explicitly affirmed and made public. Unlike beliefs, they can violate social conventions and thus be criticized for being unseemly or inappropriate. But both claims and beliefs about the specific ways in which one is superior to others, even when they are objectionable—and they may be conceited, arrogant, unjustified, laughable, crazy, or just plain silly—do not constitute snobbery. That invariably involves a sense of superiority derived from one's association with some group.

> *Def. 3. Snobbery: believing you are superior to another person in certain respects because you belong to or are associated with some group.*

As a definition this is obviously still quite broad. It could encompass all sorts of prejudices, including racism, sexism, antigay attitudes, chauvinistic nationalism, class-based condescension, religious exceptionalism, and political dogmatism. It might also apply to aggressive rivalries like those between street gangs, soccer fans, or students from neighboring schools. This is not necessarily a problem. We could make a decision to classify all these as examples of snobbery and then make distinctions between them, eventually zeroing in on whichever ones especially interest us here. Or we could use the more generic term "prejudice" as the catchall rubric and proceed to distinguish the different species of prejudice from one another, eventually isolating the one we call snobbery. In my view, questions like this do not have an objectively correct answer. Nor does it make too much difference which view we take. The second option is somewhat more in line with ordinary linguistic usage, but the first approach promises more insight into the ways snobbery is related to and overlaps with other kinds of prejudice.

In fact, if we start out thinking of snobbery as a species of prejudice, we soon find ourselves drifting back to conceiving of it as a catchall concept. The question of how to distinguish snobbery from other forms of prejudice is tricky, because while we wish to differentiate between types of prejudice, we also have to recognize how they can overlap. Snobbery based on class, for instance, has often been intertwined with a prejudice against a person's ethnicity or religion. Still, we are focusing on a sense of superiority deriving from group membership, and certain kinds of membership criteria are associated with snobbery more than others. For instance, class, wealth, education, occupation, cultural attainments, and ethnicity are more commonly a basis for taking a condescending attitude toward others than, say, the kind of computer one uses or the sort of cat one owns. Typically, the snob identifies with a group that enjoys a higher position in some social hierarchy. Think of the way U.S. senators are occasionally accused of not showing enough respect toward the House of Representatives, or the way the "popular kids" in high school look down on the "losers." If we incorporate this idea into our definition, we get

Def. 4. Snobbery: believing you are superior to another person in certain respects because you belong to or are associated with some group that places you above them in a social hierarchy.

This further honing of the definition is helpful, but the refinement we have introduced opens up another difficulty. The clause "places you above them in a social hierarchy" implies that your higher social status is a matter of objective fact. But rank is often in the eye of the beholder. High-flying go-getters look down on ivory-towered academics, seeing them as out of touch; academics look down on the go-getters, seeing them as rat-racers. Members of the medical establishment despise advocates of alternative healing, viewing them as pseudoscientists; the latter adopt a superior attitude toward the establishment, which they see as narrow-minded and corrupted by money. Perhaps what matters, then, is not the objective status of your group in some social hierarchy but your *perception* of the hierarchy. In that case, we should modify the last definition in the following way:

> *Def. 5. Snobbery: believing you are superior to another*
> *person in certain respects because you belong to*
> *or are associated with some group that you think*
> *places you above them in a social hierarchy.*

Is this definition better than the preceding one? Choosing between them is not easy, and one reason for this is that there is another subtle variable in play. We have to consider how close your perception is to the way things really are—or, for those not comfortable talking about "the way things really are," how close your perception is to the point of view that enjoys cultural dominance. Is your way of thinking broadly in line with the mainstream, or does it cut against the grain? This can make a difference.

Suppose, for instance, that you believe your family lineage dating back to the time of Paul Revere, the number of your forebears who have held high office, your considerable inherited wealth, and your Ivy League education place you in the upper social echelons of contemporary America. Who would disagree? Hardly anyone. Your view of the hierarchy and your place in it meshes with what most people take to be the way things are. And *for this very reason*, if you display a superior air you will be criticized for it. The very fact that your superior attitude is anchored in real privileges provokes resentment and an impulse to resist or contradict.

If, on the other hand, you are a hard-up poet, despising bourgeois philistines from your unheated garret, or you belong to some tiny religious cult whose members condescendingly pity all who have not been saved, you could just as reasonably be accused of having a superior attitude and of looking down on the world. But the rest of the world won't care. We won't accuse you of snobbery; we'll simply be amused and label you an eccentric—deluded, but harmless.

This issue of whether one's attitude toward others is under-written by social reality is important. It helps to explain why the label "snob" sticks so much more readily to some people than to others. Consider two stereotypical caricatures from the long-running culture wars in the United States. In the blue corner we have the fancy-suited, East coast–educated, Chardonnay-sipping, Brie-eating, whale-saving, gym-visiting, Europhilic, secular, liberal Democrat. And in the red corner we have the baseball-capped, gun-toting, deer-hunting, burger-eating, flag-waving, tax-hating, redneck Republican. According to the standard account, the liberals look down on the rednecks, viewing them as ignorant and unsophisticated. They consider a conservatism based on God, guns, and antigay sentiment to be intellectually backward, and they chortle over George W. Bush's malapropisms and Sarah Palin's obvious ignorance.

Aware that they are objects of condescension and contempt, the rednecks accuse the liberals of snobbery and elitism. Yet they certainly do not admit to being inferior. True, they may know less about Italian wine and French cheese. But when it comes to the things that really matter—for instance, God, guns, taxes, individual freedom, traditional Christian morality, support for the military, and patriotism—they see themselves as occupying the higher ground, and from there they look down on the effete elite. On a different hierarchical scale, they claim to be the "real Americans"; those at the other end of the political-cultural spectrum are, relatively speaking, "un-American."

Thus both sides are convinced of their superiority on the axes that matter most to them. What we could do with here, to illustrate both the pervasiveness and the perceptivity of snobbery, is an Escher-style drawing in which everyone is managing to look down on someone else without anyone's being at the bottom.

In the end, I view Definition 5 as preferable to Definition 4 because I believe it is useful to see even inverted snobbery as a form of snobbery. The guy who assumes that his working-class roots, or his minority status, or his physically demanding occupation makes him superior to Waspy yuppies is essentially doing the same thing as the more conventional, upper-crust snob. He is implicitly claiming a kind of superiority because of his association with some group. The fact that his belief goes against rather than with the grain of social reality suggests that it may be more an affirmation of the will than of the intellect, but that does not make it less inherently snobbish. It does, however, explain why it tends to be viewed as less objectionable. Those who occupy objectively lower positions on the socioeconomic totem pole are thought to be less able, and hence less likely, to hurt those they despise.

So is Definition 5 adequate? I would say no, and for a fairly obvious reason. Consider the following examples of people believing themselves superior:

- An army captain believes he is better able to command his unit than are members of lower rank.
- A judge believes she has a better grasp of the law than do the jurors to whom she gives directions.
- A chemistry teacher assumes that as a qualified teacher with a degree in her subject she typically knows more about chemistry than her students do.

According to Definition 5 these could count as examples of snobbery. The army captain, the judge, and the teacher each assume a specific kind of superiority over other people with whom they are interacting. And this belief is supported by their perception (probably a correct perception in these cases) that in virtue of title, qualifications, and experience they occupy a higher rank—belong to a higher-ranking group—in an established social hierarchy.

Yet these beliefs seem to be reasonable, and we would not normally call the people holding them snobs. This shows that our definition needs to be honed further. How? Well, there is one essential feature of the concept of snobbery that we have not yet captured—a very obvious feature, in fact. The word "snob" is pejorative. It invariably carries an implicit criticism.[9] In this respect it is similar to a word like "pervert": it is impossible to use in a completely value-neutral way. You cannot seriously say to someone, "You're a pervert!—no criticism intended." And similarly, it is hard to call someone a snob without implying that she is guilty of some failing. The word "snob" does not just describe: it also accuses.

Our definition of snobbery needs to capture this aspect of the concept. If it fails to do so, then its net will be cast too wide, catching beliefs and actions we would not want to call snobbish.[10] But it is not good enough to just tag onto the definition a final clause that says "and you're at fault." We need to identify the failing in question more precisely than that. Having done this, we will be in a better position to distinguish between objectionable and acceptable claims concerning superiority.

My suggestion is that the failing lies primarily in the fact that the assumption of superiority is unjustified, or at least goes beyond what is justified. This gives us

Def. 6. Snobbery: believing without sufficient justification
that you are superior to another person in certain
respects because you belong to or are associated with
some group that you think places you above them in
a social hierarchy.

The introduction of the clause "without sufficient justification" distinguishes this definition from the previous one. The new definition, which is the one I will work with from this point on, may not be perfect in the sense of applying to every instance of snobbery and to nothing that could not be called snobbery.[11] But it accords with the way we normally use the term, it incorporates the important observations and distinctions discussed above, and it clarifies the concept's pejorative nature.

What is objectionable about snobbery?

As we have just observed, the concept of snobbery is both normative and negative. It contains a criticism of someone's character, his conduct, or his way of thinking. Our next task is to try to pin down exactly what is objectionable about snobbery. Here we should immediately distinguish between something's being displeasing to us and something's being morally objectionable. It may annoy me that you are better at tennis than me, that you can predict my behavior, or that you go to church; but these are not traits or actions I can reasonable criticize you for. Similarly, as we shall see, some aspects of snobbery may be displeasing without being blameworthy. In general, understanding why we are annoyed by something is a psychological issue; deciding whether and why something is morally objectionable is a question for normative ethics, and this will be our main focus in what follows.

The final revision made to our definition offers one lead regarding what might be objectionable about snobbery: the fact that it usually involves an unjustified belief. This may not be all that people object to, but it is likely to be one of the main things that raises hackles. So let us consider it more closely.

The snob, according to our definition, believes one thing *because* of another thing. The word "because" here is ambiguous. It could refer to what *causes* the snob to hold his or her belief, as when I say that Pat believes in the value of scholarship because she comes from an academic family. Her heritage influences, perhaps even determines, her belief, and mentioning it may *explain* why she holds it. But it doesn't *justify* the belief; it doesn't give anyone else a reason to share that belief. Alternatively, the word "because" could refer to the *reason* the snob holds his or her belief—that is, the consideration that justifies the belief, that makes it reasonable, at least in the snob's own mind, even if he or she would never say it out loud.

Reasons and causes can seem to overlap. An aristocratic upbringing may *cause* the Count of Condescension to look down on tradespeople, and he may also believe that his superior education and more rigorous moral training *justify* this attitude. It does not usually make sense to criticize a person for being exposed to some ideological influence; that is generally beyond his control. Aristocrats and the offspring of fat cats (fat kittens?) do not choose the circumstances into which they are born any more than the rest of us do. So it is hardly fair to blame them for being exposed to certain environmental influences. All we may reasonably criticize as far as causes are concerned is a person's unwillingness to reflect on the influences at work on her so as to make the effects of these influences—her beliefs, attitudes, prejudices, habits, and traits— things she consciously chooses to embrace or reject.

Such unreflectiveness may sometimes be one of the things we object to. But it is not necessarily present wherever snobbery is on display, and it is not what makes the snob's belief in his or her superiority unjustified. If belief in superiority is *unjustified*, this must be due to a failure of reasoning; there must be something wrong with the *inference* that sees group membership as indicating some sort of superiority. This, I suggest, is the primary target of the criticism contained in the charge of snobbery (which is not to say that it is the only thing about snobbery that people dislike).

It will help if we place before us a few concrete examples. Imagine someone saying any of the following:

i. "I'm sorry, but I find it hard to take seriously the opinions of anyone who employs the locution "Tha dunt 'ave nowt left"[12] to inform me that I no longer possess anything."

ii. "I think we can safely assume that someone who decorates his living room with pink plastic-framed pictures of puppies did not graduate from a first-tier art school."

iii. "Wealth is best entrusted to those who have the wisdom, acquired over many generations, to manage it fruitfully."

Each utterance expresses a snobbish attitude. And each involves an inference from some fact or datum about a person (whom we can call the "victim") to some sort of evaluative judgment. Let us make these explicit:

Datum		*Evaluative judgment*
i. the way a person speaks (here this includes accent, vocabulary and grammatical structure)	→	an appraisal of her opinions
ii. a person's home decor	→	a supposition about the quality of his education
iii. a person's socioeconomic status	→	an assessment of his sagacity

Every inference can be formulated as an argument with premises and a conclusion. If we take (i) and flesh it out, imagining it being applied to someone, we get something like this:

Premise 1:   You speak a nonstandard, strong regional dialect of English.
Premise 2:   People who speak that way are ignorant.
Conclusion: Therefore, you are ignorant.

Let us take this as a representative sample of snobbery and subject it to close analysis, putting it under the microscope, so to speak, to see what we can learn.

The first premise states a fact that is indisputably true. The second premise offers a generalization that is obviously not true since there are many counterexamples. The conclusion is validly drawn: that is, *if* both premises were true, the conclusion must also be true. But although the argument is valid, it is unsound since one of the premises is false.

There are plenty of things here that the victim might find annoying or objectionable.

1. the truth of the first premise (if she is embarrassed by the way she speaks)
2. the falsity of the second premise
3. the generalizing tendency behind the second premise
4. the falsity of the conclusion
5. the truth of the conclusion (if it happens in this case to be true)
6. the uncomplimentary nature of premise 2
7. the uncomplimentary nature of the conclusion
8. the sense that she is being looked down on
9. the sense that she is trapped in a socially inferior position by beliefs such as premise 2

I have couched these possible sources of displeasure in general terms so that they can be applied easily to other examples of snobbery. Their relative importance will obviously vary depending on the details of the situation and the parties involved. So, too, will the degree to which the victim's objections are justified. But some tend to be more common and more legitimate, as a closer examination will reveal.

The first premise reports a datum. One can imagine its being mistaken: for instance, the snob might misidentify a dialect, just as he might think a person is poor when in fact she is well off. But assuming it is true, the victim cannot reasonably object to anyone's holding a true belief about her. We might not like some fact about ourselves—that we have a certain accent, that we are poor, or fat, or have a parent in prison—but we are what we are. And we may not like the fact that others notice or know these things, but that is not usually any sort of failing on their part that we can reasonably hold against them.[13]

Exactly the same points apply to the conclusion of the argument. Like the first premise, it could well be true: you may be ignorant, unsophisticated, foolish, boring, or crass. And this would understandably be something you do not like being reminded of. But you cannot reasonably *criticize* someone for holding true beliefs. In normal circumstances, we all accept the epistemological imperative to try to believe what is true while rejecting what is false. You can dislike certain things about yourself; and you can be unhappy about other people's noticing them. You can wish that others were more charitable in their interpretation of your actions, even that they were more susceptible to being duped by you. But holding true opinions about one's fellow human beings, while it may sometimes indicate that a person is cynical, or suspicious, or untrusting, or coldhearted, can rarely, if ever, be deemed a moral failing in itself.[14]

What about the second premise? In the example we are focusing on, and in many parallel arguments one could construct, the premise is false. Strong regional dialects do not necessarily indicate ignorance; poverty does not prove that a person lacks wisdom; being foreign-born does not entail untrustworthiness. So one might readily conclude that it is the *falseness* of such ideas that gets our backs up. The snob is at fault for believing falsehoods.

This seems plausible initially, but I do not think it can be the whole story, or even the main story. The fact that the snob entertains false beliefs is not the main thing we find objectionable in snobbery. Consider this argument:

Premise 1: You have an honest face.
Premise 2: People with honest faces are honest.
Conclusion: Therefore, you are honest.

Here, too, the second premise, taken as a universal claim, is obviously false; so the argument is unsound in exactly the same way as the earlier example. But presented with this sort of thinking, we are less likely to be annoyed, or if we are annoyed it will be for a different reason. We may accuse one who thinks this way of being foolish, naive, or even irresponsible. But for various reasons—because the quality being attributed is positive, because the prejudice is not thought to harm any particular group (although this assumption is questionable), because the attitude is associated with a trusting, good-hearted nature—most of us, most of the time, will not see holding a false belief of this sort as a moral failing.

The same argument shows that it cannot be the *falsity* of the conclusion that we primarily object to. Who gets offended when he learns that someone has incorrectly supposed him to be well-traveled, or highly qualified, or good at mathematics?

A similar argument shows that it cannot really be the generalizing tendency itself that we find objectionable. We love to generalize, especially about people. Americans are brash. Americans are generous. Brits are reserved. Brazilians love soccer. Moldovans are gloomy. Californians are laid-back. Computer scientists are nerdy. Coal miners are tough. The Amish value family. Teenagers are difficult. The Japanese have a strong work ethic. Parisians love their pets. Israelis are rude. New Yorkers are rude. Muscovites are rude. It is hard to get through a day without encountering—or offering—a generalization of this kind.

Our tendency to generalize is certainly open to criticism. Nearly all our generalizations about specific groups of people are, strictly speaking, false, many of them are downright stupid, and some are pernicious. Even seemingly positive generalizations can be harmful. For instance, the claim that black people are naturally good athletes arouses the suspicion that beneath the apparent compliment is a subtext suggesting that they are more physical than cerebral. And in recent years we have become more aware of how our willingness to generalize may feed and be fed by dubious stereotypes, which in turn feed and are fed by our prejudices. Nevertheless, most of the time we find false generalizations about some group we belong to fairly easy to tolerate, especially if we see them as harmless. So generalization in itself cannot be what we mainly object to in snobbery.[15]

Summing up what we have learned so far, it seems that if we were the victim of implicit reasoning such as that laid out above, we might be annoyed by the truth or falsity of the premises, and by the truth or falsity of the conclusion. But where the snob's beliefs are true, we cannot really criticize; and where they are false, what displeases us is not so much their falsity as their content and their possible consequences. This brings us to the other aspects of the argument we might find annoying or objectionable.

The second premise asserts that people who speak a strong regional dialect are ignorant, and the conclusion says this about the victim. Now most people are happy to admit that they are ignorant of specific information or even of entire fields of learning that they are not expected to know anything about. But the adjective "ignorant" applied to a person in a general way is nearly always uncomplimentary; ignorance is generally viewed as a kind of inadequacy. This is presumably the main reason why the victim of the argument would be displeased. In addition, group solidarity with others who speak as they do (or who share their ethnicity, their geographical origin, their social class, etc.) may also be a reason for resenting the general assumption that everyone who speaks a certain way must be ignorant.

The derogatory nature of the belief is responsible for two other things the victim might reasonably find objectionable. The first of these is the feeling of being looked down on. To be sure, there are some who relish their inferior status as an easy way to secure for themselves some sort of identity, rather as the youngest child may play up being the "baby" of the family. It is also true that within hierarchical societies and institutions individuals may sometimes find it reassuring to see those above them affirm their superiority. This can bolster their confidence in the leadership as well as lessen any anxiety caused by uncertainty over their own place in the hierarchy. Even so, in communities where some form of egalitarianism is generally professed, being regarded as inferior threatens one's self-respect and goes against the moral ideal of equal respect for all.

The other objectionable aspect of derogatory beliefs is the role they play in preserving existing inequalities. When snobbish attitudes are in line with the prevailing social hierarchies, the victims justifiably view these as oppressive. Like stereotypes, jokes, or loaded language, prejudicial beliefs can exert—and can be felt as—a form of downward pressure on the victims, frustrating attempts at social advancement.

The upshot of all this is that snobbery can be either annoying or objectionable in a number of ways. Exactly how important each factor is will vary according to circumstances. One could construct a pie chart showing the various sources of displeasure experienced by victims of snobbery, but it will obviously vary from person to person and case to case.

As noted earlier, we can distinguish between what merely annoys and what is reprehensible. Yet when we try to identify what

Figure 3.1. Sources of displeasure

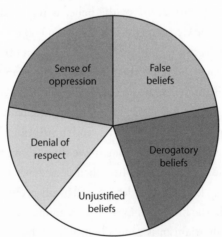

is objectionable about snobbery, we find that these are often hard to disentangle. Where the reasoning is flawed but the conclusion reached is complimentary (even though it may be false), our critical faculties tend to lie dormant. Uncomplimentary conclusions, on the other hand, prod us into action, especially if we think them false. Then we examine the reasoning much more closely and criticize unsound inferences. When the false and derogatory conclusions occur in a social and historical context that gives them an oppressive function and power, then the snobbery alarm sounds—we feel not just slighted, but wronged, and our displeasure expresses itself as indignation.

The arrow of inference

Moral philosophy would be easier if everything could be divided into good and bad, right and wrong, guilty and innocent, with clear-cut boundaries between the categories. It is rarely so, of course, and snobbish attitudes are no exception. We have identified an unsound inference from an unjustified generalization to a derogatory conclusion as the morally objectionable element at the heart of typical instances of snobbery. But the justifiability of a belief is also not an all-or-nothing affair but a matter of degree. The same goes for the reasonableness of an inference.

A useful way of grasping these complexities that also reveals more about what we find objectionable in snobbery is to conceive of the inference involved metaphorically, as an arrow in flight. As illustrated in figure 3.2, there is even a connection between the trajectory of the arrow and the reasonableness of the inferences. Sticking with the same example as before, we can represent a series of inferences along the arrow's trajectory.

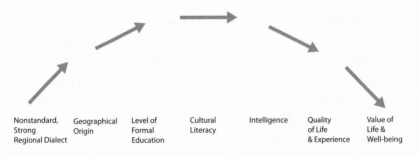

Nonstandard,   Geographical   Level of   Cultural   Intelligence   Quality   Value of
Strong   Origin   Formal   Literacy   of Life   Life &
Regional Dialect   Education   & Experience   Well-being

Figure 3.2. The arrow of inference

I start with a datum, a plain, unarguable fact: you speak a nonstandard, strong regional dialect. A dialect includes accent (pronunciation and stress patterns), vocabulary, grammar, and syntax. We are not talking here about a faint burr or twang, but about a way of speaking that people unfamiliar with the dialect can barely understand without subtitles. From hearing you speak I infer that you hail from a particular place. We all do this regularly. The only time it might cause annoyance is when a mistake is made owing to the listener's lack of discernment, as when, say, a Yorkshire accent is mistaken for a Lancashire accent, or a New Zealander is mistaken for an Australian.

Now I make another inference: given the way you speak, I assume you didn't receive a college education. Is this justifiable? Here, too, I would say yes. Immediately, some people will protest. You shouldn't judge a book by its cover, they will say. You should meet so-and-so: he has a Ph.D. in astrophysics yet sounds like Lady Chatterley's gamekeeper.

But this protest is misguided. Four points need to be stressed.

First, the inference rests on an uncontroversial sociolinguistic observation. Institutions of higher education demand that those who attend them speak and write something fairly close to standard English. Hence it is normal for people who speak a non-standard dialect to modify their mode of speech in the direction of standard English during the time they are in college.

Second, when we say that an inference is justifiable, we mean that it is reasonable. And when we say it is reasonable, we do not usually mean that the conclusion is completely beyond doubt.[16] We mean, rather, that given everything we know, the belief we arrive at is *probably* true.

It cannot be emphasized enough that even where an inference is natural, reasonable, and unobjectionable, we are not usually dealing with certainties, only with probabilities. This point should be constantly kept in mind. Even our first inference is not certain. Dialect is not an infallible guide to regional origin. You could be faking it as a joke. You could be an actor staying in character between rehearsals. Your mode of speech could be an affectation that eventually stuck. These are all possibilities, but they are unlikely. Ninety-nine times out of a hundred, when a person speaks a strong regional dialect, it is a reliable guide to where she grew up.

To appreciate that the inference from dialect to level of formal education is merely probabilistic, yet still reasonable, consider the following scenario. You listen to two people speaking for a minute each. One sounds like a BBC newsreader, the other like Lady Chatterley's gamekeeper. You are told that only one of them is college-educated, and you have to bet one thousand dollars on which one it is. If you are correct, you double your money; if you are wrong, you lose the lot. How do you bet? The question is a no-brainer. You back the newsreader. Anyone who backs the gamekeeper is an idiot. Anyone who says she wouldn't know what to do or how to decide is a disingenuous idiot. She implies that she might as well choose whom to bet on by tossing a coin, and that is an absurd denial of obvious social and socio-linguistic realities.

Third, the justifiability of any belief in this sort of everyday context is a matter of degree. An assumption or an inference can be more or less reasonable and hence more or less justifiable, for reasonableness, like probability, is not an all-or-nothing affair.

Fourth, it is impossible to interact with people in a normal way without making probabilistic assumptions of this sort.[17] We constantly make on-the-spot judgments about whether someone is likely to be acquainted with a certain city, know a piece of music, understand a joke, sympathize with a point of view, respond to some news with gladness or sadness, catch a cultural reference, or be familiar with a name, a word, or a piece of information. I assume my students are more likely than their grandparents to have heard of Coldplay. When I converse with a colleague, I expect him to catch an ironic remark about our employer that would be missed by an outsider. When I attend a philosophy conference, I assume the participants are unsympathetic to white supremacist organizations. Teachers, if they want to be effective, have to make different assumptions about such things all the time according to whether they are teaching twelve-year-olds or sixteen-year-olds, first-year college students or graduating seniors.

This last point is important. It shows that there is nothing inherently wrong with making assumptions about people when we meet them. We all do it all the time. Some people might claim that they try to avoid doing so, but their position is naive. Suspending all assumptions about the people we meet and interact with is neither possible nor desirable. Stereotyping can no doubt be harmful at times; but probability-based generalizations also facilitate social interaction.[18] Those who issue blanket condemnations of such generalizations fail to appreciate this point. The moral issue is not how we might avoid ever making assumptions about people, but how justifiable our assumptions are and what their effects are likely to be.

This is all clearly relevant to the next inference on the arrow's flight path. What should we say about the supposition that a person with a strong regional accent is likely to be less culturally literate than someone who speaks like a public radio newsreader?

The step could perhaps be defended as an implication of the previous inference. After all, aren't people who go to college usually more culturally literate than those who don't? Isn't that one of the supposed benefits of getting a college education? Shouldn't college graduates have something to show for all that debt? This is true; but the argument is weak since the general knowledge of many college graduates is put to shame by that of self-educated individuals.

Nevertheless, it is undeniable that one sort of assumption we readily make about people concerns the level and kind of cultural literacy we expect them to possess. If a new academic colleague asks me what the topic of my next lecture is, I might say something like, "Kant's critique of the ontological argument." If the person serving me in a coffee shop asks the same question, I will perhaps say something like, "Why the eighteenth-century German philosopher Kant thought that you can't ever prove that God exists." Here I make a spot decision, taking into account the whole context of the exchange, about how much the person I'm speaking to is likely to know about the topic and adjust what I say accordingly. Car mechanics, doctors, journalists, and police officers do the same. Is there anything wrong with that?

I do not think there is. Nevertheless, some who might be willing to concede the reasonableness of the previous inference about formal education may feel uncomfortable condoning assumptions about a person's cultural literacy. This is understandable, and the discomfort has several sources. One is simply the lower probability of the inference's being correct. A generalization about the cultural literacy of folks with strong regional accents is more likely to be false than an assumption about their level of formal education. There are more exceptions.

Another reason for viewing the inference with suspicion is the prevailing idea that cultural illiteracy is more shameful than not having gone to college at all. Attending college involves major investments of time and money; it can be difficult going on impossible for people growing up or living in disadvantageous circumstances. Self-education, on the other hand, is an ever-present option for most people in our society. Public libraries, print media, radio, television, and the Internet offer ample resources for anyone interested in becoming better informed about anything.

A third problem is that the concept of cultural literacy is ill-defined and tends to be loaded in favor of certain sorts of knowledge. Champions of cultural literacy seem to privilege fields such as history, literature, philosophy, and the arts, while downplaying other areas like sports, popular culture, or technology. Why isn't understanding how to read circuit diagrams, computer programs, or knitting patterns considered important compared to a passing acquaintance with Homer, Jefferson, and Mozart? In short, the concept of cultural literacy is sometimes used self-servingly by culture snobs to support their own claim to superiority.[19]

These are all excellent points. Still, it cannot be denied that we all do make spot assumptions about what the people we are interacting with are likely to know. Moreover, as we noted earlier, this is not usually any sort of moral failing: effective communication depends on our doing so. Indeed, our ability to gauge what needs to be explained and what can be taken for granted is often impressively subtle.[20] Overall, then, I would argue that the inference from the way a person speaks to the kind of thing one expects her to know *may* be reasonable, provided we remain alert to the possibility that we could be mistaken, and to the risk that we are harboring pernicious prejudices.

Clearly, the legitimacy of the inference we have been focusing on is controversial. From this point on, though, the inferences tracked by the arrow become ever more obviously objectionable. The next inference the arrow passes through is one that most of us will immediately criticize. The belief that a strong regional dialect implies anything about a person's general intelligence seems obviously mistaken. Here we have clearly moved into the land of the unjustifiable inference.

Thick accents and dull-wittedness have, of course, often been associated in representations that draw on stereotypes. The country yokel sitting on a wall, sucking on straw, staring into space, speaks with a country voice. Comedians frequently make use of these associations. Monty Python, for instance, used a loud, ungainly man with a knotted handkerchief on his head and a heavy Northern accent to personify a certain kind of blockheadedness.[21] But the upper-class twit with plums in his mouth is just as likely to be ridiculed as any peasant. As far as stereotypes are concerned, regional accents do not have a monopoly on stupidity. Nor does received pronunciation enjoy exclusive rights to intelligence; the quick-witted slum kid is also a familiar character in picaresque novels and films.

The logical basis for objecting to this inference is thus quite simple. A person's dialect is an unreliable indicator of her intellectual qualities. It is as if we were to infer someone's capacity for love on the basis of her occupation. But as we noted earlier, it is not just the unsoundness of the inference that we object to. There are other aspects of the underlying attitude that also displease.

Most obviously, there is the fact that weak intelligence is universally regarded as a defect. More subtly, low intelligence is generally seen as a more integral feature of who one is than is a trait such as ignorance. True, certain kinds of ignorance are seen as reprehensible; decent citizens of a modern society are expected to keep themselves moderately well-informed. But ignorance can be remedied. Intelligence levels, by contrast, rightly or wrongly, tend to be viewed as more or less fixed. Anyone who doubts this or who is inclined to protest that he doesn't think this way should ask himself whether, if he had to choose, he would prefer to be ignorant or unintelligent.

Another problem with the inference concerning intelligence is the concept of intelligence itself. Like the concept of cultural literacy, it comes weighted. In a scientific culture, general intelligence has come to be closely identified with certain sorts of intellectual ability, particularly the ability to think abstractly. This is the kind of intelligence paradigmatically represented by chess masters and rocket scientists, and it tends to be found most readily among those who enjoy the benefits of a good formal education. But intelligence of some sort is required for many tasks: raising children, appraising other people, repairing a machine, pitching a baseball, preparing a meal, building a house, enhancing self-awareness. Associating a way of speaking with intelligence or stupidity overlooks this.[22]

Finally, we will perhaps raise a suspicious eyebrow at anyone who seems unduly concerned with such things as a person's intellectual ability or cultural literacy. Very often, the motive underlying this sort of interest is to boost one's self-image through a reassuring comparison with someone else. But ideally, if we are going to concern ourselves with what someone's speech, dress, or appearance tell us about her, it might be healthier to focus on such matters as what we might learn from her or ways we could benefit her rather than on how we compare with her.

Following the arrow's flight further, we encounter the idea that people whose speech is heavily vernacular (or who exhibit other signs of coming from the lower classes) have less interesting inner lives. The quality of their subjective experience—of sensory pleasures, of the arts, of intellectual pursuits, of historical events, of friendship—is assumed to be inferior. Nowadays, hardly anyone would dare to voice this opinion; its antiegalitarian, antidemocratic thrust is too strong. In the past, though, it was a fairly commonplace view across the social spectrum. Shakespeare's Hamlet, for instance, casually dismisses "the groundlings, who for the most part are capable of nothing but inexplicable dumbshows and noise."[23] Nietzsche, who prided himself on being "untimely," had no qualms expressing his view that "noble souls" experienced things in a richer, deeper way than did plebeians—an attitude that can be traced back to the classical authors he so admired. Poets like Homer, Aeschylus, and Sophocles take princes and kings as their heroes in part because they assume there is some correspondence between a person's stature in the world and the greatness of his heart.[24]

The sort of inference we are here talking about is not usually a direct deduction of spiritual capacity from a person's way of speaking. Rather, limited sensibility is taken to be associated with or to follow from the qualities inferred earlier: lack of education, poor cultural illiteracy, low intelligence. And the realization that any one of these inferences is mistaken can stop the arrow in its flight.

Ultimately, the trajectory of the arrow of inference takes us to the idea that the lives and well-being of some people are less valuable than those of others. This is the logical—or better, the illogical—terminus of the inferential train. Or, to put it another way, it is the poison on the tip of the arrow. I believe this devaluing of a person's life, happiness, and experience is, at bottom, what we find most objectionable about snobbery in any form. It is a form of indifference or contempt that was once expressed much more openly, but which in a modern culture dare not speak its name. Yet we dimly suspect its presence behind and beneath many instances of snobbery we encounter.

We have been attending to one particular example of snobbery involving responses to a person's way of speaking. This was the sample we selected to put under the microscope. But snobbish reactions can be triggered in a thousand ways, by a person's appearance, clothes, occupation, possessions, tastes, or sundry bits of information about her. Each of these constitutes a distinct platform from which a different arrow of inference is launched; yet each arrow points toward the same ultimate conclusion—the belief that some lives matter less than others. This is where the hail of arrows converge. This is what we most dislike about snobbery in any form. It is what excites our fear—and our guilt.

The egalitarian axiom

The idea that the life and well-being of every human being is, at some fundamental level, equally valuable is a profound ethical assumption. It is not a conclusion that we usually try to support with arguments and evidence, and which could be overturned by new discoveries. Rather, it is a normative axiom—some might call it a "self-evident truth"—that is central to a large family of moral outlooks. But it is not as obvious as one might think.

In Western civilization the earliest expression of the egalitarian axiom is in the Hebrew Bible, where every human being is understood to be one of God's children, sharing a common ancestry and "made in God's image." Of course, the idea was immediately contradicted: God, it turns out, loves some of his children more than others; his instructions to Israel about how to deal with the Canaanites, as well as the Torah's rules concerning the rights of slaves, women, and Gentiles, can hardly be called egalitarian. Nevertheless, early Judaism planted a seed that would eventually produce a remarkable flower.

Until modern times, the default way of thinking was not egalitarian. The great mattered more than the small, masters more than slaves, men more than women, princes more than peasants, squires more than serfs. Hence there was little discussion of snobbery until social forces began to challenge these assumptions. The rise of capitalism, increased social mobility, the English, American, and French revolutions, Enlightenment and Romantic ideals, the abolitionist and suffragette movements, and universal education all breathed new life into the egalitarian axiom, which was most famously, though inadequately, expressed as the proposition that "all men are created equal." Concurrently, the concept of snobbery emerged as one for which people had a use.[25] Indeed, the period from the late eighteenth century to the mid-twentieth century could reasonably be called the Great Age of Snobbery, particularly in countries like Britain and France. This is when the untroubled acceptance of hierarchy characteristic of premodern times clashed continuously with rising egalitarian attitudes, a conflict documented and explored repeatedly in English literature during this period in novels like *Pride and Prejudice*, *Vanity Fair*, *Jude the Obscure*, and *Howards End*.

Antiegalitarian attitudes did not exactly perish overnight. A snobbish attitude continued to be acceptable in many settings, provided it accorded with one's objective circumstances. Employers looked down on their servants; management looked down on workers; seniors looked down on frosh. "Do you realize to whom you are speaking?" was a question that had some bite, that could be used to intimidate an upstart. Gradually, though, at least where egalitarianism officially prevailed, airs of this sort came to be generally condemned. So few today will admit to harboring the outlook underlying them, even in the dark recesses of their superior soul. For all that, traces of the blatant snobbery of earlier times remain commonplace. Contemporary news media and government policies still often subtly communicate the idea that the suffering of nonwhites matters less than that of whites. There are many households where the assumption persists that a man's wishes take priority over those of women and children. Nationalism, especially in times of war, is often accompanied by a lopsided valuing of some lives over others: witness the Israeli-Palestinian conflict.

Snobbery's antiegalitarian thrust is neither the only nor the most obvious thing about it that is morally objectionable. The unreasonable inferences it rests on, its oppressive function, and the denial of respect it implies are also grounds for criticism. But its violation of the egalitarian axiom is perhaps the most profound reason why most people today object to it. This is not to say that every little instance of snobbish manners betrays some deep-seated, unforgivable moral failing. It is just to point out that snobbish attitudes implicitly clash with an ethical principle that has become fundamental to an enlightened modern outlook; and we moderns are acutely sensitive—perhaps sometimes oversensitive—to any hint that the egalitarian axiom is not being respected. So although most of us are guilty of snobbery at times—after all, the satisfaction of feeling superior is just too cheap and easy to resist—snobbery is pretty much universally condemned since we are all egalitarians now, at least in theory.

Snobbery about things versus snobbery about people

I argued earlier that, on the basis of certain information or impressions, the snob typically makes inferences about people that are uncomplimentary and go beyond what is reasonable. There is no sharp line dividing what is reasonable from what is unreasonable, although many inferences are clearly one or the other. In general, the less probable or the more uncomplimentary the inference, the more cautious one should be about drawing it.

Fine, someone might say. That seems plausible, and we should all try hard not to fall into objectionable ways of thinking about people. But there is a problem. It is not easy to avoid making assumptions about people that are likely to give offense, and often the conclusions we draw, although disparaging, seem perfectly reasonable.

Take another example of snobbery mentioned earlier. I see that a person has decorated his bedroom with large murals of idyllic country scenes in which puppies and ducklings play together in a green meadow under a blue sky. "Something tells me," I remark, "that the occupant is not a trained connoisseur of the fine arts." My observation sounds arrogant and condescending. Yet isn't it true that virtually no one who studies fine art seriously would decorate his rooms in this way (unless, perhaps, he was trying to be ironic or make some sort of statement by embracing kitsch)?

The problem stems from the fact that there are, broadly speaking, two kinds of snobbery:

- snobbery about *people*, including their attributes, such as age, nationality, or education; and
- snobbery about *things*: for instance, wine, music, furniture, or vacation spots.

Few people in our society today will admit to being a snob in the first sense, a snob *simpliciter*. To say "I am a snob" without qualification means that you look down on people you consider your inferiors in terms of class, wealth, occupation, and the like. This is the kind of snobbery that contains within itself the poisonous idea that some people's lives and well-being are worth less than others'. Yet many of us will cheerfully "confess" to being a snob in the second sense, in our attitude toward particular things. "Call me a snob, " people say, "but . . .

- . . . I am simply not going to eat baked beans on toast
- . . . as far as I'm concerned, hip-hop is not music
- . . . I do not consider Bud Lite a beer
- . . . Florence is just more interesting than Fargo
- . . . a twelve-dollar haircut looks like just that
- . . . there's no way I am going to buy my wedding dress at a thrift store
- . . . Agatha Christie is simply an inferior writer."

When we say "I'm a snob about X . . . ," our words are really a form of shorthand. We are saying, in a slightly provocative, slightly tongue-in-cheek way, with some anxiety about our ability to support our position, and a dash of guilt about its antiegalitarian implications, something like this:

"I believe some sorts of X really are better than others. I can appreciate the difference between better and worse Xs, and I care enough about X to exercise discrimination, making choices that express my preferences and my values."

And so we assert that the *New York Times* is more intellectually stimulating than the *National Enquirer*, that Italian shoes are more elegant than shoes mass-produced in China, and that Twinings tea tastes better than Lipton.

In all such cases we can usually come up with some plausible justification for our position that points to the objective qualities of the things in question. When we support our preferences in this way, we are fending off the charge of snobbery. We are trying to extricate ourselves by uncoupling the suspected link between preferences and prejudices. Although we don't despise people who spend their vacations playing slot machines in Las Vegas or eating deep-fried Mars bars on the beach at Blackpool while reading Spider-Man comics, we nevertheless believe that Venice, asparagus oreganata, and Proust meet certain criteria of superiority.

But things are not so simple. Things are signs. They have symbolic force and a social meaning. And what they say much of the time is: I belong to this group, not to that one.[26] Moreover, this message is one that people are usually aware of at some level, and it often provides an ulterior reason for their preferences.

I prefer antique furniture to modern furniture. Why? Because it is better made. The wood is solid, not veneered particleboard; the grain is more beautiful; the parts are held together with skillfully crafted joints; the designs are more pleasing, and so forth.

Chapter 3

Some or all of this may be true. But beneath the rationale is my identification with a certain class—the kind that tend to have antique furniture in their homes. And who are these people? They are people who can afford to buy it (the well-off) or people who have inherited it (the well-established). The former in fact go antiquing in part so that they can present themselves, and conceive of themselves, as the latter. The same point applies to all sorts of things, from houses to silverware. My taste for the venerable expresses a desire to identify with those who can boast deep historical roots. And this desire is fueled by a more profound desire for identity and social standing that helps to bolster one's sense of legitimacy and entitlement. You, on the other hand, prefer the sleeker, plainer look of modern furnishing. Your cabinets are Ikea; your coffee table is glass and steel. This tells the world that you identify with members of a different group: the technologically empowered whose status derives not from their past but from their cutting-edge importance in the contemporary world.

Similar observations can be made about countless other things. I form my sentences carefully, eschewing redundancies, profanities, and loose constructions. I say I do this because I value precise thinking and efficient communication; but my practice also serves to identify me as belonging to the educated classes. A friend wants her children to attend brand-name colleges. Her rationale is that they will receive a better education and be more intellectually stimulated there than at less prestigious institutions. But is it just a happy unrelated accident that their admission to an elite college also places them (and by extension the whole family) among the upper social tiers as well as in the "most talented" category?

These observations are not reductionist. To point out that my preferences have meanings other than the official justifications I offer does not mean that these justifications are false or insincere.

My rationale can be sound. Perhaps I am right; perhaps vinyl records really do reproduce music more accurately than CDs or MP3 players. But my preference for vinyl unavoidably signifies more than just my belief that this is true. It also identifies me as someone with a discriminating ear, someone who cares enough about music to opt for a more expensive and less convenient system; perhaps, also, as someone who is underwhelmed by the digital revolution and associates in spirit with an earlier period.

We are not always fully conscious of these ulterior meanings that our words, actions, possessions, and choices may carry. Ferreting out the snobbery is a matter of determining to what extent the rationales we offer are rational and to what extent they are rationalizations. Sometimes the snobbery can be exposed by scientific methods. I claim that the earthy structure and fruity yet reticent nose of a 2001 Château de la Maltroye Chardonnay marks it as clearly superior to some cheap Australian plonk marketed to the masses. But a blind taste test exposes me as unable to tell the difference without the label to guide me. Dieter Flury, first flautist for the Vienna Philharmonic, upheld excluding women and non-Europeans from the orchestra on the grounds that

> [t]he way we make music here is not only a technical ability, but also something that has a lot to do with the soul. The soul does not let itself be separated from the cultural roots that we have here in central Europe. And it also doesn't allow itself to be separated from gender.[27]

And the empty yet noisome pretentiousness of his talk about "soul" is exposed every time applicants to the orchestra who are not white males come out tops in blind auditions.

Ulterior snobbery can be made apparent in other ways too. One obvious indicator is a discrepancy between a person's expressed opinions and her actions, or between two sides of her behavior. I sneer at cheap tools, making a point of purchasing only professional quality, oil-quenched, chrome-vanadium wrenches made in Germany. Yet when my car needs fixing, I take it to a garage and pay others to do the work. Every morning I buy the *New York Times*, haughtily rejecting any substitute on the days when it is not available; yet I only ever read the sports pages. In such instances, the motive for what I do seems to be a desire to belong to, or to be seen as belonging to, or to see myself as belonging to, a certain group, even though objectively my claim to membership is dubious. Here snobbery and self-deception prop each other up quite effectively.

Another clue that snobbery may be in the air is when a person cannot offer any convincing justification for his preferences. Dismissing sweet corn or oats as fodder for animals rather than food for humans; insisting that ending clauses with prepositions is something one should abstain from; objecting to certain ways of pronouncing words even though communication is not impeded: prejudices of this sort that float free of attempted justifications often betray an underlying interest in distinguishing one group from another, ranking them, and identifying with those that enjoy higher standing.

Of course, sometimes a person's rationale for her preferences is quite plausible. Hondas are statistically more reliable than Yugos; the *New York Times* really does offer better coverage of international affairs than does the *New York Post*. Often, though, we cannot determine precisely to what extent a preference is genuine and reasonable and to what extent it is motivated by snobbery. We just have to form judgments about the plausibility of the justification being given in light of what we know about the person and the sort of thing under discussion.

Sliding from thing-snobbery to people-snobbery

Specifying the exact degree to which a preference for one thing over another is snobbish is not usually all that important. More significant, and more troubling, is the tendency for snobbery about things (which we may view as acceptable) to bleed through into snobbery about people (which we generally condemn).

Consider the example already used of our attitude toward the news media. I candidly admit to holding views on this front that some will call snobbish. I think the so-called quality newspapers offer a broader, more thoughtful, and more thought-provoking coverage of events than that provided by the tabloids. While I may have my criticisms of the BBC or NPR, I believe the journalists working for these organizations provide reports that are more fair-minded, informative, and insightful than those one typically encounters on Fox News or commercial talk radio. But is it possible to think this and not consider myself superior to tabloid readers or devotees of Rush Limbaugh and Bill O'Reilly? Can I avoid thinking of myself as smarter than them?

There are actually three questions here concerning the slide from a position about things to a view of certain people:

1. A *logical* question: Does the slide necessarily involve an unreasonable inference?
2. A *psychological* question: Is the slide from snobbery about things to snobbery about the people associated with them avoidable?
3. An *ethical* question: Is the slide necessarily objectionable?

In my view, the answer to all three questions is no. But each question deserves to be examined separately.

> Does the slide necessarily involve
> an unreasonable inference?

To a large extent we have already dealt with this question. Snobbery about people, according to the definition proposed, generally involves an unjustified inference. The difficulty, as indicated
by the arrow of inference metaphor, is that there is no sharp line
dividing reasonable from unreasonable inferences. Rather, there
is a spectrum running from the perfectly reasonable to the de-
spicably fallacious, with a gray zone in the middle where controversy is likely to arise.

Those fearful of ever making potentially offensive assumptions about people can resolve to eschew all inferences that are
not completely certain. So even though someone is wearing a
Yankees shirt and a Yankees cap, they hold off from inferring
that this person likes the New York Yankees. Perhaps the clothes
were gifts she feels obliged to wear; perhaps she buys her clothes
at thrift stores and is indifferent to logos. But pledging total ab-
stinence in this way is an extreme policy that is both unrealistic
and neurotic, akin to the resolve never to talk about other people
for fear of falling into the sinful practice of malicious gossiping.

At the other end of the spectrum is a cavalier willingness to
traffic in stereotypes that have little or no basis in reality. Men
who own Dobermans have aggressive personalities; adults who
read children's literature are escapists. Inferences of this sort are
terribly weak and serve only to sustain unthinking prejudices.

The middle ground—following Aristotle, one might talk of
the "golden mean"—involves inferences that are not completely
certain and may sometimes be uncomplimentary. But neither of
these features necessarily makes an inference unreasonable. They
do, however, underscore the need to be careful, to deliberate be-

fore we deduce. There is no algorithm to ensure that one will always stay on the path of what is reasonable, never making a false step. All we can do is try to be informed, aware of circumstances, sensitive to nuances, and self-critical.

Is the slide psychologically avoidable?

This is a more complex question. Jesus says, "Judge not, lest you be judged,"[28] but the tendency—some would say the temptation—to form value judgments about people, their particular actions and attributes as well as their overall worth, is widespread and deeply entrenched. This is understandable. Success in life involves understanding and coping effectively with one's environment. For millions of years human beings have looked at the sky for signs of impending storms, at the land for signs of a water source, at plants for signs of nutritional value, at animals for signs of danger. And in the same way we look at people for signs of strength, weakness, friendliness, hostility, health, sickness, anger, cruelty, compassion, intelligence, stupidity, and sexual attraction toward us.

We are descended from people who were good at doing this. Those who failed to notice signs of hostility got killed; those who failed to register sexual attraction failed to mate. Appraising people is an especially important part of coming to understand and deal successfully with one's environment. And that involves asking questions about their character, their probable past, their likely responses to what you say and do, whether they should be trusted or feared, whether they are likely to be useful or a burden, and so on. Evolution has hardwired us to think about such matters.

Moreover, in trying to answer these questions, we naturally consider all the evidence at our disposal, which means not just what we see them do and hear them say, but everything else we learn about them also. If we hear they went to Harvard, we tend to assume they must have some sort of intellectual talent. If they drive a Rolls Royce, we assume they wish to impress people with their wealth. If 50 percent of their CDs are Spice Girls albums...

Unfortunately, this natural and defensible tendency to assess others is often entwined with a propensity to judge them according to criteria that we ourselves satisfy rather well. I'm good at fighting, so I rank others according to how well they can fight; I'm proud of my expensive and fashionable wardrobe, and this leads me to look down on the shabbily dressed. The motivation here is no mystery: we use a self-serving measuring stick as a cheap way of giving ourselves an ego massage. Strictly speaking, this need not be snobbery as defined earlier, since the superiority one feels may be individual rather than group-based. But here, too, there is no sharp line, and we commonly warm our egos by thinking of ourselves as belonging to some select group.

Much depends, though, on whether or not we see the things or attributes in question as central to a person's identity, as what confers worth upon them. This is what determines the steepness of the slide from judgments about things to judgments about people. You may raise an amused eyebrow at my passion for lumpy cornmeal mush topped with lashings of bacon grease. But this won't affect your overall view of me or my worth unless you think that gastronomic taste is the true measure of a person—a rather rare and obviously stupid point of view. I may be a neat freak in my own house, yet happily free from any prejudice whatsoever against slovens and slobs. Yes, you're a slob, I say, but so what? Tidiness and personal appearance are trivial matters compared to your warm heart and stimulating conversation.

It is different, though, when we regard something as close to or indicative of the core of a person's identity. If I place a high premium on artistic creativity, I may find myself subtly grading people according to their artistic abilities, fawning over some supposed genius while snubbing those I view as lesser talents. If I view the world through partisan political spectacles, I may find it hard to avoid feeling a degree of contempt for those who lap up propaganda from the other side. To engaged partisans, a person's politics matter. When they encounter or think about someone, it is one of the first considerations to come before their mind.

This point about how central to a person's identity we think something is also helps us understand another reason why snobbery will produce different reactions in different "victims." One reason, discussed earlier, concerns whether the snob's sense of superiority conforms to objective hierarchical realities (as when the rich look down on the poor). Where it does, the victims are more likely to be aggrieved; where it does not, they can afford to be merely amused. Here we have another consideration: how much agreement is there between the snob's values and the victim's values, both of which include their view of what is central to a person's identity? The further apart these are, the easier it is for the victim to be indifferent to the snob's attitude (putting aside concerns over the possible practical consequences of this attitude).

To take just one example, staunch egalitarians will not be troubled by the haughty mien of aristocrats, since they reject the idea that one's breeding is relevant to one's worth. They may be angered by the pernicious effects of such snobbery; but being annoyed, frustrated, or angry is not quite the same experience as being offended. In general, for us to take offense we must have some respect for the person denigrating us, some desire for his good opinion.[29]

Which attributes people view as central to a person's identity obviously varies among different cultures and subcultures. The

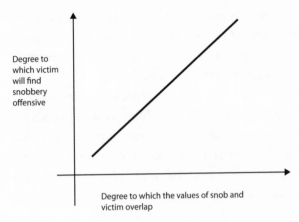

Degree to
which victim
will find
snobbery
offensive

Degree to which the values of snob and
victim overlap

Figure 3.3

Swiss tend to identify themselves strongly with the locality they
are from. In cities like Glasgow and Milan, which soccer team one
supports is very much a part of one's identity. Religious affiliation
matters more in Israel than in Canada. Dress seems to be more important in Hollywood than at conferences of ceramic engineers.

What is thought to matter most about a person also changes
over time. Family lineage was hugely important in many ancient
societies: witness the long genealogies provided in the Bible, in
Homer's *Iliad*, and in other ancient texts. Marital status used to
be more central than it is today, especially in the case of women;
hence the distinction between "Miss" and "Mrs." in the traditional
forms of address. Until quite recently in our own society—and in
many parts of the world still—an unmarried woman's virginity
was of paramount importance. "Innocence" was her first virtue;
once it was lost, she was "soiled goods." Today, in modernized societies, such things as education and occupation have largely dis-
placed sexual purity, both as the sort of thing others are first interested in, and as primary building blocks of a woman's self-image.

Three key points emerge from the preceding remarks: (1) not all attributes are equally central to a person's identity or worth; (2) which attributes we consider central is historically and culturally relative; (3) we tend to place a higher premium on those attributes we pride ourselves on possessing in good measure.

These points relate to the question before us: is the slide from snobbery about things to snobbery about people psychologically avoidable? The people we identify as card-carrying snobs are the type who shoot down the slide easily, often, and whooping as they go. They positively keep an eye out for opportunities to treat things in the world as further evidence of their own superiority over others. If we are honest, most of us secretly enjoy such opportunities, at least some of the time.

But while the slide may be unavoidable, it can—to extend the metaphor almost painfully—be made less slippery and less steep. By keeping in mind the three points just made, we can cultivate in ourselves a certain restraint. We can ask ourselves: Does the thing or attribute in question—reading habits, clothes, furniture, musical tastes, and the like—really tell me something about who a person is? Am I just uncritically buying into my own culture or subculture's assumptions about what matters most? Am I lured by the prospect of smugness-inducing comparisons? Questions like these will not block the slide entirely. Nor should they, since some of our inferences from things to the people we associate with them are legitimate. But here again, asking them can help us become more self-aware and self-critical.

Is the slide morally objectionable?

At one level, this question has an easy answer. We built into our definition of snobbery the proviso that snobs believe themselves superior to others *without sufficient justification*. We also argued that snobbery invariably carries the insinuation that some people's lives and happiness count for less than those of others. If we subscribe to even a modest version of ethical rationalism, we will object to the first of these features. And if we are good, modern egalitarians we will object to the second. So any tendency that produces snobbish attitudes toward other people can be criticized on these grounds.

Unfortunately, hypersensitivity to any hint of antiegalitarianism sometimes leads to a knee-jerk, wholesale condemnation of anything that is thought to have a snobbish tinge to it, and accusations of "elitism" start flying around. But as with blanket condemnations of gossip or rudeness, this response is too crude and takes in too much. It is a mistake to advocate never talking about others for fear of "gossiping," or to fetishize manners to such an extent that one cannot recognize when rudeness might be acceptable. And similarly, it is a mistake to forgo expressing or arguing for our tastes, preferences, considered opinions, and values merely out of a fear that we might appear snobbish or be tempted onto some slippery slope.

What we need, therefore, is a way of distinguishing between beliefs and attitudes that are objectionable because snobbish and those that are defensible but tend to get wrongly tarred with the same brush. To facilitate this I propose drawing a distinction between snobbery and elitism.

Elitism

In everyday discourse the terms "snobbery" and "elitism" are often used interchangeably. A snob is an elitist and vice versa. The definition of snobbery arrived at earlier is intended to stay fairly close to ordinary usage, but the following account of elitism will not do this quite so well. So in drawing a distinction between snobbery and elitism I do not claim to be accurately mirroring a difference in the way people ordinarily use these words. Rather, I am using a linguistic distinction to forcibly distinguish two different ideas.[30] In effect, I am co-opting the term "elitism" to designate a family of beliefs and attitudes that are widely distrusted but which can include many reasonable and even meritorious ideas. For while elitism, as I will use the term, sometimes overlaps with snobbery, it does not always do so.

As with snobbery, one can have an elitist attitude toward just about anything: colleges, music, literature, food, politics, sports, fashion, and so on. Clearly, elitism involves the idea that some things are better than others, but this does not tell us very much. Everyone except out-and-out nihilists thinks that. To gain some initial purchase on the way the notion is commonly understood, let us look at a concrete example.

Consider these statements:

a. I like all kinds of music equally.
b. I prefer classical orchestral music to brass band; that's just my personal taste.
c. Brass band is better than classical.
d. Classical is better than brass band.
e. Classical is better than brass band, and people who think otherwise must be aesthetically challenged.

Which of these is likely to be labeled elitist? Obviously (e), but also (d). The person who affirms (b) might be described as having elitist tastes or tendencies, but (b) is only a statement about subjective preferences, whereas (d) is a value judgment advanced in the form of an objective statement. So the person who asserts (d) is much more likely to be described as an elitist.

And what about (c)? Would we call someone who proclaims the superiority of brass band music over classical music an elitist? I would say no. To be sure, he is offering a value judgment in objective form. But to call him elitist would be odd given the relative social standing of classical and brass band music. To hold that brass band music is superior to classical is to assert something at odds with an outlook commonly associated with the elite.

These considerations suggest that elitism involves at least the following features. Your view of x is elitist if

1. you think that some kinds of x are objectively better than others; and

2. your view conforms to the perspective associated with an elite.

Both conditions deserve further elaboration.

Regarding (1), there is no need to suppose that claims of this sort commit one to the existence of some metaphysical realm of objective values. "Objective" here simply means that the judgment is not *just* an expression of subjective preferences or tastes. If I assert that chess is a better game than dominoes, I mean that it is better according to certain criteria (e.g., complexity, variety, skill level required, opportunities for creativity, beauty, excitement, depth of pleasure experienced by participants, spectator interest, and so on). You can disagree with me in two ways. You can agree with my criteria but hold that dominoes satisfies them better than chess does. Or you can hold that we should judge games by other criteria, or by a different ordering of criteria. For instance, you might argue that dominoes is better than chess because it is easier to learn, incorporates an element of luck, and allows for more sociability.

Where the criteria are agreed upon, most judgments about which of two things is superior will be uncontroversial. Virtually every professional chef would, I assume, agree that vegetable curry with rice is a better entrée than a deep-fried Mars bar. Just about every historian holds that Lincoln was a better president than Harding. Where common criteria are used, disagreement emerges only if the things being compared enjoy close standing: French cuisine and Italian cuisine; Pelé and Maradona; George Eliot and Jane Austen.

If there is no agreement about the criteria, disputes are unlikely to be resolved. This is because neither side will be able conclusively to prove the superiority of their criteria. Any such proof requires some agreed-upon common ground, and that is precisely what is often lacking in these cases. If I judge novels primarily by their popularity and you judge them mainly by their stylistic originality, we are probably not going to agree any time soon over how to rank *The Da Vinci Code* and *Lolita*.

But that does not mean that discussions about which criteria should be preferred are pointless. Some of society's most important conversations are at that level: Should foreign policy serve national interests at the expense of global interests? Should school meals reflect what kids like to eat or what is nutritious? Should each human being be viewed as having the same value and entitled to the same rights as every other person? Should a society be judged by how close it comes to realizing a blueprint laid out in an ancient scripture? Changing the criteria by which we form our conclusions is a more fundamental reorientation in our thinking than just changing our opinion about whether someone or something satisfies our current criteria of merit. That is why, even when it does occur, change at that level tends to be a more laborious process. But it does sometimes happen, albeit slowly, and when it does the value of such conversations becomes apparent.

The second condition—to be elitist a view must conform to the perspective associated with an elite—also needs a little elaboration. To be called elitist, it is not enough for a view simply to be one that an elite share. After all, just about everyone, including members of the elite, agrees that David Beckham is a better soccer player than the Dalai Lama, yet we would not describe this belief as elitist. To say that a view is "associated with an elite" implies, at a minimum, that it is in competition with alternative views and draws a higher proportion of its adherents from an elite group than do competing views.

Three further points are worth making here regarding this second condition. First, the group designated by the term "elite" can be defined in various ways: for instance, by wealth, power, education, or status. To a large extent, of course, these attributes tend to hang together, so we sometimes talk of *the* elite, thereby loosely designating the upper echelons in our society where such attributes tend to intersect. But it would be a mistake to think of the elite too narrowly. Two centuries ago only a tiny percentage of the population had university educations, significant accumulated wealth, and good prospects of holding high office. Today, many more enjoy these advantages.

Second, in addition to *the* elite there are also elites within particular fields, professions, and organizations. Because of this, one might sometimes describe a view as elitist because it accords with the outlook of the elite within a restricted field such as medicine, theater, soccer, or computing. The view that John Ashbery is a great poet, or the belief that books published by Knopf are more reliably high quality than those put out by less prestigious trade presses, is elitist in this restricted sense.

Third, unlike snobbery, elitism as I am characterizing it cannot be inverted. It makes sense to talk about inverted snobs who think themselves better than others even though (or even because) the latter stand higher in the social pecking order. But this cannot happen in the case of elitism if we stipulate that to be elitist one's view must conform to the outlook associated with the elite, or at least with the elite in a particular field. So no matter how fervently you believe in the objective superiority of Froot Loops over muesli, your preference cannot be called elitist.

The two conditions set out above encompass elitist thinking fairly well. But we should recognize that the term "elitism" is also occasionally used to describe a view that is simply critical of or disparaging about something associated with the lower socioeconomic sections of society. For instance, people may find themselves called elitist for criticizing diets heavy in fatty foods and soda, or for complaining about people whose yards are full of scrap cars, or for dismissing blockbuster movies like the Rambo series that seem to be little more than delivery systems for representations of violence. Here, the view expressed may be widespread and not especially associated with an elite.

The categories of opinion identified here—for instance, views associated mainly with an elite; views critical of things associated with lower socioeconomic groups; views embraced by the majority—have overlapping boundaries that shift over time. Thus there was a time when much of the musical establishment disparaged jazz, which was clearly associated with people lower in the socioeconomic hierarchy. Gradually, though, jazz won so much respect among the musical cognoscenti that nowadays a taste for jazz (over, say, country, or brass band) may even carry a whiff of elitism. These changes happen for various reasons, and noticing how and why they occur can tell us quite a lot about broader social movements. For instance, the intellectual elite today contains more scientists and social scientists and fewer classicists and theologians than in the past. This shifts our notion of what conforms to elite opinion, at least in some areas. Or again, in a field like music the boundaries between elite taste and nonelite taste have become considerably less sharp over the years. Today, the finest practitioners of folk, pop, rock, soul, blues, and jazz are acclaimed and honored by both the musical elite and the political establishment to an extent that would have been inconceivable a hundred years ago.[31] This obviously reflects all sorts of profound social changes—in education, in race relations, in political consciousness—that have taken place and are continuing today. In general, the long-term shift seems to be toward a leveling of social distinctions, and thus a shrinking of the domain marked out as conforming to elite opinion (as opposed to a widespread view that the elite also happen to share). But the trend has not been uniform, neither across fields nor over time. For instance, it has been much less noticeable in the critical appreciation of literature and the visual arts than in the world of music. Exactly why this should be is a fascinating question.

Often, of course, people express their preferences not as objective truths but as mere matters of taste. You happen to find show jumping more interesting than NASCAR, but you insist that you don't despise or disparage the latter. Everyone to her own taste, you say. In such cases, your critics may not be able to produce hard evidence that you hold elitist beliefs, and according to the way we have defined elitism, you do not. But you may still be accused of having elitist tastes and tendencies. To some people this accusation need not matter very much; they can either shrug it off or cheerfully admit its truth. But there are times and places where such an accusation can be very damaging. In China during Mao's Cultural Revolution, for instance, to be suspected of elitist tastes even in matters such as food or hairstyle could lead to exile in a labor camp.[32] And even in contemporary America, politicians running for office who carry elitist baggage feel the need to prove themselves true sons of the soil by eating hot dogs in diners, clearing brush with a chain saw, or going duck hunting before breakfast.

For while preferring sailing to bowling or Camembert to Kraft might seem trivial, the snobbery-alert patrol that watches over politics in the United States and many other places see it as the visible sign of a stain that runs deep. Elitist tastes indicate elitist tendencies in one's thinking, which means one holds elitist views, which inevitably foster snobbish attitudes, which involve implicitly violating the egalitarian axiom and looking down on the very people that the politician is supposedly seeking to serve. Or so goes the reasoning. Often this sort of accusation is made cynically by critics like Rush Limbaugh who will throw any kind of mud at those they disagree with if they think it will advance their own political agenda. But others may honestly believe there is something to this sort of guilt by association. An elitist preference in some insignificant area is then viewed the way the police view traces of fertilizer in the garage, as evidence of something far more sinister than an interest in gardening. Distrust of elitism in others can even extend to anxiety about one's own elitist tendencies.

Now it is not my intention to argue that all forms of elitism (as defined here) are acceptable. They are not. But some are, and it is important to be clear about this. It is elitist, in the sense given earlier, to hold that internationally renowned professional orchestras tend to offer the finest renderings of classical works. Or that the work of visual artists acclaimed by the contemporary "art world" (i.e., artists, curators, critics, and scholars) is generally more interesting and important than conventional representational art used to illustrate get-well cards. Or that a gifted student is likely to benefit more from going to a selective college than from attending a community college. Or that whole wheat bread is more nutritious and has a more interesting flavor than Wonder bread. Such beliefs are certainly not self-evident truths; they can be reasonably challenged. But they can also be reasonably held and supported.

When the term "elitism" is used as a near synonym for snobbery, it, too, packs a pejorative punch. Usually, this is because the elitist is thought to be making certain unwarranted assumptions without much critical reflection—for instance, that graduates from the highest-ranked medical schools make the best doctors. This indicates where elitism, even as we have defined it, overlaps with snobbery. But the idea that elitism in any form indicates or entails snobbery is misguided, and this is just the sort of confusion that the philosophical analysis applied to everyday life can help to dispel. For although snobbery and elitism may be connected psychologically and sociologically, neither logically entails the other, at least not as we have explicated the two concepts.

In fact distrust of elitism, whether in others or in ourselves, arises out of a tangle of anxieties. We worry that the relativity of tastes means we will not be able to justify our preferences, which means they will stand exposed as mere expressions of snobbery. We worry that elitism conflicts with our commitments to equality and democracy. Most of all, perhaps, we worry that elitist views in one area reflect or will lead to snobbish attitudes that, as we argued earlier, conflict with some of our most cherished moral principles.

Anxieties of this kind can lead people to renounce value judgments wholesale. They then declare that all art, all music, all literature, all food is, objectively speaking, of equal worth, and reduce all differences in evaluation to differences in subjective taste. This is an easy way to avoid any hint of elitism, but at the same time it invites the strong suspicion that one is neither sensible nor sincere. It is one thing to be self-critical; it is another thing to be so filled with self-suspicion or concern for political correctness that one refuses to offer honest normative judgments.

Yes, if I think that the *International Herald Tribune* is much superior to the *Daily Rag*, then I am likely to infer that *Tribune* readers are more politically informed than *Rag* readers. Appraising people on the basis of everything we observe about them is, as we noted earlier, something that comes naturally to us. My view of the media here is elitist. But this need not entail snobbery toward the tabloid readership. Snobbery involves unreasonable inferences to uncomplimentary conclusions about people, and a tendency to undervalue their lives and experiences. That is something quite different, which can, and should, be avoided.

And yes, some will say it is elitist to favor political candidates who are informed, intelligent, articulate, and wise over those who are unimpressive in these respects but who have the common touch and can claim to be closer to ordinary people. But there is surely nothing objectionable about this point of view, nothing unreasonable, or antidemocratic, or antiegalitarian. There are even instances where too much concern for not appearing elitist can lead to positions contrary to the interests of the people supposedly being slighted. The case of lottery tickets is a good example of this. People with low incomes buy the majority of state lottery tickets and spend a higher proportion of their income on them than do better-off players.[33] It may be elitist to say that they are spending their money unwisely, but does that mean one shouldn't say it? It is, after all, true.

In its worst forms snobbery contains much that is morally objectionable. It can hurt, humiliate, and oppress. Although in the West people began to label certain attitudes snobbish only with the advent of modernity, the attitudes in question are in some ways a hangover from the long portion of human history in which rigid social hierarchies were considered normal and necessary. "Snob" becomes an insult or a criticism as some form of moral egalitarianism becomes more popular. Calling someone a snob can thus serve a valuable critical function, reminding him and everyone else that we are trying to move away from that older society in which a person's worth is determined by his social status and toward a better world in which every human life is accorded equal value.

Inevitably, though, such terms will sometimes be thrown around too readily, too often, and without sufficient thought or discrimination. When that happens, perfectly reasonable inferences and defensible value judgments are wrongly criticized, and people back away from making them. This approach of automatically distrusting any point of view that *might* be accused of being snobbish or elitist certainly makes things simpler, but it also makes our thinking less intelligent and less honest.

Marx's critique of ideology taught us to look out for the class interests that underlie people's beliefs; and we certainly should continue to be alert to the ways elitist views may serve the interests of the socioeconomic elite. At the same time, just because a practice, a point of view, or a cultural product is favored by the elite does not mean there must necessarily be something wrong with it. It can still be enlightening, amusing, beautiful, stimulating, edifying, or true. Snobbery, as we have defined it, is objectionable; but the way to avoid it is not to eschew entirely any thought, word, or deed that might conceivably be thought snobbish. The better solution is to cultivate humility, self-awareness, and a willingness to think hard and honestly about these matters. And let's face it, the snobbery-alert patrol won't be out of work any time soon. They can expect to be gainfully employed at least until the end of the next millennium, or until we realize an egalitarian utopia—whichever comes sooner.

And again and again the human race will decree
from time to time: "There is something at which it is
absolutely forbidden henceforth to laugh."
—Nietzsche

4 "That's not funny—that's sick!"

Humor, like dance, music, and morality, is a cultural universal.
In every human society people find certain things funny and
deliberately say or do things to make those around them laugh.
Humor is also viewed positively by almost everyone. True, one
might encounter the occasional puritan or zealot who distrusts
laughter and seems to lack a sense of humor. But most normal
people would hate to live in a mirthless environment. A sense
of humor is usually high on any list of desirable traits we look
for in a partner or friend. And our own capacity to be amused
is, quite literally, one of the things that makes life worth living.
We delight in our physiological senses; but I suspect most of us
would probably choose to be blind or deaf rather than face the
prospect of a life in which we would never again find anything
funny, never again feel inclined to laugh at something someone
has said or done.

The things we find comic are many and varied. They include

- jokes
- riddles
- puns
- caricatures
- mimicry
- mime
- surprises (a jack-in-the-box popping up)
- absurdities (a man wearing a toilet seat as a necklace)
- incongruities (a child speaking like an adult)
- insults ("It's great that you love nature despite what it did to you")
- representations of various kinds of misfortune (accidents, embarrassment, loss of control, weakness, stupidity, ignorance, and failure)
- transgressions (dead baby jokes that violate our normal notions of moral decency)
- talk about sex, body parts, and toilet functions

There is probably no situation that could not be found amusing by someone, somewhere. But that just testifies to the diversity—some would say the perversity—of human beings and their cultures. From the standpoint of normative ethics, the key issues concerning humor involve questions such as these: Should some sorts of humor be condemned as morally objectionable? If so, why? Should finding certain things funny be viewed as a moral failing? For that matter, should being able to find certain things funny be viewed as a moral virtue? These will be our guiding questions here. But in order to tackle them we need first to review the leading explanations of why human beings laugh, as well as our reasons for valuing humor, and a sense of humor, so highly.

Why do we laugh?

Why do human beings laugh? This question is ambiguous. It could be understood in at least three ways:

1. What features of jokes or amusing situations prompt us to laugh?
2. What psychological mechanism is called into play by the things we find amusing?
3. What evolutionary process led to the phenomenon of human laughter and our capacity for humor?

The first question has often been posed by thinkers seeking to identify the essence of humor, a key feature that all amusing phenomena have in common. The second question sees humor as a possible avenue of insight into human nature. Philosophers and psychologists who have sought to understand humor and laughter have typically focused on (1) and (2). The third question has been asked only more recently as the popularity of evolutionist thinking has grown.

The evolutionary question is certainly fascinating and has produced some ingenious hypotheses. Perhaps the simplest view is that laughter originated in the cry of triumph let out by a victorious hunter or warrior. As Stephen Leacock puts it, "The savage who first cracked his enemy over the head with a tomahawk and shouted 'Ha ha!' was the first humorist."[1]

More subtle is the "false alarm" theory, which notes that we typically laugh after some gradually built-up expectation is resolved in a nonthreatening way. This happens, for instance, when we hear the punch line of a joke, when we are saved from danger, or when the monster threatening us with outstretched talons turns out to be a tickling monster. The theory suggests that laughter began as a specific kind of signal from an individual to the rest of the group that what had seemed threatening was in fact harmless.[2]

A variation on the false alarm theory is the idea that smiling and laughing evolved as ways of indicating that an apparent act of aggression was intended playfully rather than seriously. This is the function it still serves in rough-and-tumble play and when it accompanies practical jokes or teasing. It lets everyone know that the safety catch is still on. Along related lines, Robert Provine speculates that laughter originated in the sort of panting that accompanies boisterous play (including sexual play), and eventually came to symbolize the playful state itself.[3]

The essentially social nature of laughter would also seem to give it evolutionary value. We rarely laugh alone, but in groups laughter is contagious. This indicates that it has a bonding function, promoting solidarity and trust within a group. At the same time, the fact that smiling bares one's teeth suggests the possibility that it evolved from what was initially an aggressive display.[4] This idea hooks up both to the idea that laughter accompanies the transition from feeling threatened to feeling safe, and to the theory that it is prompted by feelings of superiority (see below).

Evolutionary accounts such as these can certainly suggest things to look for when we are trying to understand what amuses us today and why.[5] Nevertheless, these latter questions are distinct from the question of origins. In the Western philosophical tradition many accounts of the nature of humor have been offered, often presented as explanations of laughter, but three have been especially influential.[6]

Laughter expresses feelings of superiority

This is the oldest theory, suggested by Plato, taken up by Aristotle, and given its best-known expression by Hobbes.[7] It is easy to see its appeal. So much humor involves someone being represented as suffering a misfortune or exhibiting some kind of failing. Consider, for instance, the clown with outsized ears and a big red nose who slips on a banana skin, sits on a hot plate, or gets a pie in the face; jokes about people who are ignorant, stupid, ugly, impotent, humiliated, immoral, sick, or about to be eaten by cannibals; true reports of people who have harmed themselves in ways so ridiculous as to qualify for a "Darwin award"; or simple teasing, where we typically suggest that a person is inadequate in some way.

The superiority theory coheres easily with the evolutionary accounts of laughter that see it as originating in displays of aggression or in the triumphant roar of the victor over the vanquished. An obvious weakness of the theory, however, is that it does not seem to fit cases where the laughter is entirely good-natured, as when two friends meet each other unexpectedly. Nor does it apply in any obvious way to neutral sorts of humor like simple wordplay. Nor does it easily explain the many occasions where we laugh at ourselves.[8] A more sweeping criticism of the theory is that it generalizes from the kind of humor that is popular mainly among men and overlooks the typically less aggressive sort of humor preferred by women.[9]

Laughter is a reaction to incongruity

This theory was first articulated by Kant in the late eighteenth century, although earlier writers on humor had noted that surprise was often an important ingredient. Incongruity is a broad term covering many things, including absurdity, impossibility, strangeness, inappropriateness, irrelevance, ambiguity, and unexpectedness. The theory certainly seems to offer an important insight into what it is in so many jokes, witty remarks, comic routines, and other humorous situations that prompts laughter. Take a simple joke:

> Two cannibals are eating a clown. One says to the other, "Does this taste funny to you?"

The joke hinges on the ambiguity of the word "funny" which can mean "unusual" as well as "humorous." The incongruity lies in the application of the first of these senses to a piece of food being eaten, suggesting that something could have a humorous taste, which is absurd.

In a lot of humor the incongruity is so obvious as to require no analysis: animals dressed as humans; adults acting like children; Greek philosophers in togas strolling around a soccer pitch (a famous Monty Python sketch); someone who is supposed to be respectable (for instance, a priest or a rabbi) breaking the rules; a person revealing herself to be fantastically stupid. The list is endless.

The incongruity theory seems to catch more in its net than does the superiority theory, applying to slapstick as well as to simple puns. But stated in general terms—as it usually is—it does not seem to explain very much. The problem is that not all incongruity is funny, only some. If the cannibal eating the clown had said, "Does this taste metaphorical to you?" there would be incongruity but no joke. We laugh only when the incongruity is significant in some way, when it fits the situation and gives us some sort of intellectual satisfaction.

Laughter is a release of nervous energy

This is the view made famous by Freud in *Jokes and Their Relation to the Unconscious*. Freud's basic idea is that when we laugh, we are discharging surplus psychic energy that is suddenly no longer needed. The energy can be cognitive or emotional, but his theory seems most plausible when the energy in question is being used to repress thoughts, feelings, and desires surrounded by social taboos. In this respect jokes are similar to dreams, a place where forbidden desires surface into consciousness.[10] For Freud, the forbidden desires are primarily sexual or aggressive, and this certainly helps to explain the high proportion of jokes that concern sex, body parts, bodily functions, and victims of cruelty, violence, accidents, and other misfortunes. But one can easily extend the basic idea to include the constraints imposed by other social norms or even by reason itself. A lot of humor involves violating expectations established by logical thinking (cold baths are a lot nicer when the water is warm) or by our experience of a familiar order, either natural or social. (Q: Why do elephants sit on marshmallows? A: To avoid drowning in the hot chocolate.) This theory also fits quite well with some evolutionary accounts of laughter since cackling over a vanquished foe or laughing from relief at the removal of danger can also be understood as expending suddenly superfluous energy. Like the other two theories, though, it seems to capture one aspect of humor rather than provide a key to the whole. Many jokes and humorous routines involve a buildup of tension that is released when the punch line is delivered; but just as many are not of this sort. And while humor certainly gives us a safe form of transgression, if Freud's explanation of laughter were correct we would expect the people who are normally the most repressed to be the ones most prone to explosive laughter; yet the reverse seems to be true.

There are, of course, other accounts of humor. Max Eastman argues that humor is a form of play in which we are able to adopt a disinterested attitude toward matters that we would normally take seriously.[11] Henri Bergson argues that humor typically involves an incongruous mixing of the human and the inhuman, as when a person is represented as a thing controlled by mechanical laws.[12] Most theories, like those discussed above, are open to the charge that they fail to cover every form of humor or humorous situation. But we do not need to view the various theories as exclusive or even as competitors. They typically highlight important, though not necessarily universal, features of humor or laughter, and thereby, in conjunction with one another, deepen our understanding of a phenomenon that remains somewhat mysterious despite its familiarity.

The value of humor

It is reasonable to assume that any attribute of human beings or feature of human society that is found in every society must have proved valuable in some way. It must have helped people—both individuals and communities—to survive and flourish. This is true of our ability to empathize with others, our capacity to cry, and our tendency to gossip, as well as our enjoyment of music, dance, and storytelling. So we may assume it is also true of our capacity for laughter and the pleasure we take in jokes, funny stories, slapstick, teasing, absurdity, and the like.

But in what ways is humor beneficial? Identifying at least some of its possible benefits will provide us with a suitably broad, holistic perspective from which to address the problem of determining what our attitude should be to humor that could be considered morally objectionable. Here, then, are some of the main reasons we value humor.

Humor gives pleasure

Most obvious of all is the simple fact that under normal circumstances humor is something we enjoy. Comedy, jesting, bantering, joking, silliness, and countless other varieties of lightheartedness give us pleasure, and we value such pleasurable experiences for their own sake. In this respect, as John Morreall argues, humor may be compared to works of art, and our enjoyment of humor to aesthetic experiences.[13] We think of happiness as necessarily involving pleasure, and a life devoid of pleasure cannot be considered happy.

Humor promotes health

The Bible tells us that "a merry heart is a good medicine,"[14] and some recent research into the therapeutic effects of laughter seems to bear this out. Research findings are perhaps not as conclusive as the champions of laughter therapy assert. But there is evidence that laughter boosts the immune system, activates the cardiovascular system, and lowers stress.[15] The release of endorphins that accompanies laughter may also reduce cravings for food and drugs. And it is reasonable to suppose that humor carries indirect physical and psychological benefits by facilitating social interaction.

Humor creates and strengthens social bonds

Humor is inherently social. We laugh far less when we are alone than when we have company. Laughter is contagious, which is why television comedies often come with laugh tracks. It is also cohesive, helping people to feel more comfortable with one another, even when they are meeting for the first time.

Humor socializes

Through humor we learn important information about our society, and not just while we are growing up. Who we are, what we value, what we despise, what we pride ourselves on, what we are ashamed of, what is expected of us, what is acceptable, what is taboo—we glean a good deal about such matters from the kind of humor we witness and participate in, as well as from the sort that is frowned upon and discouraged.

Humor reinforces a sense of community

Along with its socializing function, humor also makes people aware of what they have in common. As Henri Bergson observes, "laughter always implies a kind of secret freemasonry, or even complicity, with other laughers, real or imaginary."[16] It is an interesting fact about many jokes that they work only if the assumed knowledge or point of view that they rest on remains unstated. Somehow, letting this information remain implicit makes a difference. Consider this joke:

> A Saudi, a Russian, a North Korean, and a New Yorker
> are walking down the street. A pollster approaches them,

clipboard in hand, and says, "Excuse me. What is your opinion on the current meat shortage?"

"Shortage?" says the Saudi. "What is a shortage?"

"Meat?" says the Russian. "What is meat?"

The Korean looks especially confused. "Sorry," he says, "but what is an opinion?"

It is the New Yorker, however, who looks most confused of all. "Excuse me?" he says. "What is 'excuse me'?"

To understand this joke, one must know that Saudi Arabia is a rich country, that many Russians have experienced serious economic hardships in recent times, that North Koreans are subject to ideological indoctrination by their government, and that New Yorkers have a reputation for being rude. But anyone who explained all this before telling the joke would lessen its impact on the listeners: half the air would already have escaped from the balloon. In part this is because the element of surprise is diminished; but it also because we enjoy the sense of being in the know. The joke-teller assumes we have the background understanding, and when we laugh along with others, our common grasp of things is confirmed. All of this is pleasing.

The joke contributes to a sense of community in other ways too. Although the punch line targets New Yorkers, it is New Yorkers who will probably enjoy it the most. True, rudeness, is not considered a virtue. But New Yorkers can feel that they, more than anyone, are able to appreciate just how "true" the joke is. And they can take pride in the well-defined identity that is their own, an identity in which their famed rudeness is seen as an inevitable side effect of the fast, crowded, urban, modern, dynamic, take-no-prisoners-and-suffer-no-fools character of their beloved city. They can also enjoy the contrast evoked between their situation and that of the other figures in the joke. People not from New York, on the other hand, can enjoy the slight boost the joke gives to the idea that they and their communities occupy higher moral ground.

Humor enlightens

Because so much humor works by presenting us with some kind of incongruity, it frequently offers novel perspectives on familiar things; and these can yield insight into situations, theories, cultural developments, and people, including ourselves.[17] Here is a philosophical example:

> Q: How does one behaviorist greet another behaviorist?
> A: "You're feeling fine. How am I?"

The joke effectively (and wittily) brings home just how radical a change it would be to our normal ways of thinking and speaking if we took seriously the idea that we do not have "inner" subjective states to which we enjoy some sort of privileged access. Another example, which I admit is unlikely to produce guffaws but which happens to be a personal favorite:

> A tourist in Rome asks another tourist how to get to the Colosseum. "Oh, it's fairly easy," says the latter. "You go down this road, take a left, and walk on about half a mile. You can't miss the Colosseum. It's directly opposite the souvenir shop."

Momentarily seeing the great monument take second place in a person's thinking to the souvenir shop, and recognizing that this inversion is quite conceivable, tells us something about contemporary culture, tourism, and our attitude toward history.

Cartoons are especially good at providing this sort of jolt to our thinking.

Humor is wit-sharpening

Bantering, especially the kind that involves back-and-forth teasing, is essentially an intellectual contest. Engaging in it presumably brings cognitive benefits just as playing a sport yields physical benefits. More generally, because a key ingredient in much humor, especially jokes, is a moment of surprise, "getting" a joke of almost any kind involves quickly making unexpected connections. The sort of cognitive shifts and lateral thinking required constitute a kind of intellectual calisthenics.

Humor is a way of tackling difficult issues

One familiar way of communicating a complaint to someone while reducing the likelihood of his being hurt, offended, or annoyed is to wrap the criticism in humor. So we ask the person who is not helping with the chores what her last servant died of. Or we tell the driver who has parked three feet from the sidewalk that we can walk to the curb from there. We also use humor to address in an indirect way important topics that can be hard to confront directly, such as sex, marriage, sickness, and death. It is surely significant that so many jokes concern such matters.

> Doctor: About your chest X-rays. I've got good news and
> bad news.
> Patient: What's the bad news?
> Doctor: The X-rays show that you're dying of lung cancer.

Patient: So what's the good news?
Doctor: Did you see that hot little nurse who brought
      them in?
Patient: Yes.
Doctor: I'm screwing her.

Humor is a tool for social criticism

George Orwell remarked that "[e]very joke is a tiny revolution."[18] In authoritarian societies where criticism cannot be expressed straightforwardly or publicly without risk, jokes about the government, the police, the official media, and so on, often constitute an important channel of underground criticism. The mere act of repeating them can be a rebellious gesture, especially when the consequences of doing so may be dire. This is one sort of situation where the "release" value of humor is especially evident. But even in open societies, humor performs an indispensable critical function. Socrates famously defended his critical, questioning ways by arguing that he prevented Athens from becoming sluggish, likening himself to a biting gadfly. But his contemporary, the comic playwright Aristophanes, could have claimed this role with equal justice. And today it is the cartoonists and the comedians who often provide some of the sharpest criticism of the way we live and the way we are governed. Nor should the criticism be thought trivial or superficial just because it is delivered with or through humor. According to Louis Rubin, a leading scholar of American humor, in "the basic American humorous situation . . . humor arises out of the gap between the cultural ideal and the everyday fact, with the ideal shown to be somewhat hollow and hypocritical, and the fact crude and disgusting."[19]

Humor toughens us up

Self-pity is an ever present temptation to anyone afflicted with the human condition. Each of us is exposed to and will inevitably experience loss, failure, misfortune, frustration, sickness, and death. Humor, which as we have just noted often deals with such things, helps to keep us from being overwhelmed by their attendant miseries and anxieties. It does for us what parents do for their children when they see them take a painful tumble and make light of it before the bawling starts. The availability of the amused standpoint means that the analgesic properties of humor are already circulating in our blood when misfortune strikes. And showing that we can take a joke and laugh at our weaknesses indicates to others an underlying strength.

Humor can make us more self-aware and self-critical

For many people, the most entertaining humor is the kind in which some group they belong to is targeted in a nonhostile way, usually by fellow insiders. Much Jewish humor is of this sort.

Abe: Heard this one? Cohen and Goldstein go into business . . .

Sol: Oh, give it a rest! Why does every joke have to be a Jewish joke? Why can't you, just for once, tell a joke about some other ethnic group?

Abe: OK, OK, I get the point. So, Yamamoto and Suzuki are going to their nephew's bar mitzvah . . .

Many of the best New Yorker cartoons serve a similar function, aiming their darts at the lifestyles, anxieties, foibles, and obsessions of the chattering classes from whom the magazine draws most of its readership.

Simon Critchley takes this point a little further and gives it a philosophical twist. Humor, he argues, raises our awareness of contingency: that is, it enables us to see in a fresh light things that we take for granted, regard as natural, or assume to be necessary.[20] For instance, a comic might raise a laugh simply by pointing out the strangeness of the following exchange: A man in a café points to an empty chair and says to the woman sitting nearby, "Excuse me, is anyone sitting in this chair?" "Yes," says the woman. "Oh, sorry," says the man and walks away. When Lenny Bruce makes an entire routine out of reiterating an offensive word until its meaning drains out of it, we are left asking ourselves how a certain arbitrary noise ever came to have so much power over us.

Humor offers us a way of seeing our practices and conventions through alien eyes. This can have a liberating effect insofar as conventions are constraints that we unthinkingly accept. Even reason itself is a kind of constraint: hence the pleasure we take in zany humor. (Groucho: "Outside of a dog, a book is a man's best friend. Inside of a dog it's too dark to read.") In some Asian philosophies, this sort of liberation is seen as a precondition of enlightenment; hence the absurdist character of much Taoist and Zen humor.[21]

Pursuing the connection between humor and self-awareness still further, Critchley argues that humor underscores the "eccentricity" of human beings—that is, the radical difference between ourselves and the rest of nature.[22] We alone are able to reflect on our identity and situation; we alone are aware of our ultimate fate. To be sure, this sort of philosophical detachment may not have any obvious evolutionary value for the species; but it could prove beneficial to certain subgroups, particularly that select band who make a living from teaching philosophy.

Objectionable humor

For all the reasons just given, humor is generally a good thing, and only blood descendants of John Calvin would want a world without it. Yet most people would agree that humor can sometimes be objectionable; so let us take a look at the kinds of humor one might object to.

The unfunny

Probably the most common criticism of remarks or actions intended to amuse is that they are simply not funny. A lot of people respond this way to puns, possibly from bitterness at their not being endowed with the punning gift. Very often, attempted humor is unfunny simply because it is puerile; we might laugh at it if we were six, but we aren't, so we don't. This is not a moral objection, however. A puerile sense of humor can be tiresome at times; we might think its possessor would be more attractive or impressive without it. But parents don't warn their children to be wary of such people. Silly or tedious jokes are no worse than cheesy poetry, and having a taste for them is hardly a moral failing.

The inappropriate

Sometimes we disapprove of humor because we consider it inappropriate in a particular situation. A string of knock-knock jokes inserted into a eulogy, for instance, or someone's toasting a newly married couple with crude jokes about marital problems, would normally fall into this category. A subspecies of the inappropriate is the tactless. Telling a joke about a guy getting fired to a friend who is upset over having just been laid off would show a disturbing lack of empathetic consideration. But there is nothing much that one can say in general terms about such circumstances: there are no specific rules of appropriateness relating specifically to humor that one can construct or consult. We must simply be familiar with the relevant prevailing conventions and exercise good judgment.

The hurtful

The kind of humor that is most obviously objectionable from a moral point of view is the kind that causes unnecessary and undeserved pain to a particular person or group of people who are present. In ordinary, everyday circumstances, raising a laugh at someone's expense by taunting, insulting, belittling, or humiliating her is a form of bullying. The schoolteacher who amuses the class by making cruel jokes about some child's appearance is essentially doing the same thing as the playground bully who enjoys throwing his weight around.

The wrongness of this sort of humor is situational. The taunts and insults may be quite witty in themselves, the way "yo mama" jokes sometimes are. But directed at real people who have done nothing to invite or deserve them, they are like a slap in the face. Humor of this kind can be condemned both because it causes needless pain (the utilitarian reason) and because the victim is being treated as simply a means to the humorist's own ends (the Kantian reason). As we noted when discussing rudeness, there may be occasions when raising a laugh at someone's expense serves some worthwhile purpose: a teacher may embarrass a student who has fallen asleep in class, or require late-arrivers to sing a song; a quick wit may successfully shame a bully. But in such cases the victims are not innocent; that is the special circumstance that permits the general rule to be suspended.

The importance of "innocence" in determining what is acceptable and what is off limits is clearly indicated by our attitude toward humor at the expense of public figures. For cartoonists, and comedians, it is always open season on politicians and celebrities. These victims are fair game since they have chosen to be public figures and must accept the slings and arrows of the humorists as part of the price they pay for their elevated status. The same rule applies to contestants on a talent show such as *American Idol*. They know in advance that they may be ridiculed by the judges: the humiliating forthrightness of the judges' remarks is, after all, one of the reasons for the show's popularity. But some things remain off limits: for instance, the children of the public figures. So while Bill Clinton—whom no one ever accused of innocence—probably set a record for the number of jokes inspired by a U.S. president, the satirists generally refrained from making off-color jokes about his daughter, Chelsea.[23]

The ideologically unsound

Some humor rests on attitudes we consider morally reprehensible. Of course, what one considers ideologically objectionable will depend on one's ideology.[24] Po-faced advocates of prohibition might see nothing funny in representations of drunkenness. Some Christians may disapprove of jokes about Jesus. But what comes to mind most readily here are jokes that express forms of racism, sexism, sexual prejudice, or cultural arrogance. This is not necessarily because these are especially common. It may be that we automatically think of such examples because there is greater agreement today about the wrongness of, say, racist humor, than about the impropriety of jokes mocking some religious or political doctrine. And that is because—as we have noted elsewhere—some version of egalitarianism, accompanied by an associated commitment to universal rights, has increasingly become part of the intellectual bedrock of the mainstream political culture in modernized societies.[25]

The tasteless

Tasteless humor is the kind that seeks to generate laughter out of something that prevailing notions of moral decency tell us is not a proper subject for humor. We can distinguish here between the sick and the gross. Gross humor takes as its subject matter things we find aesthetically disgusting such as vomit or excrement. Most of it is puerile and is neither especially funny, nor interesting, nor morally objectionable. It may, of course, be objectionable to make gross remarks in a certain setting, such as at a medal ceremony. But there seems to be no reason to condemn gross humor as morally reprehensible except, perhaps, insofar as it uglifies our culture.

Sick humor is different. Classic examples include dead baby jokes, Helen Keller jokes, jokes about accident victims like Princess Diana, jokes about uses for dead cats, and jokes about people suffering from some illness. What is distinctively "sick" about sick humor is not the fact that it makes fun of suffering or misfortune: a lot of humor does that. What makes a joke "sick" is the way it transgresses norms of conventional moral decency, either in its subject matter or in the callous attitude the joke presupposes or expresses. Take this example:

Q: How do you stop a baby falling down a manhole?
A: Stick a javelin through its head.

If one finds this funny, it is partly because of the bizarre visual image conjured up, partly due to the absurdity of forestalling a threat to the baby by a method that would kill the baby, and partly because the problem—admittedly one that is highly contrived—is solved in a way that scandalously ignores normal ethical constraints. (The prevailing consensus among professional ethicists is that sticking javelins through the heads of babies is morally suspect.) Just as "blond" jokes involve hyperbolic stupidity far beyond anything one might conceivably encounter, sick jokes usually express an indifference to misfortune and to common moral norms that is somewhat fantastic in relation to our everyday experience.

What distinguishes humor that is deemed inherently unsound or sick is that it will be thought objectionable even when there is no victim immediately present to feel the jab of the jest. In these cases the moral issues are raised more by the *content* of the joke than by the immediate situation in which it is told. This is the sort of humor that raises interesting questions from the standpoint of normative ethics; so this is the kind of humor we will be concerned with from this point on.

What do we object to in sick or unsound humor?

There are two main reasons for objecting to the sort of humor we have described as sick or unsound. The most obvious objection is that such humor often causes harm. Admittedly, the harm is not directly inflicted on some target that is present, but people can be harmed indirectly. Unsound jokes that express prejudices of some sort, for instance, may help perpetuate existing inequalities and injustices by reinforcing negative perceptions of ethnic minorities, women, gays, or other disadvantaged groups.

The causality at work here can be subtle and complex. The problem is not that people hear an antigay joke and immediately head off to find some gays to beat up. As Merrie Bergmann observes in a discussion of sexist humor, a sexist joke is never an isolated event; it will always belong to a widespread pattern of instances in which women are demeaned or disparaged.[26] This point applies generally to other jokes that express prejudices. Humor of this sort is like pollution in the air: we all breathe it in. In some places it is more concentrated, and here the effects are worse. Communities where crude antigay humor flourishes are more likely to see blatant prejudice and hostility directed against gays. But everyone's thinking is affected. Negative stereotypes can promote distrust, fear, anger, contempt, dislike, or indifference directed toward those targeted. They can foster fear, doubt, anxiety, and self-hatred in those being demeaned. And the telling and retelling of jokes expressing prejudice conveys the message to anyone within earshot that such prejudices are acceptable, as does the action of laughing at them.

This objection—that the humor is injurious—seems to apply more to unsound than to sick humor. An argument can presumably be made that sick jokes subtly foster contempt for the afflicted and callousness toward suffering, thereby diminishing our reserves of sympathy toward those who suffer. But in this case the causal track from jest to tangible harm is circuitous and rather faint. Indeed, some have even argued that dissolving the pity we naturally feel for those we view as unfortunate could be a good thing since it helps us to see and treat them as equals.[27]

The other main reason for disapproving of sick or unsound humor concerns not its consequences but its source: those who traffic in it are thought to reveal some sort of failing within themselves. Often, the main thing revealed is just that the humorist holds false beliefs. He or she believes, for instance, that Jews are obsessed with money, or that gay men are more likely than heterosexuals to molest children. Now holding false beliefs, even of this sort, is not always viewed as a moral failing. We make allowances in the case of children or of people who have spent their lives immersed in an environment where such beliefs are commonplace. Darwin's belief that women are by nature intellectually inferior to men, or Lincoln's doubts about the intellectual and moral equality of blacks and whites, are not generally held against them as unpardonable moral blemishes. But we do not so readily forgive false beliefs like these in our contemporaries whom we expect to be better informed.

More significant, though, is the idea that sick and unsound humor evinces, and perhaps reinforces, failings within the humorist that have more to do with character. Racist jokes, for instance, may reveal various kinds of resentment, hostility, arrogance, or contempt. Sick humor perhaps gives us a glimpse of depravity lurking in a person's depths. We suspect that people who tell sick jokes are insufficiently sympathetic and good-hearted, and so we suspect that they are more likely to hurt us and less likely to help us when we are in need.

This last point underscores the fact that although we can easily make an abstract distinction between what humor reveals about people and what consequences it promotes, in the real world these are linked, and we see them as linked. Where there is anger, bitterness, or contempt, there is also danger, for our character traits find full expression in our behavior toward others. To take just one example, research among college students showed that males who enjoyed sexist humor reported themselves as more likely to be sexually aggressive, while women who enjoyed sexist humor tended to be more accepting of interpersonal violence.[28]

We might also note here that there are two further reasons why we might *dislike* sick or unsound humor, although these are not, strictly speaking, objections to its content.

When someone tells you a joke, she reveals, among other things, something about her view of you, and you may find this objectionable. When I tell you a joke in the normal way, it is reasonable to assume both that I think it funny and that I expect you will too. I presuppose that you share something of my beliefs, attitudes, or sensibility. As we noted earlier, this is one of the ways humor promotes social cohesion. But if the mind-set in question is one you disagree with or disapprove of—say, one that is racist or heterosexist—you are likely to view my assumption as insulting.

You may also dislike what your response to a joke tells you about yourself. It is possible to disapprove of a joke, even to be insulted that anyone would think you would be amused by it, and yet find it funny. In this case, part of what you object to may be the way the joke disturbs the dark sediments of your own thoughts, attitudes, prejudices, desires, and feelings. Your internal chuckle is an unpleasant reminder of the gap between these subterranean impulses and the ethical standpoint you officially endorse.

There are thus plenty of reasons why we might dislike and disapprove of sick or unsound humor. Yet, as we saw earlier, humor in general is valuable in many ways, both personally and socially. So as we take up the normative issue of what our attitude should be toward humor that conventional morality condemns, we find ourselves once again trying to balance two perspectives. For what we think objectionable at the micro level according to the norms of apple-pie morality may be contributing to or signifying a certain kind of cultural health when viewed from a wider, more holistic vantage point.

The normative appraisal of dubious humor

What should be our attitude toward sick or unsound humor? One response is just to denounce it all as morally wrong. This keeps things simple, and it yields an easy rule to guide one's conduct when dubious humor is flying around: if in doubt, don't laugh. But as with blanket condemnations of gossiping or rudeness, this is too simple. It is safe, but thoughtless. And it overlooks the possibility that at least some sorts of objectionable humor may have a positive role to play.

Option B is to go to the other extreme and argue for blanket acceptance of any kind of humor whatsoever. Nothing is sacred. Anything goes. Anyone time-traveling from the early days of radio or television to look in on twenty-first century comedy would probably think that this must now be the rule, even in the mainstream media. Publicly acceptable humor today is much less straitjacketed than it used to be: adultery, masturbation, oral sex, bestiality, necrophilia, race relations, and the prospect of nuclear annihilation or environmental disaster are all grist to the comedian's mill. But the time-traveler would be wrong. There are still lines that no humorist anywhere near the mainstream would dare to cross. Making light of the Holocaust, the 9/11 bombings, or any fairly recent tragedy; comedy that rests on offensive stereotyping of ethnic minorities; and jokes that implicitly approve of crimes like rape or child abuse, for example, are considered beyond the pale in mainstream circles, and few believe it would be a good thing for this sort of humor to become commonplace.

The obvious "third way" would be to formulate some general principles to serve as guidelines in determining whether or not a given piece of dubious humor is morally acceptable. But this is remarkably difficult to do. A natural starting point might be to draw a line between humor that carries harmful consequences and humor that is merely judged to be in bad taste. Harmful jokes are the kind that cause pain to or hurt the interests of individuals, social groups, or society as a whole. Tasteless humor, by contrast, has no victim or injured party: it just causes noses to wrinkle in disgust. But this apparently straightforward distinction cannot be made sharp, nor can it yield clear criteria for isolating unacceptable humor.

One problem—not the most serious, perhaps, but still significant—is that for some people the tasteless is never *merely* tasteless but is invariably harmful insofar as it befouls the culture. It might be compared to the sort of unsightly architectural structures that spoil a landscape; no specific individual is a victim, exactly, but everyone is worse off. Aesthetic issues are not usually viewed in ethical terms, but where people's quality of life is significantly affected, it is reasonable to think in this way.[29]

A more obvious difficulty is that, as we noted earlier, a good deal of humor has a target. Much of the time what we laugh at are people's failings, misfortunes, eccentricities, and so on. To try to isolate whatever is likely to injure or offend someone somewhere would not leave much to jest about. It doesn't really make much sense to say that we may make jokes, but we should avoid anything that disparages people who are ignorant, stupid, old, sick, poor, privileged, rich, fat, or neurotic, or that picks on identifiable groups such as academics, engineers, doctors, lawyers, priests, and politicians, or, for that matter, men, women, Jews, Gentiles, Catholics, Protestants, whites, blacks, gays, straights, and so on. Humor that doesn't eat meat becomes anemic. So if we want our culture to be one in which humor flourishes, we have to accept that there will be victims.[30]

Thus there is no clear-cut general formula that we can use to determine whether or not a given instance of humor is morally acceptable. Here, as elsewhere, we have to exercise *phronesis*—practical wisdom—factoring in and weighing up all sorts of variables. But although we may not be able to construct an algorithmic formula, we can still try to identify the more important considerations and say something about how they should be taken into account. We will do this by taking a closer look at the types of humor we classified earlier as "unsound" and "sick."

Unsound humor

If asked what kind of humor is ideologically unsound, many people will probably think immediately of jokes that are blatantly racist, sexist, or antigay. It is often assumed that our world is awash with such jokes, but this is questionable. Undoubtedly there are many communities, defined by some combination of age, class, region, religion, education, profession, gender, race, ethnicity, sexual orientation, or political opinions, where jokes resting on crude disparaging stereotypes are common. But to a large extent such humor tends to stay in these cultural sinkholes.[31]

Any scholar who says this obviously invites the standard charge of being hopelessly out of touch, cocooned away in some ivory tower. But in response, I invite readers to call to mind, say, five jokes that denigrate black men as lazy, dirty, obsessed with sex, or prone to crime. Or to call to mind the last time they heard that sort of humor on television or from the mouths of public figures. True, you can easily find such jokes on the Internet; but then you can find pretty much anything on the Internet. My point is simply that across wide swaths of our culture today, humor of that sort is largely absent. So much is this the case that even when seeking to analyze humor one can feel uncomfortable just relating examples of it for illustrative purposes. One fears that one will be suspected of harboring the offensive attitude, or accused of irresponsibly spreading the poison.

In Michael Moore's film *Roger and Me*, the television celebrity Bob Eubanks is shown telling the following joke:

You know why Jewish girls don't get AIDS?
They only marry assholes; they don't screw them.

This joke manages to convey an insulting view of Jewish men, reinforce the false idea that AIDS is primarily a "gay plague," express a callous attitude toward AIDS victims, and pick up glancingly on the stereotype of Jewish women as frigid. It succeeds in being both sick and unsound at the same time. The fact that Eubanks tells it may be viewed as evidence that jokes of this sort circulate like schools of fish in the dark waters below the surface visible to polite society. But it is surely also significant that Eubanks tried to prevent this clip from being included in the film and was forced to make a public apology on *Entertainment Tonight*.

If one does dive into the humor of crude prejudice, the most striking thing is perhaps how unfunny most of it is. The joke just cited, however distasteful, arguably contains some degree of cleverness. But a good deal of willfully offensive humor is frankly puerile. Dark-skinned people are likened in dozens of roundabout ways to pieces of excrement; Mexicans are ridiculed for being poor and eating only rice and beans; gays are portrayed as sex-obsessed, and often the whole point of a joke about gays is simply to conjure up an image of anal intercourse or same-sex fellatio.

Many jokes of prejudice, as we might label them, are little more than vehicles for the expression of prejudice. Their point is to shock. For instance:

> What is the difference between a black person and a snow tire?
> A snow tire doesn't sing when you put chains on it.

The joke carries the implication that black people are well suited to slavery or the chain gang. But since slavery is no longer a live political issue in the United States, the real force of the joke lies in the unabashed way it expresses a disparaging view of black people. The analogical connection is forced and silly. Anyone enjoying this joke today would be amused largely by the sheer transgressive character of the attitude conveyed, an attitude toward black people that no longer dare speak its name in polite society.

It is not always easy, though, to be clear about why one finds a joke unfunny. Quite a lot of jokes occur in many variations; they are shells into which one can pour different content. Most people will have heard a variation on this one:

> What do you call a hundred lawyers at the bottom of the sea?
> A good start.

The same joke has presumably been told about blacks, Jews, Mexicans, Gypsies, Brits, Germans, Democrats, Republicans, socialists, and gays. In some cases we laugh; in other cases we do our Queen Victoria impersonation and are not amused. Yet the structure of the joke is identical, so the difference in our response must be entirely due to how we view the attitude being expressed.

Here is a joke I would probably not tell at a feminist philosophy convention:

What do you call a woman with two brain cells?
Pregnant.

Yet here is one that nobody I know would object to:

What do you call a man with half a brain?
Gifted.

Why the difference? Obviously jokes will receive different responses from audiences with different ideological leanings. But the wider social and historical context is also relevant. For millennia women have been denied equal rights and opportunities. An important aspect of this oppressive treatment, and a common rationalization of it, has been the idea that women are less intelligent than men. So humor that rests on this stereotype is more suspect since if it does anything to reinforce a sexist prejudice, it is harmful. Jokes that disparage men, on the other hand, are considered innocuous since men have not been systematically subjugated by women. Indeed, such jokes could even be viewed as culturally beneficial insofar as they chip away at patriarchy and the idea, absorbed by both men and women, of male superiority.

This point can be generalized. The moral dubiousness of a joke is inversely proportional to the social standing of those it targets. The more powerful the "victim," the less likely we are to object; the more vulnerable the victim, the more questionable the humor. This is surely why no one ever worries much about jokes that insultingly stereotype Americans, Germans, the British, or the French. In the contemporary world such people are taken to represent the rich, the powerful, and the privileged (even though many of them are none of these within their own society). Stereotyping Jews, Mexicans, African Americans, or gays, on the other hand, immediately opens one to the charge of picking on those who have already been victimized by life itself, of kicking people when they are down.

The point just made is fairly obvious, but it can be accepted only in a loose way. Once we press on it a little, we find there are all sorts of tricky complications. For instance, one venerable way of poking fun at men has been to imply that they are bossed around by women. Thus:

> A Jewish boy returns from school and excitedly tells his mother that he has been given a part in the school play.
>
> "That's wonderful!" she exclaims. "What part is it?"
>
> "I'll be playing the Jewish husband," says the boy.
>
> "What?" says the mother, obviously annoyed. "You go straight back and tell the teacher you want a speaking part."

Few would see this sort of joke as objectionable. Yet it is possible that laughing at men for failing to be assertive subtly reinforces the very norms of masculinity that have oppressed both women and men for so long.

Equally problematic is the apparent double standard that operates regarding jokes about the stereotypical deficiencies of men and women (or other groups unequal in power). There are those who laugh readily at jokes making fun of men while scowling suspiciously at jokes targeting women. Yet this inconsistency could be accused of indirectly encouraging just the kind of stereotype feminists have long criticized, the notion of women as the weaker sex who need to be protected from insults in a way that men do not. In that case, the critique of supposedly unsound humor may be as open to criticism as the humor itself.

About stereotypes

We noted above that the most obvious objection to unsound and sick humor is its potential to do harm. The harm can be direct or indirect, subtle or crude, and it can be suffered by the victim, the humorist, the audience, or the community at large. In the case of unsound humor, as we have just observed, the harm is often thought to arise out of its reliance on negative stereotypes.

Stereotypes and thinking in terms of stereotypes have a bad reputation. Some might even argue that a good reason for a blanket condemnation of all unsound humor is that it promotes these alleged evils. But this is misguided. As we noted in our discussion of snobbery, thinking in stereotypes is in fact something we all do all the time. We can't help it. It's a kind of thinking that has been hardwired into us in the course of our evolution, and we could never survive without it. What, after all, is a stereotype but a general idea of some type of thing to which we assume specific instances will conform.

I come across a bright red and yellow toadstool in the woods; it may be harmless, but I stereotype it as possibly poisonous and leave it unpicked. I see a converted railway carriage with a red neon sign over the door that reads "Joe's Cafe"; I assume this is a place where I can probably buy a BLT sandwich but will not find sweet potato gaufrettes with duck confit on the menu. I ask a well-dressed middle-aged man for directions in downtown Toronto and do so in English, unthinkingly assuming that he speaks English too. I select a cantaloupe at the grocery store by presuming that if it looks healthy on the outside, it won't be rotten on the inside. I decide to buy a Honda rather than a Yugo on the grounds that it will probably be more reliable.

In each of these cases I make use of stereotypes. I assume that qualities often associated with a certain class of things will be found in the particular instance I encounter. Of course, I could be wrong. The toadstool may be harmless; the Honda may be a lemon; Joe's Cafe may be a gourmet French restaurant sporting a humble exterior as a humorous, postmodern gesture. But to be reasonable, and useful, an inference only needs to be probable; it does not need to be certain.

Granted, though, that thinking in stereotypes is both unavoidable and useful, it may still be objectionable in certain instances.[32] What people usually object to are negative stereotypes of certain groups such as ethnic minorities, the aged, country folk, the disabled, gays, or women. Jokes targeting such groups obviously rely on these stereotypes: for instance, on the notion that women are poor drivers, that Jews are avaricious, or that gays are sex-obsessed. Here again, though, this is a problem only in relation to certain groups. We don't object to *all* negative stereotypes. Consider the following news item:

> The Harvard Psychology Department has announced that in future it will use lawyers rather than rats in all its behavioral experiments. Four reasons were given. (1) There are more of them. (2) There is no danger that the researchers will become fond of them. (3) They clean their own cages. (4) There are some things rats won't do.

The joke rests on a negative stereotype of lawyers, but of course no one minds since lawyers are not seen as vulnerable: they can take it. True, some lawyers may be offended; but who cares?

As we noted earlier, it is always open season on those seen as privileged.

There is one kind of negative stereotype appearing in countless jokes that illustrates well the complexity of determining the moral acceptability of humor. From time immemorial, people in almost every culture have found stupidity funny, and it is common for some alien group to be stereotyped as stupid and made the butt of jokes. Thus the English tell Irish jokes, Canadians tell Newfie jokes, Germans tell Polish jokes, and people everywhere today tell blond jokes, such as this one:

> A blond walks into a library, goes up to the circulation desk, and cheerfully asks for a hamburger with fries. The librarian points to the books on shelves all around them, to the people sitting at desks reading, and says, "I'm sorry, this is a library."
>
> The blond is confused for an instant, but then the penny drops. "Forgive me," she says, and, leaning over toward the librarian, whispers, "Could I have a hamburger with fries, please."

Do such jokes express, foster, or reinforce negative stereotypes and harmful prejudices? One could, of course, protect oneself against this charge (except insofar as the prejudice is against stupid people in general) by saying "dumb guy" instead of "Newfie" or "incredibly stupid person" instead of "blond." But it is an interesting feature of such jokes that doing this makes them less funny.[33] Why this should be so is hard to say. Part of the explanation might be that we derive satisfaction from making the connection ourselves between the type mentioned and the behavior described. But perhaps more important is the simple fact that some group is being put down and we enjoy the taste of blood.

And of course, when someone else is ridiculed, our own superiority is indirectly affirmed.

One could also argue that the extreme nature of the stupidity represented, the utter implausibility of anyone's being *that* dumb, takes the edge off the insult. Yet this is not always true; it depends on who is being targeted. And gross exaggerations of some still-vulnerable ethnic group's supposed laziness, filthiness, or criminal tendencies would not be redeemed on this score. As we have already noted, historical circumstances are relevant. If Irish jokes are less objectionable than they used to be, this is surely in large part because in places like England and America Irish people are less oppressed and victimized than in the past, so the jokes matter less.

In fact, though, it is not just that improved circumstances toughen one's hide; the very proliferation of jokes about the stereotypically stupid blunts the edge of the knife. To a large extent the blond joke or the Polish joke has become a genre rather than a weapon. Their purpose is not to insult a specific group, or to express contempt for them; their purpose is just to be funny.[34] The Newfies, Poles, or blonds are little more than part of a joke delivery system, the tray on which the joke is served, similar to the "mama" in "yo mama" jokes. The *form* of a yo mama joke —"Yo mama is so fat she needs her own postal code!"—is an insult directed at someone's mother; but the real point of the joke is simply to display one's wit.

Sometimes a targeted minority can take over an offensive stereotype and wield it in self-defense. The African American comedian Redd Foxx once asked a predominantly white audience, "Why should I be wasting time with you here when I could be knifing you in an alley?"[35] And in some circumstances a group can even come to relish the genre that may once have been offensive. In 1978, the election of Karol Wojtyla as the first Polish pope (and the first non-Italian pope in over four centuries) triggered a new round of Polack jokes. For instance:

Why are they building a pub behind the Vatican?
So the pope will have somewhere to cash his paycheck.

Did you hear that the pope is planning to wallpaper the Sistine chapel?

Asked what he thought about the abortion bill, the pope said, "Pay it."

Did you hear that Pope John Paul II thought he was Pope John Paul the eleventh?

Are these jokes demeaning to people of Polish descent? Some scholars think so, but others disagree.[36] Lydia Fish, for instance, denies that these jokes should be taken seriously as expressions of anti-Polish prejudice, pointing out that they were being told and enjoyed by members of the Polish community. At the time, she argues, these jokes became "a real source of ethnic pride, a sort of humorous gloating that 'one of our boys made it.'"[37] This sort of disagreement between scholars underlines the point that determining the significance of allegedly unsound humor, and appraising its likely effects, can be a complicated affair.

Just how complicated it can be is well illustrated by Elliott Oring in an interesting analysis of blond jokes. Some people see jokes that rest on the stereotype of the sexually promiscuous dumb blond as demeaning to women; indeed, this is a common feminist criticism of them. According to Oring, though, the criticism is misguided. Blond jokes, like other cycles of jokes, form a "joke script." And the target of the jokes is not always what it seems.

Joke cycles are not really about particular groups who are ostensibly their targets. These groups serve merely as signifiers that hold together a discourse on certain ideas and values that are of current concern. Polish jokes, Italian jokes, and JAP jokes are less comments about real Poles, Italians, or Jewish women than they are about a particular set of values attributed to these groups. The attributions, while not entirely arbitrary, are, for the most part, not seriously entertained.[38]

The real focus of blond jokes, Oring argues, is not women as such. That interpretation leaves unexplained why blonds are picked on rather than brunettes, why of all negative traits, stupidity and promiscuity should be highlighted, and why blond jokes are as popular with women as with men. In his view, the ulterior purpose of the jokes is to express contempt for values that are opposed to the needs of the modern workplace.

As women have moved into the workplace and into positions of power in the public sphere, they must be dissociated from images of ineptitude and sexuality. The workplace is theoretically and semiotically a world of rationality, calculation, organization, and cool efficiency. It is not a world that can accommodate stupidity or the disruptive forces of sexuality. In other words, women in the workplace should not in any way suggest that they are reminiscent of the dumb blond.[39]

Now this analysis of blond jokes does not necessarily legitimize them entirely. It plays down the idea that they perpetuate harmful stereotypes, but it calls attention to ways in which they add to the pressure on women to conform to an existing ethos. It does show, though, how the role of stereotypes in humor may not be as obvious as we sometimes think.

The upshot of this discussion of stereotypes is not that they are never objectionable, nor that jokes never play a part in promoting stereotypes that are injurious. But concerns about political correctness can easily make us too censorious. They can also blind us to the ulterior significance of the humor in question. Stereotypic thinking is not inherently wrong. Jokes that rely on stereotypes, even negative stereotypes of particular groups, may be harmless. Only when the stereotype is taken seriously and the group in question is socially vulnerable do we really need to worry.

Appraising unsound humor

The main point that has emerged so far is that any moral appraisal of humor thought to be ideologically unsound has to take into account many variables. The most important of these are the following:

- the content of the humor
- how much harm it actually does (or is likely to do)
- the occasion
- the identity of the humorist
- the known (or assumed) opinions and attitudes of the humorist
- the identity of the audience
- the known (or assumed) opinions and attitudes of the audience
- the extent to which the "victim" is vulnerable to oppression today

- the background historical circumstances of the victim
- the history of the sort of humor at issue

What makes things so difficult for the normative ethicist is that these variables are continually shifting. So the same joke can have a different meaning at different times, to different groups, and on different occasions. The following joke was told to me by a Jewish friend:

> What's the definition of an anti-Semite?
> Someone who dislikes Jews more than is necessary.

This could prompt laughter when told between Jews or between anti-Semites. But the nature of the laughter would be different—in one case self-deprecating, in the other aggressive—for the meaning of the punch line would be understood differently.

Or consider this one:

> How many men does it take to open a bottle of beer?
> None. It should already be open when she brings it to you.

Told among men in a community where women are still viewed as subservient, the joke may bolster the attitude it expresses. Told by a man to a mixed company of progressive-minded, twenty-first-century, politically correct liberals, the joke has a very different force. It is presumably intended and likely to be received ironically. The humor largely lies in the teller's affecting an outmoded and politically incorrect attitude. And far from reviving or supporting this attitude, the joke, if anything, underscores the fact that everyone present rejects it.

We see here what we have already noted in earlier chapters: the fact that contemporary cultures lack homogeneity, along with

the fact that we live in such fast-changing times, greatly compli-
cates the normative appraisal of behavior. One last example that
illustrates this very well is the comic stereotyping of gay men as
effete and narcissistic. Before the 1960s this would usually have
been a straightforward expression of sexual prejudice, one of the
many ways that homophobic attitudes throughout society were
encouraged. At a time when gay rights was not on most people's
political agenda, the oppressive impact of this sort of caricature
went unnoticed by many. As the campaign for gay rights gained
momentum, the offensive caricature became subject to criticism,
and progressive-thinking audiences started to view it with distaste. Eventually, however, as the gay community becomes more
confident and more accepted within the cultural mainstream,
the humorous use of the old stereotype can sometimes reappear
but in a less objectionable light. Of course, in some contexts it
may still function oppressively. But in a production such as the
2001 Broadway version of *The Producers*, the gay characters are,
in effect, caricatures of caricatures; and the New York audience,
gay and straight, is able to enjoy them precisely because in this
particular time and place the stereotypes have become relatively
harmless. Indeed, laughing at them now arguably reinforces not
the old prejudices but the new spirit of toleration and sense of
common community.

Changing times can change the significance, the impact, and
the moral acceptability of a joke. This is a source of anxiety for
many of us today. We do not wish to be or be thought prejudiced
or insensitive, but neither do we want to put ourselves in a hu-
morless straitjacket of political correctness for fear of occasionally making a mistake. Here is a joke I like to tell on the first day
of a logic class.

A guy working in his backyard sees his new neighbor next door and goes over to introduce himself. On learning that the new neighbor is a professor of logic at the university, he's impressed, but a little confused.

"So what is logic, anyway?" he asks.

"Let me explain," says the professor. When I look over at your yard, what do I see? A dog kennel. From that I infer you have a dog. Given you have a dog, I next deduce that you have kids, since they're always the ones who persuade their parents to get a dog. Your having kids entails that you have a wife, and from that I infer, naturally, that you are heterosexual. That's logic."

"That's brilliant!" says his neighbor, and goes away suitably impressed. Later that day he gets talking to his friend across the street.

"You should meet the new guy next door to us," he says. "He's one sharp cookie. He's a professor of logic."

"Logic? What's that?" asks the other.

"You don't know? Ah, well, let me explain. Do you have a dog?"

"No."

"FAG!!"

In my opinion this is an excellent joke. But some people may be made uncomfortable by it. They perhaps hear the politically incorrect word "fag" and worry that any joke that uses the word must be expressing an attitude sympathetic to the views of people who use the term for real, as a term of abuse. Obviously, this is not the case. The butt of the joke is the homophobe who is shown to be an illogical fool.[40]

Still, some might argue that regardless of the joke's content, the mere utterance of the word "fag" is reprehensible since it subtly legitimizes an epithet that should be flushed from the language. Isn't this, after all, why I would not tell a similar sort of joke that made fun of racists but used the word "nigger?" This argument has some plausibility, but I do not think it is correct. For one thing, the term "nigger" has a unique position in the language at present. The problem with using it is not that doing so necessarily encourages racists; the problem is that when uttered in certain contexts the word has the status and discomforting force of an extreme obscenity. Even caged within quotation marks it can still shock.

There is also a more theoretical point to be made here. The taboo against using terms like "fag," "nigger," "kike," "dago," and so on, has probably served a useful purpose. It expresses a disavowal of prejudice, a disavowal that one hopes will become increasingly widespread. But there is a basic distinction, well known to philosophers of language, between *using* a word and *mentioning* it. It is offensive to refer to Japanese people as "Japs." There is nothing wrong with making the observation that some people refer to Japanese people as "Japs." In this latter case the word in question is being mentioned rather than used. If we are to talk intelligently and intelligibly about cultural and linguistic matters, we have to be able to do this. Thinking that even the *mention* of an offensive word does harm is a mistake, an attitude that almost smacks of superstition, reminiscent of the way characters in J. K. Rowling's Harry Potter novels refer to the evil Voldemort as "He-Who-Must-Not-Be-Named."

When we appraise humor in which offensive words appear, the mere appearance of the words is not in itself grounds for criticism. Everything depends on how they are being employed. In the 1960s, when the comedian Lenny Bruce identified members of his audience as "niggers" or "kikes," his purpose was to call attention to the words themselves rather than to racial features of the people in question. He was provoking the audience to ask the question: why should we let words have such power over us? What he was doing, therefore, was more like *mentioning* the epithets than actually using them in the normal way to express prejudice, hostility, or contempt.

Our anxieties go beyond the use of certain words, of course. People may worry that a joke about Jews is anti-Semitic, especially when it plays off a stereotype. But it all depends on a host of variables. This joke seems to be generally regarded as funny and inoffensive:

> A priest and a rabbi had an ongoing argument over
> whether Jesus was really Jewish. One morning the rabbi
> buttonholes the priest and gleefully shows him an article
> in a theology journal. "Here you have it," he crows, " a
> conclusive demonstration that Jesus was indeed a Jew.
> Four points which taken together constitute a conclusive
> proof. He lived at home until he was thirty. He went
> into his father's profession. He thought his mother was a
> virgin. She thought he was God!"

But what about this one?

> Have you heard about the Jewish sports car? It doesn't
> just stop on a dime, but turns around and picks it up.

Many people would consider this joke offensive. Why the different appraisal? Both jokes rest on stereotypes; but the second one rests on the stereotype of the avaricious Jew, and there are at least three reasons why this might be considered more objectionable. First, avarice is generally viewed as a moral failing; the traits ridiculed in the first joke, by contrast, are not vices that are likely to provoke hostility. Second, the avaricious stereotype is not accepted by Jews as having any basis in reality, so it comes across as hostile rather than self-deprecating. And third, this is a stereotype that has played a part in the tragic history of the Jews, for it has been used to incite and justify hostility, persecution, violence, and murder.

Perhaps underlying these objections to the joke about the Jewish sports car is the idea that to find it funny one must, in some sense and to some extent, endorse the negative stereotype it relies on. But this is not obviously so. David Benatar, for instance, in a discussion of the way humor employs negative stereotypes, denies precisely this point. He offers as an example the following joke:

Q: Why do Jewish men like to watch pornographic movies backwards?

A: They like to see the prostitute giving the money back afterwards.

According to Benatar he can—and does—enjoy this joke even though he is perfectly confident that he does not buy into the stereotype of Jewish miserliness underlying it.[41]

Even more anxiety-inducing are jokes about the physical features—the noses, eyes, lips, genitalia, and so on—of racial groups. Very often these are simply crude and puerile expressions of contempt or hostility. But they don't have to be. Here is a joke discussed by Laurence Goldstein:

How do you stop a black man from jumping on the bed?
Stick Velcro on the ceiling.[42]

Many people's immediate reaction to this joke, before they have time to reflect on it, will be suspicion. The joke raises a laugh out of a physical feature of black people. Because so many jokes that do something similar are offensive, our first response in this case is understandable. But I would say it is mistaken. The joke is admittedly childish; but it is also creative, and that is what makes it funny. To be sure, as Goldstein notes, one could accuse the joke of reinforcing demeaning ideas of black men as infantile, or of getting a laugh out of the image of one stuck in a ridiculous position. But these points strike me as somewhat forced rationalizations of an instinctive distrust of the joke. We hear a joke that references a racial characteristic and our automatic assumption is that there must be something suspect about it; we then scratch around until we find something that looks as if it will serve to justify our suspicions.

To conclude these reflections on humor suspected of being ideologically unsound, the most striking point to emerge is just how complicated the normative appraisal of humor can be. With so many factors to consider, and with the relations between these in a state of continual flux, it is not surprising that some people opt for a take-no-chances approach, eschewing or even condemning whatever might conceivably give offense. But this is a mistake. While it is obviously true that some kinds of vicious humor can be harmful, it is also true that granting a limited license to risky humor can be beneficial. Ideological correctness tends to be unresponsive to changing times. It applies prefabricated formulae to situations unthinkingly, like a computer running a program. Humor—especially risky humor—is one of the means through which we become more aware of how things stand historically in the complex interplay between our ideological assumptions and the changing circumstances in which they operate. Monitoring our response to humor is a way of taking our cultural temperature.

Humor is also, of course, a vehicle for self-criticism:

Pat: This current obsession with political correctness is crazy!

Kim: You mean "psychologically challenged."

When we laugh at ourselves, we loosen the straps of our ideological straitjackets. This is surely a good thing. And it is another good reason for allowing ideologically risky humor some license. If we are so cautious that we always stay safely within the lines provided by principles of political correctness and moral respectability, we deprive humor of one of its most valuable functions, a function it shares with philosophy—making us think again and anew about the things we take for granted.

Sick humor

The other kind of humor we identified earlier as morally suspect is the kind that is routinely called "sick." But what are we saying when we describe a joke as sick? Obviously, the term is strongly pejorative. It goes beyond saying that the joke is in bad taste, suggesting, rather, that it should be classified with the utterances of the mentally disturbed or criminally insane. The implication is that a healthy mind would not come up with a joke of this kind, would not pass it along, and would not find it funny.

Jokes described as sick are usually about such matters as sickness (naturally), disabilities, pain, death, old age, the victims of accidents, of crimes, or of natural disasters, criminals, criminal actions, or sexual activities generally regarded as deviant such as bestiality or necrophilia. They typically express what seems to be an amoral attitude by making light of things we regard as an occasion for sympathy (e.g., dead babies) or disapproval (e.g., rape). The cynicism conveyed can actually be a motive for telling sick jokes. While the primary motive behind most joke telling is to make people laugh, thereby giving the teller the satisfaction of being the cause of this valued effect, a secondary motive often at work is that of self-presentation. Through their humor jesters project a certain image of themselves as, say, progressive, conservative, cheap, hedonistic, clever, or naive. When we tell sick jokes, we unavoidably convey a measure of cynicism since we show through our actions that we don't regard some sacred cow as all that sacred. Our willingness to transgress challenges the authority of the lines we are crossing.

As with unsound humor, most sick jokes are just puerile:

What is red and silver and walks into walls?
A baby with forks in its eyes.

When they tickle the more sophisticated funny bones, this is usually because they involve some kind of imaginative wit or ingenious wordplay. But in most instances, what is funny about the "sickness" is the transgression of conventional moral norms. This is the moment of incongruity that many take to be necessarily present in all humor. Sick humor typically depicts or assumes a callousness that is funny both because it is exaggerated to the point of absurdity and because it is unexpected. There is a shocking contrast between what we naturally take to be the correct moral attitude and the kind of mind that would be amused by what is described. The discovery that we ourselves possess this sort of mind provides a secondary shock. It also creates a bond between humorist and audience. We noted early on that one function of humor is to promote social cohesion. Sick humor can do this in a particular way by incriminating the listener along with the teller. Anyone amused by it shares in the humorist's amoralism, and a rapport is established between people who see themselves mirrored in the other's cynicism.

The transgressive nature of sick jokes is surely one of the main reasons they are especially popular with children: to them transgression is thrilling. Of course, it may also be that children usually have less understanding of certain sorts of suffering, so their readiness to laugh may evince a failure of empathetic imagination. Then again, childhood suffering seems capable of generating callousness as easily and as often as it produces sympathetic sensitivity.

The transgression of norms can be viewed as a kind of originality, and in other spheres—most obviously the arts—this is generally considered a virtue. In everyday moral life, however, we tend to praise predictability. It may not make people more interesting, but it generally makes them less threatening and more trustworthy. So sick humor, like provocative art, can set up a nervous tension between our admiration for the cleverness behind it and our unease at what it points to or unearths within us.

But what sort of people are we that we find sick humor amusing? Why *do* we find the morally shocking funny? Well, if laughter is indeed rooted in the cry of triumph expressing a sense of superiority, that presumably indicates that some part of us often feels pleasure when we encounter vulnerability: the experience enhances our own sense of health, strength, and supremacy. This is an insight Nietzsche exploits to great effect wherever he applies his theory of the will to power. The pleasure in question can be aroused in many ways: by infants, lapdogs, defeated opponents, executions, someone else's failed marriage, and every kind of schadenfreude. Here is one source of the pleasure offered by sick humor; and from a Nietzschean perspective, far from being "sick," such humor is grounded in what is natural. It is natural to relish health, vigor, and mastery. If anything is "sick," Nietzsche argues, it is the bad conscience we suffer from when we find ourselves enjoying our sense of superiority.[43] It is sick in the sense of being contrary to our natural impulses.

Transgression is also an element in most people's fantasies. According to Freud, "jokes evade restrictions and open sources of pleasure that have become inaccessible."[44] Like dreams, jokes offer a form of substitute gratification of our often unconscious desires, and this is another reason why sick humor might thrive. Dead baby jokes, for example, may express the thought, common among young people, that babies are a nuisance, a hindrance that one would be better off without.[45] At the same time, sick humor can also provide an outlet for unconscious anxieties. This might help explain the popularity of genres such as the "Mommy, mommy" joke among children ("Mommy, mommy, what's for dinner?" —"Shut up and get back in the oven.").

These explanations of why sick humor amuses us may strike some as resting on rather dismal views of human nature. But there is no reason to suppose they tell the whole truth about what we are, or that they plumb our psychological depths while familiar qualities like sympathy or altruism are comparatively superficial. Human beings are morally complex. As David Hume elegantly puts it, there is "some particle of the dove, kneaded into our frame, along with the elements of the wolf and the serpent."[46]

Our reaction to sick humor is accordingly complex. Pleasure at the spectacle of vulnerability is usually combined with anxiety at both our own callousness and our ability momentarily to put aside conventional moral norms. Finding ourselves amused by sick humor is also likely to produce a pang of guilt, a response worth investigating briefly.

As we observed when discussing gossip, an interesting and important component of our moral heritage is the saintly ideal, the ideal of a perfectly pure heart. Kant describes such a person—one who only ever wants what is right—as a "holy will." In Christian cultures the ideal is commonly associated with Jesus. It also figures in myths and legends, perhaps most famously in the story of Galahad, the only one of King Arthur's knights who was pure enough to attain the Holy Grail. To be pure in heart is not simply a matter of always doing the right thing; it is also, and more importantly, a matter of always having morally sound thoughts, feelings, and desires. It means being above selfishness, envy, petty rivalry, cruelty, contempt, illicit desire, and so on.

One assumes that such saintly types would not find sick jokes funny. The perfectly good heart is so dripping with kindness and compassion that no spark of morally dubious humor can kindle a smile. Our own amusement reminds us of our distance from this ideal, so it is accompanied by a moment of self-criticism, experienced as guilt. Such feelings should not be ignored, but nor should they always be our guide. The saintly ideal may sometimes serve a valuable purpose, but it should not be the only or even the main benchmark against which we judge ourselves. No doubt it would be good in many ways if most of us were less callous and more humane than we are (although comedians would find it harder to make a buck). But our ethics has to be one tailored to flesh-and-blood human beings trying to get by in a complex world, not to saints.

An analogy may be useful here. Moralists celebrate love and frown on illicit lust. But this Manichaean attitude is simpleminded. Romantic love grows out of sexual desire. Evolution has programmed us to feel this, and we are not programmed to stop feeling it once we have found a special companion. So to condemn lust, as orthodox Christian morality does, is foolish. We should accept it, even be grateful for it, as a key component of romantic love and one of the things that makes it possible. The case of humor is similar. It commonly involves the thought or spectacle of someone else discomforted or rendered vulnerable. We are more or less programmed to enjoy such situations, and if we were not, we would probably be living in a world without laughter—or, more likely, in a world without us, since we would have been selected out long ago. So it is misguided to lacerate ourselves over what we find funny. This is not to say that we have no responsibility whatsoever for our feelings;[47] but common sense tells us that our inner states are less easy to control than our actions.

Should sick humor be discouraged?

The conventional moralistic response to sick humor suggests that it should be discouraged. When parents or teachers hear a child telling jokes about Helen Keller or the victims of some natural disaster, they typically disapprove and may well feel some obligation to convey this to the child. This attitude is understandable. There are several cogent arguments for discouraging sick humor, all resting on the idea that it does some sort of harm. Sick humor may

- cause pain to those whose misfortunes are targeted;
- cause pain to others whose pain is related to those targeted;

- negatively affect the character of the joke-teller, fortifying any tendencies to callousness and cruelty;
- negatively affect society at large in the same way;
- weaken the power of the conventional moral norms that sick humor transgresses.

These look like powerful objections to any kind of sick humor. Yet as with some of the other alleged vices we have examined, what may be ugly or discomforting when seen close up can have an important role to play in our wider cultural economy. As Peter Berger observes, "the social order is enhanced by allowing a place within it of counterthemes, counterworlds."[48] And Bernhard Greiner, a historian of comedy, sees comedy as establishing a counterworld to everyday life.[49] From this perspective, sick humor could be viewed as a kind of counterpoint to our society's leading moral melody.

So before we condemn sick humor too readily, we should ask whether we would really prefer a world in which only morally healthy humor flourished, and where sick jokes were either never told or never found funny. Should this be our ideal?

This is surely one of those cases where we need to be careful what we wish for. As we have seen, humor is essentially transgressive: it challenges authority; it overturns reason; it violates taboos. It is also commonly directed at misfortune, weakness, stupidity, incompetence, and failure of all kinds. These are the aspects of humor that give it its bite. Without them, it would be tediously insipid and lose much of its social value. Of course, humor can be transgressive without being sick and can target failure without picking on excruciating misfortune. But it is possible to be disgusted by specific jokes while recognizing them as by-products of a culture whose vibrancy and self-awareness make them inevitable.

This does not mean we have to laugh at jokes we consider sick. We may choose to distance ourselves from them. But it does not follow that we should wish to rid the world of them. The sick humorist may not be greatly admired; but then there have always been jobs that are valuable, even necessary, yet not much respected. Humor is an important constituent of our culture, to be valued for its contribution alongside science, literature, the arts, political debate, television, public parks, sports, journalism, or food. To expect it to keep its transgressive character while never crossing the line of moral respectability is unreasonable.

We might think of sick humor as like a pungent spice that by itself would burn the tongue but without which the soup would be bland. It may even in some ways be a sign that a culture is healthy, just as our anxieties about rudeness may be a symptom of cultural dynamism. For it perhaps indicates a historical trajectory away from a society constrained by traditional notions of the sacred and the taboo.

This is not to say that any and every kind of humor is morally acceptable; obviously it is not. As with gossiping or rudeness, when humor causes undeserved harm to those who are vulnerable, either directly or indirectly, that is a good reason for criticizing it. But we should not leap onto our moral high horse too quickly. Nor should we be too hard on ourselves for what we find amusing. The lines of acceptability with regard to humor, as with social etiquette, are constantly in motion. So to those who earnestly peer at everything through moral spectacles, who are instantly suspicious of anything that might cross some line of political correctness or moral probity, the message is simple—lighten up!

5 Why Should I Respect Your Stupid Opinion?

You have been called for jury service. The trial is complex and much hangs on the relative credibility of different witnesses, particularly those offering expert testimony regarding whether a certain medicine is likely to produce aggressive behavior as one of its side effects. A professional psychiatrist called by the defense testifies that in his opinion this effect is very likely. During cross-examination, however, the wily prosecuting counsel manages to unearth a surprising, seemingly irrelevant, but nonetheless startling fact about this "expert": he believes that aliens from space landed in the Nevada desert around 1965 and now effectively control all branches of government using advanced mind-control technology. The "expert" has in fact published several articles arguing for his views in the journal *Alien Watch*, and is a founding member of MASA (Mankind Against Space Aliens).

When the jury eventually retire to deliberate, it is not long before these beliefs become the focus of attention. One juror refers to the expert as "that nutcase who believes in UFOs." Another calls him a "crank." A third describes him as "cuckoo." Inevitably, his beliefs about aliens damage the credibility of his other testimony in the eyes of some jurors, even though he undoubtedly has the requisite qualifications to be considered a legitimate expert on the side effects of certain medicines.

One juror, however, playing the role of Henry Fonda in *Twelve Angry Men*, resists this wave of skepticism. "Did anyone notice," she says, "that the expert called by the prosecution wore a crucifix around her neck? This 'expert' may well believe that a man called Jesus walked on top of the sea, changed water into wine, came back to life after being executed, and ascended to heaven on a cloud. I hate to be awkward, but to my way of thinking these beliefs are even more incredible than the idea that space invaders landed in the desert. After all, the belief about aliens— unlike orthodox Christianity—doesn't assume anything supernatural or contrary to the scientific view of nature."

Listening to the debate, you feel yourself pulled in two directions. On the one hand, you can't help agreeing with those inclined to question the judgment of someone who believes the government is controlled by aliens from outer space. On the other hand, supposing for the sake of the argument that your general outlook on the world is thoroughly secular, you sympathize with the view that many orthodox religious beliefs are just as implausible. So you find yourself astride a paradox. You consider both sets of beliefs equally incredible, yet you think of only one as giving grounds for impugning the wisdom of the believer.

This little scenario raises many questions. Is it reasonable to allow what a person believes in one field to affect how we receive her opinions on other matters? Are religious beliefs that posit miracles on a par with other beliefs that run counter to mainstream, scientifically informed opinion? What makes a belief rational? Should the acceptability of a belief be affected by how long it has been held or by how many people share it? These are intriguing issues, but my main focus here will be on the notion of *respecting* another person's beliefs. In particular, what does it mean to respect someone's beliefs? When and why should such respect be given? When and why might it be withheld?

The default position for most of us in a modern, pluralist, liberal democracy is that we should respect other people's beliefs. Respectfulness is a virtue, and it is associated with tolerance, which everyone agrees is a good thing. To not respect someone's beliefs is generally viewed as a failing; it can be hurtful or alienating, and evinces a closed mind. But this common response is too simple. Not all beliefs are worthy of respect, and withholding respect is sometimes in order. There are different kinds of respect, and a belief may deserve some of these but not others.

Already, alarm bells may be ringing in some readers' minds, since it is often assumed that respect for a person's beliefs is inseparable from respect for him as a person; so to deny the former is to withhold the latter. But I will argue that this view is mistaken. Moreover, it supports an attitude that, in the name of respect and tolerance, sometimes condones intellectual slovenliness.

Being willing to withhold respect from certain beliefs is a corollary of thinking critically—a quintessential modern virtue. This is why it is an attitude that many of the pioneering minds responsible for shaping the modern era were willing to express, and express boldly. Most often, they did so with reference to the orthodox dogmas of established religions. Thomas Jefferson, for instance, wrote that "the day will come when the mystical generation of Jesus, by the supreme being as his father in the womb of a virgin, will be classed with the fable of the generation of Minerva in the brain of Jupiter."[1] Elsewhere he described the final book of the New Testament as "merely the ravings of a maniac, no more worthy, nor capable of explanation than the incoherences of our own nightly dreams."[2] John Adams called Christianity "a system of holy lies and pious frauds."[3] Voltaire declared it to be "the most ridiculous, the most absurd, and bloody religion that has ever infected the world."[4]

More recent heirs to the Enlightenment tradition also believe there is a time and place for this kind of blunt honesty. Freud held that "religion is comparable to a childhood neurosis."[5] Bertrand Russell described it as "a disease born of fear."[6] Arthur C. Clarke expressed himself only a little less directly when he said, "I have encountered a few creationists and because they were usually nice, intelligent people, I have been unable to decide whether they were *really* mad, or only pretending to be mad."[7] Usually, the argument of these critics is that the beliefs they are dismissing are utterly implausible, given everything else we know about the world, and are obviously inconsistent with other beliefs their proponents hold. But sometimes the negative practical consequences of giving such beliefs a free ride is also emphasized. Thus Richard Dawkins, after the terrorist attacks of 9/11, wrote:

> Many of us saw religion as harmless nonsense. Beliefs
> might lack all supporting evidence but, we thought,
> if people needed a crutch for consolation, where's the
> harm? September 11th changed all that. Revealed faith
> is not harmless nonsense, it can be lethally dangerous
> nonsense. Dangerous because it gives people unshakeable
> confidence in their own righteousness. Dangerous be-

cause it gives them false courage to kill themselves, which automatically removes normal barriers to killing others. Dangerous because it teaches enmity to others labeled only by a difference of inherited tradition. And dangerous because we have all bought into a weird respect, which uniquely protects religion from normal criticism. Let's now stop being so damned respectful![8]

Respect for persons

The term "respect," when used to describe an attitude, has three main senses. It can denote a sort of *esteem*, as when I say that I respect your guitar playing. It can indicate *deference*, as when we speak of respecting someone's rights. And it can signify that we *recognize* and accept something on its own terms; we might say, for instance, that we respect some other culture's traditions, indicating thereby that we will refrain from imposing our own value judgments on them. This last sense, although the hardest to explicate precisely, is closest to the word's etymological root. Our word "respect" is derived from the Latin *respicere*, which means to look back at, or to look at again. This suggests considering or examining something carefully, paying it proper attention, which in turn implies trying to set aside one's prejudices and see the thing as it is in itself. Conversely, to not show respect is to be dismissive, deciding quickly and in light of one's own preconceptions, desires, or interests that something is of little value.

Many things can be objects of respect: laws, rights, skills, virtues, opinions, offices, traditions, institutions, environments—the list is endless. But the kind of respect that is most commonly expected, demanded, and discussed is respect for persons. Since one of my goals here is to clarify the relationship between respect for beliefs and respect for those who hold them, we need to consider briefly what this latter notion involves.

Respect for persons takes two main forms;[9]

i. the sort of respect we think all human beings are entitled to in virtue of their humanity;
ii. the sort of respect that individuals may enjoy—or even claim—in virtue of their particular qualities, experiences, achievements, or position.

Let us look at these in turn.

It is a fundamental tenet of nearly all modern moral and political philosophies that every human being is always entitled to a measure of respect. Various attributes have been identified as the ground of this entitlement, including the fact that we are all created by God in his image, free will, rationality, self-consciousness, natural empathy, and our capacity for feeling. Kant offered an especially profound articulation of this principle, to which most subsequent thinking is heavily indebted. According to Kant, humans are distinguished from the rest of nature in being endowed with reason, which means we can reflect on and deliberate between alternative courses of action. The freedom that our rationality gives us means that we possess a special kind of intrinsic worth—Kant's term is "dignity"—and respect for persons is an acknowledgment of this. Whereas we readily impose our will on most things—animals, plants, landscapes, artifacts—using them to attain our goals with little or no thought for how our treatment affects them, in our dealings with other human beings we generally avoid doing this. Kant even declares the fundamental principle of morality to be that we should respect other people's autonomy by never treating them merely as things to be used for our own purposes.[10] This is what underlies our condemnation of obvious wrongdoings such as murder, rape, theft, blackmail, kidnapping, assault, and so on. But we are also following this principle in a small way every time we use words like "please" and "thank you." These expressions are, at bottom, a shorthand acknowledgment of the fact that the person addressed has a choice over whether to do our bidding.

There are, of course, occasions when we have to impose our will on others. Parents must control their children; psychiatric nurses need to restrain patients who become violent; police officers should arrest bankers running Ponzi schemes. But such cases are sanctioned by widely accepted social conventions and can probably be justified in a way that is consistent with Kant's autonomy principle.[11] Moreover, the *manner* in which control is exercised matters enormously, and, done rightly, it continues to express a basic level of respect for the person being controlled. Children should not be brainwashed or humiliated; prisoners should not be tortured or deprived of basic necessities. There are parameters that constrain how we treat even criminals who have forfeited many of their rights, and these indicate our commitment to the idea that the basic respect due to every individual in virtue of her humanity is inalienable.

Obviously, this commitment is not shared by everyone. Throughout history and around the world today there are countless examples of callousness and cruelty where respect for the humanity of the victims seems to be utterly lacking. But hardly anyone ever tries to justify that sort of behavior theoretically. The closest anyone comes to offering a justification is when violent factions in war-torn countries point to grisly torturings and executions as merited punishments or as warnings to their enemies. But governments and political parties typically deny that they condone practices like torture, however strong the evidence that they have allowed them to happen.[12] For the idea that every person is entitled to a modicum of respect has become an undisputed moral principle for people steeped in modern, liberal ways of thinking. Even when an individual has lost an essential attribute of personhood—for instance, the ability to reason, to make choices, to desire, to think, or to will—the habit of showing respect, and the sensibility accompanying it, are hard to put aside. This habit even extends to our treatment of corpses, regardless of whether or not we believe in any sort of afterlife. We find it hard to view them as mere lumps of matter, just as we find it difficult to tear up photographs of loved ones.

Respect for persons in virtue of their humanity is expressed through the way we treat them. It is not just a matter of having a certain view of them or a certain attitude toward them; it concerns our behavior. It means granting them specific rights, addressing them in a certain way, avoiding treating them the way we treat nonhuman entities, and so on. The other sort of respect we accord to people is more a matter simply of viewing specific attributes positively: for instance, their skill at basketball, their knowledge of cars, their medical qualifications, their courage, their years of experience in a field, their political activism, or their supervisory position. This sort of respect can be won or lost. It can also vary in degree. Most importantly, it is quite independent of the first sort of respect discussed above. We may judge certain people to be in most respects a waste of space, with few admirable qualities or praiseworthy achievements, but we will still acknowledge their right to be treated as a human being rather than as a thing.

To be sure, we might sometimes say in a general way that we respect Jill more than we do Jane, and that kind of blanket statement may seem to apply to the whole person rather than to specific attributes that Jill possesses and Jane lacks. But this should not mislead us. In such cases, we are still really talking about the person's attributes, not about her basic worth as a human being. We are saying that Jill excels Jane in her possession of those attributes we especially value. Jane may perhaps be the better linguist or the more devout Muslim. But our blanket verdict indicates that we value still more highly other qualities—say, courage, kindliness, or sincerity—that Jill exhibits to a greater degree.

Respect for the *right* to believe

What we have referred to as a basic respect for a person's humanity is usually taken to include, or imply, respect for her *right* to believe what she pleases. Freedom of thought is, after all, an essential part of autonomy. But respecting a person's *right* to believe something is not the same as respecting the belief itself. This is another distinction we need to clarify before focusing in on what the latter kind of respect involves.

Pinning down exactly what respecting a person's *right* to believe something involves is not, in fact, as easy as one might think. Presumably it includes not making any beliefs either required by law or illegal. It must also rule out trying to force people to hold or deny a belief by methods that undermine their autonomy, such as hypnosis, drugs, or surgical interference with their brains. And it would also seem to exclude threatening to harm them in some way—physically, materially, or socially—unless they conform to some approved way of thinking. It makes little sense, after all, to tell me I have the right to think what I want, but that you'll bust my kneecaps if you discover me entertaining beliefs you disapprove of.

Yet this "right to believe what you want" is still a slippery fish. On the one hand, sanctions against *beliefs* seem to be not just wrong but silly since we cannot verify with any certainty what a person believes. Our beliefs—as opposed to our utterances and behavior—are invisible to others, at least until neuroscience develops more sophisticated forms of brain monitoring. So even though our right to hold a belief could be violated by a law prohibiting "thought crime," the application of any such law would have to be triggered by some sort of behavior such as professing the belief, participating in a ceremony, or supporting some cause.

On the other hand, there are arguably circumstances in which penalizing or discriminating against someone for his beliefs may be in order. Suppose, for example, that you are responsible for hiring the director of a public program for disturbed children and you suspect that a candidate views some sexual relationships between children and adults as mutually beneficial. Or you have reason to think he considers Caucasians to be intellectually and morally superior to other races. Or you learn that he privately supports involuntary sterilization of criminals. Would his harboring such beliefs be, by itself, a reason for not appointing the person? There are undoubtedly many who would think so. And you cannot easily avoid the problem raised by this sort of example by claiming that you are denying the person the job because of what he might say or do. His record of scrupulously correct conduct could be impeccable, and still many would regard the beliefs in question as grounds for rejecting his application.[13] But if we go along with that, we are, in effect, penalizing someone because of what he believes, which shows that many of us are in fact willing to impose limits even on a person's right to believe what he pleases.

Respect for a belief

So far we have separated out several different kinds of respect:

1. respect for a person in virtue of what she shares with all humanity
2. respect for a person in virtue of her specific qualities, achievements, or experiences
3. respect for a person's right to hold a belief
4. respect for a particular belief

A lot of people assume that both (1) and (3) entail (4); so they worry that to withhold (4) implies that one is withholding at least (1) and (3). This is perhaps what underlies much ready talk about respecting beliefs. The worry is perhaps exacerbated by the fact that withholding (4) may well involve a diminishment of (2). If I tell you that I believe my goldfish is a reincarnation of Winston Churchill, you will assume I'm joking. If I manage to convince you that I'm serious, you will probably conclude that I'm one slice short of a loaf. In other words, learning that I hold certain beliefs is likely to affect your respect for my intellect. But this reduced respect for a particular quality (2) need not affect the other kinds of respect. And the assumption that withholding (4) entails withholding (1) or (3) is mistaken, as we will see.

First, we once again need to make a distinction between respect as an attitude and respect expressed through behavior. One way of failing to respect a belief is to declare it false. Another way is to make fun of it. Another way is to insult it, describing it as "baloney," "tommyrot," "balderdash," "twaddle," "hogwash," "hooey," "blather," "bunk," "bullshit," "claptrap," "drivel," "hokum," "horse feathers," or "poppycock." (We might note in passing that the plethora of such terms indicates that denying respect to beliefs is quite commonplace in our culture.)[14] Each of these responses involves some sort of behavior that risks giving offense to those who hold the belief in question, especially when the belief is central to a person's life and identity as, say, religious beliefs often are. To respect a belief, conversely, could be understood as refraining from doing these things.

The idea that we have an obligation not to criticize a person's beliefs is foreign to a contemporary liberal outlook. There may be specific occasions when criticizing a belief someone cherishes would be tactless, rude, or hurtful; so we can allow that there may be times when silence is the morally preferable option. But in the context of any kind of public forum where ideas are up for discussion, no one can reasonably demand that his beliefs be protected from dissent.

More plausible is the principle that people's beliefs be treated with respect in the sense that they should not be ridiculed, scorned, or insulted. Here the constraint is only on the *manner* in which they are criticized. But although the principle sounds reasonable, it is surprisingly difficult to defend as a general rule. To be sure, we may agree that we should not cause anyone unnecessary pain, and insulting someone's cherished beliefs may do this. But sometimes the pain caused is not gratuitous but an unavoidable consequence of something that really needs to be said. Besides, we also cherish freedom of expression and the benefits it brings. The fact that some people may be offended by what is said hardly seems a strong enough reason to curtail free speech. Moreover, rhetorical freedom is an important aspect of the right to free speech. Very often, the critique of a belief is more powerful and more persuasive because of the way ridicule, irony, sarcasm, and wit are employed. Think of the contributions to important debates made by the likes of Swift, Voltaire, Hume, Paine, Nietzsche, and Mencken.

Those who think that when their beliefs are scorned, their rights are being violated, seem to view holding a belief as like owning a piece of property. On this view, to disrespect a person's beliefs is analogous to trespassing on or defacing her property. But the analogy does not hold. Beliefs, unlike items I own, are in the public domain. I have no more *right* to seeing them treated with respect than I have a right to not hearing people sing silly songs about the moon.[15] This is not to say that insulting a person's beliefs is never wrong. If it is done for no reason, or if the pain caused is not offset by benefits promoted, then there are good utilitarian grounds for criticizing the action. In the public discussion of ideas, though, the critic, even the vituperative critic, is usually presumed to be motivated by a concern to move people's thinking away from falsehood and toward truth, and this gives the action its justification.

So much for respect expressed through overt behavior. We can also conceive of respect for beliefs (or the withholding of such respect) as an intellectual stance or attitude. This is the kind of respect being referred to when I say something like, "I respect your faith," and it is this kind of respect that I will be primarily concerned with from here on. It is useful to approach this more subtle notion of respect by considering cases where many of us do, in fact, withhold respect. Consider the following statements:

- Homosexuals will burn in hell for eternity.
- Santa Claus lives at the North Pole.
- The earth is less than ten thousand years old.

- The Holocaust never happened.
- White people are by nature morally superior to black people.
- Men should have the right to beat their wives.
- Moses' wooden rod turned into a snake.
- Barack Obama is the Antichrist.

Each of these statements is held by some people to be true. Yet a common response—certainly my response—to assertions like these is fairly captured by the expression "hard to take seriously." This does not apply to all, or even most claims that one believes to be false. Take, for instance, statements such as "Bacon wrote Shakespeare's plays," or "Global warming is a myth." I may be convinced that these statements are false, but I will still think it worthwhile to argue against them. They are not beyond the pale. The claims listed above, however, are in a different category. Here I find I just cannot take seriously the possibility that they might be true. And this dismissive attitude seems incompatible with the notion that even while thinking the beliefs false I nevertheless have respect for them. Respect, as we noted earlier, suggests an open-minded attitude, setting aside prejudices, not making one's mind up too quickly but being willing to consider a claim on its own terms. Yet which of us would want to spend any time at all listening to or debating with someone who claims that Barack Obama is the Antichrist or that the Holocaust is a fiction?

Different reasons for respecting beliefs

If lack of respect for a claim means being closed to the possibility of its being true, then respect for a claim, logically, must mean being open to this possibility. And this seems a reasonable first explication of what it means to respect a belief. Immediately, though, we encounter difficulties. Can I not respect the tenets of someone else's religion even though I don't share the metaphysical framework to which they belong? Don't contemporary scientists respect the ideas of earlier pioneers like Aristotle and Ptolemy without actually entertaining them as possible truths? Isn't a degree of respect a necessary part of the empathy that enables us to understand and appreciate ancient mythologies, historical epochs, and alien cultures?

These questions indicate that what we have just said is too simple. Being open to the possibility that a belief is true is one kind of respect, but it is not the only kind. In fact, there are several reasons for respecting a belief. Here are a few:

- You think it is true.
- You think it might be true.
- Many people believe it.
- People you respect believe it.
- Experts in the relevant field believe it.
- It has been believed for a long time.
- There is a lot of evidence for it.
- It coheres with the rest of your beliefs.
- It is part of a belief system you value or admire.
- Believing it may have practical benefits.

Some of these reasons clearly overlap; some belong to quite distinct categories. What matters, though, is that we have to recognize several different types of respect that a belief might enjoy, including the following.

Epistemic respect: This is largely what we have been discussing so far. I grant it to beliefs that I either think are true or am willing to acknowledge might be true given the state of the evidence.

Moral respect: This is given to beliefs that express or belong to an outlook I consider morally admirable. For instance, the claim that all humans are descended from two people created as fully fledged adults by God a few thousand years ago, taken literally, is incompatible with a thoroughly secular, naturalistic point of view. So as a pretender to literal truth, it is not a claim I can honestly say I take seriously. But I can still value the moral vision of human beings and human society forming a single family that is associated with the belief, and respect it for this reason. Similar observations could apply to other articles of faith, such as belief in the law of karma or some other principle of cosmic justice, in the divine inspiration of certain prophets and texts, or in the historical inevitability of social progress.

Historical respect: I can respect a belief simply in virtue of its historical importance, the role it has played in the development of, say, a religion, a discipline, a political movement, or an entire civilization. Ptolemy's model of the solar system may now be universally regarded as incorrect, but it can still be admired for its long success in allowing accurate astronomical predictions, and its contribution to advances in science. Similar things could be said about other significant "paradigm" theories in science, such as Aristotle's physics, medieval alchemy, or psychology based on the doctrine of the four humors. Beyond science, there are countless outmoded beliefs that can also be credited with playing some sort of positive historical role. The idea that kings were appointed by God may at one time have helped societies achieve political stability. The belief that during the Eucharist wine and bread become blood and flesh prompted a sophisticated metaphysical analysis of matter by medieval thinkers that facilitated later advances in philosophy and science.

Intellectual respect: The ideas and theories just mentioned may also be admired purely as examples of remarkable intellectual achievement. Ptolemy's conclusions may no longer be credible, but the thought, creativity, and labor that lay behind them— the sheer cleverness of the way phenomena were explained and problems were resolved—are tremendously impressive. This sort of respect is due to many systems of belief—for example, systematic astrology, scriptural commentaries, and premodern cosmologies—regardless of whether one accepts the claims being made. Here we attend to the intellectual enterprise, setting aside the issue of truth, rather as we might admire the pyramids as monuments to human strength and skill while bracketing our moral view of the impulse that prompts someone to sacrifice so much life and labor on a tomb.

Aesthetic respect: Some ideas can strike us as beautiful either in themselves or as part of an entire system that we admire on aesthetic grounds. This is one of the reasons many of us today respect ancient mythologies. Beliefs about Zeus punishing impiety with thunderbolts cannot be taken seriously in a literal sense. If we met someone who really believed that a being called Zeus struck down miscreants by hurling thunderbolts at them from the top of Mount Olympus, we would probably view her as mentally ill. Yet we can and do admire the beauty and power of the entire mythological framework to which that belief belongs, and in that sense, and to that extent, such beliefs elicit our respect.

Pragmatic respect: Beliefs have uses. In general, we assume that true beliefs are more useful than false ones. But it is possible to recognize the practical value of a belief to an individual or a group while dismissing its claim to epistemic plausibility. The thought that loved ones who have died continue to exist in heaven, watching what we do and waiting for us to be reunited with them, has long been a comfort to many people. Superstitious habits, like carrying a lucky charm onto the battlefield, may have no theoretical justification, but they can still help a person perform with greater confidence. A community's faith in the truth of some legend or in their privileged relationship to a god can help consolidate their sense of identity and purpose. And we still say, "Yes, Virginia, there is a Santa Claus," because Christmas is more fun that way.

There may be other forms of respect that we show toward beliefs than the ones identified here, but I suspect these are the most important. Distinguishing between them, and especially isolating epistemic respect from the others, helps us better understand ambivalences within our attitudes toward certain kinds of belief. Minimal epistemic respect for a belief means being open to the possibility that it is true. And just as I can withhold respect from a certain belief without this implying lack of respect for the believer, or for his right to believe whatever he pleases, so I can deny epistemic respect to a belief without thereby denying it every other kind of respect. The legends about the Olympian gods, the reports of miracles performed by biblical figures, and accounts of fairies and witches are no more credible than stories about talking donkeys or Father Christmas. But this does not mean they cannot be esteemed for their beauty or their historical significance or their moral value.

Objections

It is worth pointing out at this juncture that so far much of the preceding discussion has been about the many ways that people and their beliefs may be *worthy* of some sort of respect. Nevertheless, the point of view I am staking out here obviously invites criticism. I am, after all, endorsing the idea of withholding epistemic respect from beliefs that many people hold sincerely and consider important to their lives. These include religious beliefs that are clearly incompatible with a naturalistic, scientifically informed outlook: for instance, the belief that Moses' staff turned into a snake, that Jesus came back to life after being dead for over a day, or that Muhammad flew in one night from Mecca to Jerusalem and back on a winged horse. I do not expect I can answer likely objections to everyone's satisfaction, but considering some of them may help to illuminate further the rationale for and the cogency of the position being defended.

A person's beliefs are an essential part of his identity; so my view of his beliefs must affect how much I respect the person who holds those beliefs

What the objection asserts is correct. If I learn that you hold certain beliefs, this can significantly affect my overall view of you. If you think gay men should be castrated, I will see you as bigoted and cruel. If you believe America is a perfect meritocracy, I will assume you do not think very critically. If you claim that recent unusual weather patterns were caused by the Cuban government in order to damage Western economies, I will conclude that you are a gullible paranoiac. In such instances, my respect for your moral sensibility, critical intelligence, and wisdom is reduced. This kind of thing happens all the time. Many of us speak readily of how our respect for individuals increased or decreased when we learned some new facts about their lives, their behavior, or their opinions.

But the sort of respect in question here is the sort that was identified above as respect for a person *in virtue of certain specific qualities*, which includes the beliefs he holds. This kind of respect is a matter of degree; it is given to some more than others; it can alter over time. Most importantly, though, it is not really given in a thoroughly holistic way. True, we might say things like, "I lost respect for Steve when I found out that he thinks women are less rational than men." And the form of such expressions makes it seem as if we are talking about our overall respect for Steve as a person. But really, it is our respect for particular *aspects* of the person that is diminished—for instance, his capacity for objective, fair-minded, informed judgment. Our respect for Steve's courage as a volunteer firefighter, or his skill as a dentist, or his hardworking nature need not be affected.

It is tempting to think that our respect for such aspects of an individual as her moral intelligence applies to the whole person. But this is a mistake, a sort of illusion created by the enormous importance we place on some attributes compared to others. Most of the time we value general traits that have moral relevance—for instance, good-heartedness, compassion, critical intelligence—much more than specific abilities that a person might have as, say, an artist, scientist, athlete, or artisan.[16] The only kind of respect that truly applies to the whole person is the kind championed by Kant that we discussed earlier, the kind all people are entitled to in virtue of what they share with the rest of humanity. And this is unaffected by what they happen to believe.

A variation on the objection stated above is that my approach simply fails to grasp how closely connected respect for a person and respect for his beliefs is in many societies, especially those where tremendous importance is attached to saving face or losing face. As a basic guide to Chinese culture notes:

> The concept [of "face"] is related to respect. In much
> the same way that children are supposed to listen to

their fathers' lecture at the dinner table, the Chinese
man expects to hear his opinions go unchallenged....
A man loses face when his opinion is challenged or
contradicted.[17]

Obviously, there is no question that many people the world over
do, as a matter of fact, think this way. But while some may see it as
in a sense natural, it is not necessary. We can, and often do, distinguish between our attitude toward a person and our view of his
opinions. Moreover, in many circumstances doing this is highly
desirable since it is a key ingredient in what we call objectivity.
Objective appraisal of ideas is paradigmatically represented by
the scientific method, but objectivity is recognized as a virtue in
many other contexts: for instance, in evaluating job candidates,
in grading exams, in handing down sentences, in arriving at policy decisions, and so on. Promoting and valuing objectivity is,
in fact, one of the signal features of modernity, a valuable legacy
of the Enlightenment. Drawing a distinction between the two
kinds of respect—for persons and for their beliefs—may thus be
a prerequisite for certain kinds of social progress. To insist that
respect for a person requires one to respect all his opinions can be
seen, in this light, as a reversion to premodern ways of thinking.

To deny a belief epistemic respect
is to be closed-minded

I have defined epistemic respect in terms of how likely we think
it is that a belief is true. We have most respect for claims we
view as certainties; we offer a minimal degree of respect toward
beliefs we do not share but concede to be possible within our
general framework. We withhold respect from beliefs we con-

sider beyond the pale of plausibility. As a description of many people's attitudes, this may be correct. But what about the normative thrust of what has been said? Can one justify failing to respect another person's beliefs simply because they contradict one's own general outlook? Isn't that to endorse a reprehensible narrow-mindedness?

This question can be pressed further. Thinkers like Karl Popper have drawn a sharp contrast between the scientific attitude, which is essentially fallibilist, and dogmatic ways of thinking that refuse to allow certain basic beliefs to be questioned.[18] A paradigm example of the latter would be a religious approach that says certain statements are heretical and therefore should not be uttered; certain questions are impious and therefore should not be asked. In Popper's view, no belief can be automatically ruled in or out of court so long as it can be empirically tested. We should be willing to entertain any belief as a conjectural hypothesis and then see whether it can be corroborated or falsified. To dismiss beliefs out of hand as too implausible to take seriously is thus not the way to champion science over superstition; on the contrary, the true scientific attitude is to be as open-minded as possible.

Willard Van Orman Quine's way of putting a priori and a posteriori truths on a continuum points to a similar conclusion. According to Quine, the contemporary scientific outlook forms an integrated system of beliefs analogous to a spider's web. Beliefs that are fundamental to the system, such as basic principles of logic, mathematics, and physics, are like parts of the web close to the center; they cannot be removed or replaced without massive repercussions for the entire system. Trivial beliefs on which little else hangs, by contrast, are like parts of the web that lie close to the periphery; they can be easily renounced without this disturbing the rest of the system.[19] A key feature of this account, though, is that no belief, regardless of its place in the system, is immune in principle from the possibility of revision. Just as scientists were forced to question such deeply held beliefs as geocentricity, the principle of sufficient reason, Euclid's axioms, and the Newtonian view of time, so we have to be always open to the possibility that even our most cherished and well-established beliefs may usefully be jettisoned, perhaps exchanged for ideas that from our present perspective seem quite bizarre or implausible.

These are legitimate concerns. Articulating them reveals a deep-seated tension in the modern, scientifically informed outlook. We want to affirm as important values both intellectual rigor and open-mindedness; but in the name of the former we may sacrifice the latter. Dismissing some claims as simply not worth taking seriously, it could be argued, seems to deal with the dilemma by simply grasping one of its horns.

But while the objection is correct in principle, it misrepresents the scientific approach in practice. Yes, in an absolute sense science has no critical mechanism analogous to dismissing a claim on the grounds that it is heretical or treasonous. No matter what claim is put forward, the proper scientific response is to ask after the justification—the evidence and the arguments. And if evidence and arguments are forthcoming, the implausible claims will be given a second chance. Of course, the justifications have to be the sort that science respects. Citing biblical accounts of creation as evidence against the theory of evolution, for instance, would not be seen as an acceptable form of justification. Still, the prime facie implausible claim does have some rights, so to speak, in science.

In practical terms, though, scientists, like everyone else, work within a particular theoretical framework or conceptual scheme. This constitutes a definite perspective, and that perspective sets parameters to the sort of claim they are willing to entertain seriously under normal circumstances.[20] Consequently, some claims will not be considered unless there are powerful reasons to suppose that some of science's basic assumptions need to be questioned. So from a scientifically informed point of view, the claim that the earth is less than ten thousand years old, or that Lot's wife suddenly turned into a pillar of salt, or that hanging a horseshoe above your door could help protect your home against a natural disaster, will automatically be ruled out of court as hopelessly implausible.

It should be clear from what has been said that the analysis offered here is thoroughly relativistic. Any evaluation of beliefs takes place from a particular standpoint. These perspectives enable us to make sense of the phenomena we encounter. Standpoints are distinguished from one another by their characteristic presuppositions, values, interests, and methodologies. Orthodox Marxism-Leninism, medieval Christianity, ancient Taoism, contemporary physics, Western liberalism, and Jainism are examples of standpoints from which people view the world and assess ideas. None of us occupy a transcendental standpoint, a "God's-eye point of view" from which we can determine the absolute truth of any claim or the objective merits of the different standpoints. Our judgments are necessarily and irreducibly perspectival—"ethnocentric," to use one of Richard Rorty's preferred expressions.[21]

Nor are our standpoints usually clear-cut. Often, they will be hybrid, perhaps predominantly within one intellectual or cultural tradition while incorporating elements from others the way liberation theology combines Catholic and socialist ideas. But a commitment to intellectual rigor means, among other things, striving to be clear about what our standpoint is, what assumptions it rests on, what these imply, and what they exclude. And if we are honest with ourselves, we will acknowledge that just as a cogent perspective makes certain beliefs virtually indubitable, so it will render some beliefs literally incredible. Before Copernicus, most people would have ridiculed the idea that the earth is hurtling through space at great speed. Today, the idea is a commonplace of modern astronomy. To be sure, there are still those who doubt it. The Association for Biblical Astronomy, for instance, asserts in its credal statement that

> the only absolutely trustworthy information about the
> origin and purpose of all that exists and happens is given
> by God, our Creator and Redeemer, in his infallible,
> preserved word, the Holy Bible, commonly called the
> King James Bible. All scientific endeavor which does not
> accept this revelation from on high without any reserva-
> tions, literary, philosophical or whatever, we reject as
> already condemned in its unfounded first assumptions.
> We believe that the creation was completed in six twenty-
> four hour days and that the world is not older than about
> six thousand years. We maintain that the Bible teaches us
> of an earth that neither rotates daily nor revolves yearly
> about the sun; that it is at rest with respect to the throne
> of him who called it into existence; and that hence it is
> absolutely at rest in the universe.[22]

But those who espouse such views today are regarded by the scientific community simply as risible eccentrics.

Withholding epistemic respect from a belief is therefore not necessarily an instance of closed-mindedness, at least not the sort of closed-mindedness that is harmful. It can simply be an honest recognition that the belief in question is fundamentally at odds with core tenets of one's general view of the world. This is why we do not waste time wondering if any of our economic problems might be solved by a return to slavery. It is why a headline like "Square Circle Found in Utah" elicits a smile rather than a furrowed brow.

Shouldn't a consistent relativist
respect alternative perspectives?

The position I am defending is clearly and admittedly relativistic. We determine the truth or falsity—and the plausibility or absurdity—of statements by seeing how well they fit into our prevailing belief system. Thus the geocentric description of the solar system is true relative to Ptolemaic astronomy, false relative to modern science; the biblical account of human origins is true relative to the standpoint of a biblical literalist, false relative to the Darwinian perspective. No other way of deciding what to believe is available to us. Nor can we occupy a transcendental standpoint from which we can objectively assess the relative merits of these different belief systems. The frameworks themselves can be judged only "ethnocentrically," that is, from one or another of the particular vantage points they offer. But given this relativistic outlook, some will argue, wouldn't a tolerant, even respectful attitude toward alternative perspectives be more appropriate—and more consistent—than a refusal to take them seriously?

The problem with this argument is that it fails to maintain the distinction we made earlier between epistemic respect and other sorts of respect. I can respect alternative belief systems on various counts—for their elegance, intellectual ingenuity, imaginative power, moral authority, historical importance, practical benefits, and so on. But epistemic respect is a matter of seriously considering the possibility that a claim might be true. Belief systems themselves, however, taken in the broadest sense, cannot really be shown to be true or false since they are the theoretical frameworks within which specific claims are determined to be true or false. So far as truth is concerned, it is particular beliefs rather than entire conceptual frameworks that we have to judge. One can claim that a framework has certain advantages over alternative frameworks: for instance, it may generate more accurate predictions or produce a more harmonious society, or give people a sense of purpose. But when we talk about the truth or falsity of entire conceptual schemes, we are misusing the concept of truth, extending it beyond its field of legitimate employment.[23]

Still, it may be argued, if truth is relative, why not respect the relative truth of claims that belong to points of view other than one's own—for instance, the truth of Genesis relative to the standpoint of biblical literalism, along with the truth of Darwinism from the standpoint of science. The simple answer to this is that we form our judgments about the truth of any claim from the point of view we happen to occupy. We have to. And when we encounter claims that conflict wildly with what we already believe ("the Holocaust never happened"), and the only justifications offered for those claims belong to a radically different way of thinking ("academia, public education, the political system, and the mass media are controlled by an international Jewish conspiracy"), it is more accurate and more honest to admit that, given our general perspective, such claims lie outside the parameters of plausibility.

Western science does not have
a monopoly on wisdom

Still, a critic may argue, the position I am defending unjustifiably privileges Western science over alternative perspectives. No one can deny that the scientific point of view has achieved cultural hegemony over much of the globe during the past two or three centuries. Common sense absorbs its findings. Professionals in every sphere—academics, advertisers, sports coaches, businessmen, political consultants—employ its methods. We are all hopelessly dependent on its technological fruits, from canned food to computers. But to justify withholding respect from beliefs that fail to fit in with the scientific picture is arrogant and narrow-minded. Even a hard-boiled scientist can and should recognize that other outlooks, most obviously those offered by the world's great religious traditions, offer all sorts of wisdom, insight, edification, and enlightenment.

Once again, though, we need to distinguish clearly between specific beliefs and general outlooks, and also between the different sorts of respect that we grant to these. Yes, we can readily concede that the Bible stories teach us valuable moral lessons, the Greek myths exhibit extraordinary imaginative power, the Bhagavad Gita offers profound reflective insights into the human condition, the medieval theory of humors provided a useful psychological model, and poison oracles can help people clarify their thinking prior to making an important decision. But these observations are beside the point, which is whether we—and by "we" I mean participants in modern intellectual culture—can consistently and sincerely accord *epistemic* respect to specific beliefs that contradict basic tenets of the dominant, scientifically informed point of view.

Consider the claim that every animal on the earth today is descended from a pair of animals of that same species that lived for a time on a big boat built by a man named Noah. How plausible do you think this is? True, there may be evidence that at some point in the past there was a tremendous flood, or that large parts of Mesopotamia were under water. Certainly there is some interesting overlap between the Epic of Gilgamesh and the story of the flood found in Genesis. The famous story is dramatic and memorable. Details such as Noah's learning from the olive leaf in the returning dove's mouth that the waters were abating are poetically satisfying. The symbolic suggestion that all the species on earth are bound together in the past and have common fundamental interests is highly relevant to our global situation today. But as responses to the question posed, all these excellent points are evasions. They affirm various reasons for applauding the legend of Noah and his ark, but they weasel out of giving a straight answer to a straight question: do you take seriously the thesis that all the animals in the world at one time lived together on a boat? The straight and honest answer for most people nowadays is no. Taken literally, the claim is ridiculous, no more believable than the claim that Santa Claus lives at the North Pole supervising teams of toy-making elves.

Yet people are often reluctant to speak so bluntly, and perhaps we are now in a better position to understand why. Think again about the scenario in the jury room with which we began. Beliefs about aliens controlling the government and beliefs about fabulous miracles that supposedly occurred long ago may strike us as equally unlikely, yet only the former lead us to question the judgment of the person holding them. In both cases, the reason we don't take the claims seriously is that they contradict basic tenets of our dominant conceptual scheme. But the beliefs about miracles reported in the Bible tend to provoke less derision and incredulity for two reasons.

First, they belong to a well-established, comprehensive, and internally coherent system of beliefs and practices from which they derive support. In this respect, beliefs might be compared to animals like wolves that live in closely knit groups. Integrated into a powerful group, an individual animal will appear a tough proposition, dangerous to challenge; isolated from the group, however, it will stick out as unprotected and invitingly vulnerable. Similarly, beliefs draw credibility from the system to which they belong. And just as a predator is more likely to attack an animal cut off from its group, so we are more willing to scorn beliefs that appear relatively isolated. So "Jesus ascended to heaven on a cloud" is respectable; "Elvis was abducted by aliens" is laughable.

Second, these comprehensive systems enjoy many other kinds of respect, and some of this bleeds through into the epistemic realm. Thus the fact that Christianity has been around for two thousand years, has been embraced by millions of people, continues to be a popular religion in many parts of the world, has included among its adherents so many impressive individuals, has inspired so much great literature, art, music, and philosophy, and is associated with praiseworthy moral teachings, leads us to treat its tenets with more respect than we typically show to reports of supernatural events. This transference of respect is not rationally justifiable; but it is psychologically understandable. And it surely helps to explain the double standard that we apply to, say, superstitious beliefs on the one hand and orthodox religious beliefs on the other.

Now someone might object here that I have no business projecting my own prejudices onto society at large. *I* may operate with a double standard, respecting religion while ridiculing so-called superstition; but that, the critic will say, is my problem. Other people, more fair-minded, more open-minded, and less enamored of the "scientifically informed" outlook, may be more consistent or, dare one say it, more reasonable. They will not automatically assume that whatever goes against the prevailing orthodoxy in science must be unworthy of epistemic respect. There are, after all, more things in heaven and earth than are dreamt of in my philosophy.

This objection makes a good point. A blind faith in the whole of science is a poor foundation for a supposedly modern, critical, secular outlook. But acknowledging the remarkable efficacy of the scientific method, as well as the explanatory and practical power of contemporary scientific theory, does not equate with blind faith. Moreover, it is much harder to avoid working with a double standard than the critic supposes. The respectability of some beliefs and the disreputableness of others, even though both may be equally implausible from a scientific point of view, are notions we imbibe every day from the surrounding culture; they belong to what we call common sense. Another hypothetical scenario can serve to reinforce this point.

Imagine you are hiring someone to join your departmental team. Having reduced the pool of applicants to a short list of two, you phone the candidates to arrange on-site interviews. To the first candidate you propose meeting on Friday of next week. After consulting a calendar, she tells you she would prefer not to interview on that day: it's the seventh of the month, and seven is her unlucky number. Surprised, but willing to accommodate her, you suggest the following Tuesday. This date also does not suit her since it is the eleventh, and, she explains, her horoscope for this month specifically warned her against involvements with the number eleven. Patiently, you suggest yet another date, and this option is thankfully considered free from baneful influences.

Now, you may be so open-minded as to not raise an eyebrow at this candidate's responses. But I think most people operating in a modern workplace would be more than a little exasperated at having to work around self-imposed constraints of this kind. In fact, I suspect most of us would experience exasperation mingled with a certain amount of scorn, plus more than a pinch of distrust regarding her judgment. Nevertheless, you mark the calendar and proceed to contact the second candidate. Since Friday the seventh is free, you suggest an interview on that day. But this next candidate explains that she is an orthodox Jew and therefore cannot meet on Friday since it would involve traveling after sundown and hence violate the law against traveling on the Sabbath. Nor, as it turns out, can she meet on the Tuesday since that is Yom Kippur. Eventually you find a date and time that are acceptable to her, mark the calendar, and go off to complain to a colleague over a stiff coffee.

The point of this little scenario is simple enough. The first candidate runs more risk of scuppering her chances than does the second, and the reason is fairly clear. Most of us, I believe, would feel a strong obligation to recognize the legitimacy of the reasons given by the second candidate for refusing the dates initially offered. But we would be less inclined to extend this respect to the first candidate's excuses; we may accept them, but we are likely to do so rather grudgingly, and she will probably have already damaged her prospects. But why? Her anxieties about numbers rest on the assumption that our lives are subject to forces not recognized by contemporary science. Yet her rival believes that if she catches a bus on Friday evening, the Creator of the Universe will be offended! If our reaction is different, this is surely not due to one set of beliefs' being inherently more believable than the other. Rather, it stems from the fact that Judaism is an organized religion, entrenched in our culture. This gives the beliefs it supports a measure of respectability, bound up as they are with other positive values such as cultural identity, solidarity, tradition, piety, self-discipline, and moral order. Moreover, our awareness of past injustices suffered by victims of religious persecution makes us especially wary of holding a person's religious beliefs against her. But this concern becomes weaker when the beliefs in question are not part of an accredited metaphysical system.

To sum up my response to the objection raised: the position I am defending does not presuppose that only Western science has anything to teach us. Wisdom can encompass nonepistemic forms of edification and enlightenment. But insofar as we are attending to questions about the probable truth or plausibility of the claims people make, it is difficult for any modern intellectual not to accept the overarching framework of assumptions and methodological prescriptions provided by science. Science has such prestige in the modern world that its findings, broadcast every day through the news media, are now part of the atmosphere that we inhabitants of the information age breathe. Because we are still making the transition to a thoroughly modernized way of thinking, we naturally fail to be perfectly consistent. We grant beliefs that have historical respectability and institutional support more epistemic credit than they deserve. This sort of inconsistency—this epistemic double standard—is hard to avoid. But becoming aware of it, and critiquing it, are parts of the process by means of which we can move beyond it.

Religion and science are much more
compatible than I am suggesting

A final objection to my general position is that it exaggerates the conflict between science and religion. A corollary of my argument concerning epistemic respect is that it is intellectually dishonest, or at least lazy, to embrace a general outlook that is modern and scientifically informed yet still give credence to beliefs that are completely at odds with this perspective. Against this it will be pointed out that many people, including qualified scientists, appear comfortable embracing both perspectives— the modern and the traditional, the scientific and the religious. Doesn't this indicate that perhaps the problem is not so much their intellectual slovenliness as my failure to recognize ways of harmonizing these perspectives, or at least of finding legitimate ways to make use of both?

Now, it may be possible to defend the practice of employing whichever standpoint one finds most useful for a particular task. Thus someone might adopt a hardheaded scientific point of view when trying to *predict* the weather, taking into account only such variables as temperature, pressure, and humidity, yet embrace a different set of assumptions when engaging in rituals aimed at *influencing* the weather. This could be called a sort of pragmatic perspectivism. But still the question presents itself: are the two standpoints compatible? Those who use both might say that they are not interested in that question; but that is a telling concession. In effect it amounts to giving up on the attempt to render one's beliefs consistent. From a practical point of view this attitude may be defensible; but from a theoretical point of view it is a form of intellectual suicide. Trying to work our beliefs into an internally consistent system is surely a good part of what is meant when we talk about being intellectual rigorous. Identifying inconsistencies in our thinking and trying to remove or overcome them is necessarily at the heart of any attempt to improve our thinking, at least when what is at issue is whether a particular statement about the world is literally true.[24]

Yet some will still argue that even on the strictly theoretical plane, science and religion can be rendered consistent. Believing that the universe is the product of intelligent design, for instance, or that personal identity of some sort persists after death, does not directly contradict the scientific picture. That may be so. But these are not the sort of beliefs that are at issue. More germane to this discussion are beliefs that obviously do contradict science and common sense: the sun stopped moving across the sky on Joshua's command; Mary became pregnant by means of a supernatural act performed by the creator of the universe; after death the majority of people will burn for eternity in hell. The question is whether beliefs of *this* sort deserve epistemic respect, or whether we are justified in putting them in the same box, so far as plausibility is concerned, with claims about alien abductions, Santa Claus, and fairies at the bottom of the garden.

My purpose is not to discredit all forms of religious belief. I am simply asking that we try to think hard and come clean about the way we view certain sorts of belief. And I am arguing that we are not very consistent in our treatment of beliefs that go against the prevailing scientific view of things. We treat implausible beliefs embedded in established religious traditions with far more epistemic respect than their content entitles them to, while being much readier to dismiss similar beliefs that lack the protection of organized religion.

Certainly, there are many examples of people who, although thoroughly steeped in modern, secular ways of thinking, choose to embrace religion. But in most cases I would question whether this move really involves a genuine full-blooded commitment to the truth of claims about supernatural happenings and miracles like those mentioned. Such a commitment is possible, of course, and sophisticated philosophical defenses are possible. One could argue, as Kierkegaard did in respect to Christianity, that religious beliefs are indeed absurd from any rational point of view, but that this crucifixion of the intellect is precisely what genuine religious faith requires. Or one could appeal to a self-conscious form of perspectivism that allows one to move between incompatible frameworks with a good conscience. But I suspect that many who make the move either do not feel any need to believe that reports of miraculous happenings are literally true, or choose not to dwell on any problems posed by the inconsistency between these reports and contemporary common sense.

Perhaps the most complex cases of all are those where the distinction between believing and disbelieving is not clear-cut. I am not here talking about qualifications introduced by doubt, but the stranger, harder to describe situation where a person embraces—or tries to embrace—a belief his intellect rejects. This is often a demand that late converts to an organized religion impose on themselves. For the sake of other things associated with the religion—for instance, community, tradition, identity, intellectual order, peace of mind—they try to will themselves toward taking seriously claims that they would previously have rejected out of hand. Some no doubt succeed. But in other cases it is hard not to suspect an element of bad faith.

To swallow whole a report of some miracle or other supernatural event, one needs a wide gullet. But thanks to the tremendous success of science and the dissemination of scientific reasoning, the modern mind comes fitted with a critical filter that restricts what we can swallow. Although it might occasionally appear otherwise, we are generally much less gullible than our forebears. The paranoia of the McCarthy hearings has been usefully likened to that of the Salem witch trials. But the most obvious difference between them is significant also: the latter, unlike the former, hinged on the positing of supernatural forces. Any such suggestion today would be both ruled and laughed out of court. And if a modern intellectual, who in every other respect seems to share the skeptical, critical mind-set of the age, affirms the literal truth of some big metaphysical dogma such as the virgin birth of Jesus or transubstantiation, it sticks out like a rat in the throat of a snake.

A disenchanted world

The courtroom scenario with which we began illustrates something important about our notion of rationality. "Reason," says Hilary Putnam, building on a Hegelian insight, "is both immanent . . . and transcendent."[25] In other words, some of the criteria we use to assess the credibility of claims can be thought of as timeless and universally valid; in this sense they transcend the cultures in which they operate and can be used to criticize those cultures. The demand for logical consistency, for instance, is used to criticize appeals to tradition that justify discrimination against ethnic minorities, women, or gays. But rationality is not an abstract set of rules that floats free from historically rooted ways of deciding what to believe and how to act. It is also bound up with these: it is immanent within our culture. This is one reason beliefs that accord with respectable traditions and conventions are given an easier time and are less likely to be dismissed as absurd or beyond the pale.

But the fact that we *are*, as a matter of fact, less inclined to question and criticize beliefs that enjoy the protection of cultural respectability, does not mean that this *should* be our attitude. Philosophers since Socrates have been challenging widely held assumptions and suggesting that conventional methods of deciding what is true—whether by relying on sensory evidence, appealing to popular opinion, or deferring to some authority— are inferior to a more rigorously logical approach. This inevitably makes them unpopular at times: Socrates was executed; Spinoza was excommunicated; Voltaire lived in exile. But challenging received opinion, which sometimes means withholding epistemic respect from beliefs that others cherish, is one of philosophy's critical functions.

We live in interesting times, and one of the most interesting and historically significant facets of modernity has been what Max Weber, borrowing from Schiller, called the "disenchantment" of our world.[26] The trend is gradual, but from a perspective that monitors change over centuries rather than months or years, it seems inexorable. As the tide of belief in the supernatural goes out, all sorts of superstitions and fantastical ideas are left stranded. Stories about werewolves, vampires, leprechauns, fairies, ghosts, and wizards are now little more than material for the entertainment and tourism industries.[27] Indeed, their popularity is in itself a symptom of disenchantment; they exploit our nostalgia for a premodern world we naively think of as a more charming place. Other beliefs in supernatural phenomena—in divine miracles, for instance—have greater staying power since they are supported by weightier traditions and powerful institutions. But they, too, are increasingly being left behind to keep company with dybbuks and dragons.

Recognizing this, many of those who wish to maintain the relevance of religion to modern times shift their attention to the nonepistemic value of these beliefs. Instead of insisting on the literal truth of supernatural claims, they emphasize their metaphorical power or practical significance. Besides, they say, religion is not primarily a matter of holding certain beliefs but one of embracing a form of life.[28] This move is understandable, but it is also a tacit admission that such beliefs are losing their claim to epistemic respect. Indeed, to argue that the *truth* of a person's beliefs is not all that important is actually an alternative way of failing to take those beliefs seriously.[29]

What academic defenders of religion don't like to admit—and here scriptural literalists and religious fundamentalists have a point—is that when you move away from understanding the time-honored stories about supernatural events as literally true, you hollow out the faith that attaches to them. Great cathedrals become mere tourist attractions; religious music and services become primarily objects of aesthetic appreciation. When churches seek to draw congregations by inviting them to bring along their domestic pets to be blessed, we know that organized religion is on the rocks. This is not the kind of faith that Aquinas or Luther would recognize as serious.

Again, my intention here is not to scoff at contemporary churchgoers. My point is that the corrosive effects of the skeptical, critical, scientifically informed mind-set that characterizes modernity permeates the whole culture, including the sphere of religious belief. Ultimately, it is not just belligerent village atheists who find they cannot grant epistemic respect to certain sorts of belief. Even those who like to think of themselves as more open-minded will struggle at times to avoid assuming a skeptical attitude. One last hypothetical scenario can serve to illustrate this problem.

Imagine that a candidate for a Ph.D. in anthropology is defending a thesis based on a field study of two premodern societies living in the same region. According to the mythology of one of these societies, the people from the other group are descendants of the moon god, which is why they tend to have rounder faces and paler features. One of the examiners asks the candidate, in passing, whether he knows anything about the actual historical origins of these people. The candidate cheerfully answers that he accepts the moon god story, so no further explanation is needed.

The professors sitting around the table chuckle appreciatively. "No, seriously," says the examiner. "I am serious," says the candidate. An awkward silence ensues.

This silence has the same ground as the initial laughter—incredulity that a contemporary Western intellectual could genuinely entertain as literally true a myth about a moon god. The candidate might even be in danger of failing. But why? Not because he is endorsing an idea his examiners consider false; they are used to that. The problem is, rather, that the committee would find it hard to credit that the candidate really, truly, sincerely holds the belief in question. They are likely to view him as, in effect, refusing to answer the question, as being rather like someone at a trial who is guilty of contempt of court.

Of course, the committee, familiar with the critique of ethnocentrism and cultural imperialism in the social sciences, would take it as a given that the beliefs and practices of the society being studied should be treated with respect. But whatever this means, it does not, I would argue, mean granting all these beliefs *epistemic* respect. Here the distinctions made earlier between different types of respect are useful. The absence of epistemic respect is made still more apparent if we contrast the scenario just described with one in which the candidate endorsed a familiar tenet of a mainstream religion. In that case, it is far less likely that the suspicion of bad faith would cross anyone's mind.

Conclusion

The hypothetical scenarios constructed above—the jury room, the job candidate, the doctoral defense—are all intended as vehicles to aid reflection on our attitudes toward different sorts of belief. Each highlights, from a different angle, inconsistencies many of us are likely to encounter in our own attitudes; they also indicate how hard it is to avoid these, however much we may officially be committed to open-mindedness. The difficulty, as mentioned earlier, stems from a clash between two basic values: tolerance and consistency.

I have argued that there are times when it is both appropriate and worthwhile to withhold epistemic respect from certain beliefs. Many people will automatically be suspicious of this idea because they assume it constitutes a form of intolerance. Given all the harm that has been done and continues to be done by intolerance, they will say, should we not err on the side of tolerance? But this criticism misconstrues my argument. I am not suggesting that any individual be denied the respect due to each and every human being, nor deprived of the *right* to believe whatever she pleases. Furthermore, I am happy to concede that ideas can and should be valued for many reasons other than their being true. But just as we should extol tolerance, so we should also value intellectual rigor. This means, among other things, being honest with ourselves, being willing to subject beliefs—regardless of their vintage—to hard, critical scrutiny, and striving for consistency in our thinking. It means cultivating and exercising what Nietzsche calls an "intellectual conscience."[30]

Doing so is not painless but it does have value. A concern for intellectual consistency and rigor has been one of the most profound forces driving the remarkable progress of the past few centuries that we associate with modernity. Critical thinking, which invariably involves a degree of skepticism toward previously cherished ideas, is the cutting edge that makes such progress possible. Of course, thinking critically requires open-mindedness. But perfect open-mindedness, like unrestricted freedom or absolute tolerance, is neither possible nor desirable. Even critical think-ing must occur from a particular standpoint and within certain parameters.

A commitment to basing beliefs on evidence and render-ing them logically consistent as far as possible is at the heart of a modern conception of rationality. The great thinkers of the Enlightenment saw reason as a tool that, used correctly, can im-prove our lives in two main ways. It can improve our material well-being; and it can help us become a society in which people enjoy more autonomy and suffer less injustice. I think it is blind-ingly obvious that in the modernized world tremendous progress has been made on both fronts, the material and the moral. Most of us live longer, are better fed, are better educated, receive better medical care; we enjoy pleasanter working conditions, more lei-sure, greater access to recreation and culture; and we have more control over our lives than the great majority of people who have ever lived. We live lives that most previous generations—even the upper classes—would envy.[31] The last three centuries have also seen remarkable progress in the moral, political, and social realms, in the areas of rights, freedoms, and opportunities. Uni-versal suffrage, universal education; laws advancing civil rights, workplace safety, and consumer rights; the lessening of blatant discrimination against women, ethnic minorities, and gays; the election and appointment of women, nonwhites, and gays to high office: all these developments represent obvious and signifi-cant forms of progress.

But as numerous social critics have argued, progress in the moral and political sphere has lagged behind the scientific and technological progress that has made possible the remarkable rise in living standards.[32] There are many reasons for this. The most obvious is the power of rich people to use their wealth and position to resist a more equal distribution of goods in our society. Another is deeply entrenched prejudices that remain widespread and negatively affect both individual lives and our political culture.

Constructing a more rational society means overcoming these obstacles to social progress. It means moving toward a society in which political decisions, both of electors and of government agencies, are less shaped by such forces as money, vested interests, power blocks, bigotry, ideological dogmas, and blind adherence to tradition. Instead, our choices would be guided, to the greatest extent possible, by evidence and rational argument. Of course, put like this the project sounds utopian. But we do not have to believe the utopian ideal is fully realizable; we just have to think it would be a good thing to keep pushing in that direction. Being critical and honest in our appraisal of beliefs is a part of that enterprise. For one of the tethers holding us back is our unwillingness to let go of outmoded ways of thinking. So there is something to be gained by pointing out that when it comes to reasonableness, evidence, and epistemic credibility, belief in gods and miracles is on a par with belief in leprechauns, vampires, and flying spaghetti monsters.

Of course, I am hardly the first to say this. The flying spaghetti monster is the creation of Bobby Henderson, a trenchant critic of religion, and has featured prominently in the recent debates over the so-called New Atheism triggered by books like Sam Harris's *The End of Faith,* Christopher Hitchens's *God Is Not Great,* and Richard Dawkins's *The God Delusion.*[33] Dawkins, Hitchens, Harris, and others writing in a similar vein have been criticized by many, even by fellow atheists, for their feisty attacks on religion. But while there may be valid objections to particular claims they make about institutionalized religion, they nevertheless perform a valuable service in demanding that religious doctrines be subjected to hard critical scrutiny. In effect these militant atheists are pointing out that religious beliefs have enjoyed, and still enjoy, a kind of protection from rational criticism in virtue of their historical place in our culture, but that this privileged status in the past is no reason to go easy on them now. And they focus on religious claims because they rightly see them as having far more cultural and political importance than other beliefs that are held by only a few people and are widely regarded as absurd.

The religions of the world are among humankind's greatest cultural achievements. From the beginning of civilization through to modern times, religion has been an integral and valuable part of every society. It anchored morality, ensured political stability, gave a meaningful form to everyday existence, and inspired wonderful productions in art, architecture, literature, music, philosophy, and the law. But as history moves on, it often happens that what was once beneficial starts to becomes detrimental; instead of furthering progress it begins to hinder it. This is the way Hegel described stages in the development of the human spirit. It is the way Marx viewed economic systems. And it is a perspective that applies, in my view, to at least some kinds of religious belief.

How much of an obstacle to progress are beliefs that lie outside the parameters of plausibility? That depends on the kind of belief, the way it is held, and the society in question. But in contemporary America, for instance, there seems to be some connection between the entrenchment of fundamentalist Christian beliefs and a reluctance to think afresh about matters such as gay rights, euthanasia, or abortion, to mention just some of the most newsworthy.[34] A similar point can be made about Islamic fundamentalism.

In the twenty-first century, the moral parameters of a modern outlook include a principle of equality and the idea of basic human rights. That is why we would not now entertain for even a moment the suggestion that slavery be revived: the idea is beyond the pale of respectability, not worthy of our attention. And in the theoretical domain, too, there are limits to what we can take seriously as claims to knowledge. One of these is a commitment to some form of naturalism; so claims that refer to supernatural phenomena, to entities not susceptible to any sort of empirical investigation, are off our epistemic radar, as are bizarre, unsupported assertions that contradict the mass of scientific evidence. People are free to believe what they want, of course, but not every belief deserves to be taken seriously as a candidate for truth. Withholding epistemic respect at times is one of the ways we express our current intellectual values and try to advance a little further toward a more rational society.

Acknowledgments

A pleasant aspect of writing about everyday ethical issues is that many people who are not specialists in moral philosophy take an interest in the topics and enjoy discussing them. Moreover, such discussions are often a source of new insights since everyone has experiences relevant to the issues being discussed and is likely to have reflected on these experiences. For this reason, the list of people who deserve acknowledgment is necessarily quite long. I have decided, though, that it would not be wise to be too specific in identifying particular contributions. Thanking my colleagues, neighbors, family, and friends for stimulating my thinking on rudeness, gossiping, and snobbery could easily be misunderstood! So in most cases I will content myself with simply thanking people who have helped me in one way or another, without trying to specify the exact nature of their contribution. It goes without saying that none of them should be suspected of agreeing with me on all points.

Earlier versions of the essays on rudeness, gossiping, snobbery, and respecting beliefs were presented at the Bergren Forum, an ongoing venue for public presentations at Alfred University. A draft of the essay on rudeness was also presented to the Psychology Roundtable at Alfred University, while drafts of the essay on gossiping were presented at the 49th Northwest Conference on Philosophy at Central Washington University, and to faculty and students at California State University, Sacramento. I am grateful to all who offered feedback at these events. An earlier form of "The Ethics of Gossiping" appeared in the *International Journal of Applied Philosophy* 14, no. 1 (Spring 2000). An earlier version of "The Rights and Wrongs of Rudeness" appeared in the spring 2006 (vol. 20, no. 1) issue of the same journal. IJAP's editor, Elliot Cohen, offered helpful feedback on both occasions.

Throughout the time I have been writing these essays, Alfred University has provided invaluable institutional backing. This included a sabbatical in the spring of 2004, and the Margaret and Barbara Hagar Professorship in the Humanities from 2007 to 2010. I would particularly like to thank the College of Liberal Arts and Sciences and my colleagues in the Division of Human Studies for their assistance and support.

While writing the book I have twice taught courses at Alfred on the ethics of everyday life. Teaching these courses was tremendously useful. It forced me to clarify my ideas and confront issues I hadn't previously considered. I am very grateful to all the students in those courses for their insights and critical feedback. I also benefited from the lively discussions that occurred when I presented my ideas on some of these topics at seminars for alumni and friends of Alfred University organized by AU's office of university relations.

In addition I would like to thank the following individuals: Michelle Applebaum, Gordon Atlas, Jana Atlas, Eric Baldwin, Cecelia Beach, Robert Bingham, Jim Booker, Sylvia Bryant, Emma Buckthal, Carol Burdick, Brittany Caldwell, Bill Cassidy, Dan Cherneff, Lila Cherneff, Rose Cherneff, Nick Clark, Ann Cobb, Jack Cobb, Priscilla Cobb, Samantha Dannick, Laurent Dappe, Bill Dibrell, Beth Ann Dobie, Joe Dosch, Vicki Eaklor, Debbie Edizel, Gerard Edizel, Nancy Evangelista, Victor Franco, Alena Giesche, Juliana Gray, Larry Greil, Laura Greyson, Allen Grove, Zach Grove, Rie Hachiyanagi, Brian Herbert, Shannon Hickey, Ben Howard, Amy Jacobson, Marie Komanecky, Lou Lichtman, Fenna Mandalong, Chris Mann, Stephanie Martini, Rahul Mehta, Dudley Merchant, Susan Cobb Merchant, Thomas Moran, Susan Morehouse, Geoff Nassimos, Nickelina Noel, Gary Ostrower, Tom Peterson, Becky Prophet, Craig Prophet, Rob Reginio, Simon Reid, Addison Rice, Patrick Saunders, Marilyn Saxton, Robert Shaughnessy, Nathaniel Shipley, Jeff Sluyter-Beltrao, Bob Stein, Molly Sullivan, Jennifer Templeton, Fiona Tolhurst, Hester Velmans, Francie Viggiani, Ben Waissman, Alfonso Watkins, Emmanuel Wedlock, Rayna Winters, and Justin Zeh.

There are certain people to whom I owe gratitude of a different order. Rob Tempio of Princeton University Press was the person who first suggested that I put together a set of essays of this sort, and he has been wonderfully helpful and supportive through the entire project. Chris Stout of Gehrung Associates helped draw attention to my work and thus also deserves thanks for helping to bring this book into being. Lauren Lepow's meticulous editing helped to improve the final text in numerous ways.

Acknowledgments

I learned much from my many philosophy teachers and would like to recognize in particular David Bell, Frank McDermott, George DiGiovanni, and Robert Kane.

Four close friends of long standing have been especially important to me. They are the supportively critical audience I always imagine looking over my shoulder as I write and to whom I owe a great deal. So I would here like to offer heartfelt thanks to these four: to Mark Alfino and Randy Mayes, who have made so many contributions to my thinking, and who, in countless conversations and responses to written drafts, have generously offered a stream of valuable criticisms, suggestions, and insights; to Chris Horner, who first drew me toward philosophy, and whose undiminished passion for the life of the mind remains an inspiration; and to Mark Waller for star friendship.

Finally, I must thank my family, Vicky, Sophie, and Emily, both for their love and assistance during the writing of the book and for their contributions to it. All the topics covered here have been the subject of lively conversations around the dinner table, and sharp but valuable criticism of my opinions has flowed freely. My deepest debt is to Vicky, for her expertise in sociolinguistics, her countless insights in other areas, her skills as editorial critic and proofreader, her willingness to discuss philosophy around the clock, and her loving support over many years.

Notes

Chapter 1. The Rights and Wrongs of Rudeness

1. These findings come from a poll conducted by the Public Agenda Research Group and reported on ABCNews.com, April 3, 2002. This report echoes earlier polls. In "Aggravating Circumstances: A Status Report on Rudeness in America," a report prepared by Public Agenda for the Pew Charitable Trusts, 79 percent of those polled viewed rudeness as a serious national problem, and 73 percent believed people were more polite in the past. A 1996 U.S. News and Bozell Worldwide poll found that 90 percent of Americans viewed incivility as a serious problem, and 78 percent believed the problem had grown worse over the preceding decade.

2. "When I was young, we were taught to be discreet and respectful of elders, but the present youth are exceedingly disrespectful and impatient of restraint." Attributed to Hesiod (800 BCE).

3. See John F. Kasson, *Rudeness and Civility: Manners in Nineteenth-Century Urban America* (New York: Farrar, Straus and Giroux, 1990).

4. In the Talking Heads' song "Psycho Killer," the killer tells us that he hates people when they're not polite. The killer's values may be deranged, but we can still recognize the psychological truth expressed here and identify with the sentiment: being treated with respect is of fundamental importance to most of us.

5. See Ludwig Wittgenstein, *Philosophical Investigations* (Oxford: Blackwell, 1953), sec. 57.

6. An unscientific trawling of a few thesauruses and the *OED* yielded the following list of terms closely related to "rude": discourteous, impolite, disrespectful, irreverent, uncouth, uncivil, unmannerly, impertinent, impudent, fresh, tasteless, inconsiderate, ill-mannered, undignified, insolent, loutish, insensitive, clownish, clod-hopping, ungallant, ruffianly, saucy, cheeky, malapert, ungracious, breezy, primitive, inelegant, ignorant, unrefined, harsh, curt, brusque, uncivilized, coarse, vulgar, crude, savage, ungentle, brutish, violent, tempestuous, ill-bred, common, unfashionable, inurbane, ungentlemanly, plebian, provincial, unchivalrous, boorish, unsophisticated, robust, rough, sturdy, rugged, rustic, blunt, simple. The fact that we have so many words to identify different kinds of rudeness presumably says something interesting about our culture.

7. I am indebted to Eric Baldwin for this example.

8. Cheshire Calhoun makes this point when discussing incivility. See Cheshire Calhoun, "The Virtue of Civility," *Philosophy and Public Affairs* 29, no. 3 (Summer 2000): 266.

9. Anne Lloyd Thomas, "Facts and Rudeness," *Mind* 67 (1958): 409.

10. See Randy Cohen, *The Good, the Bad & the Difference: How to Tell Right from Wrong in Everyday Situations* (New York: Broadway Books, 2002).

11. I take the question "Is the person aware that he is violating a convention?" to be essentially the same as the question "Is the violation intentional?" But to say that a person is violating a convention *intentionally* does not imply that he is violating it *purposely*. One is *purposely* rude only if being rude is part of the purpose of one's action. Thus someone who queue jumps is only being intentionally rude; someone who throws beer in someone's face is being purposely rude.

Now it could be objected here that awareness and intentionality are matters of degree, and, moreover, that they are not coextensive. So someone could be described as being aware, in some sense, that he is violating a convention, yet not so aware that the violation should be called intentional. From a theoretical point of view these are reasonable points, but I think there are practical benefits to riding roughshod over such subtleties. If someone says, "I was aware that I was breaking a rule, but I didn't really mean to do it," we are naturally and justifiably skeptical. For we suspect that in prying apart awareness and intentionality, he is trying to create for himself a moral loophole. Rather than allow this strategic possibility—both in other people and in ourselves—we should stitch the concepts together from the outset.

12. For further discussion of rudeness as a form of humor, see below.

13. I am indebted to Vicky Westacott for this point.

14. This objection was pointed out to me by Eric Baldwin and by Larry Greil. The response was suggested to me by Randy Mayes.

15. Edmund Burke, *First Letter on a Regicide Peace*, in *Selected Works of Edmund Burke*, vol. 3 (Indianapolis: Liberty Fund, 1990), p. 105.

16. One of Lenin's reasons for recommending, shortly before his death, that Stalin be removed from the post of general secretary of the Communist Party was that he was too rude. Presciently, Lenin saw this failing as grounds for doubting that Stalin would use wisely the power already concentrated in his hands.

17. A nice example of deliberately using an incorrect form of address is provided by Michael Moore in *Dude, Where's My Country?* (New York: Warner Books, 2003) when he addresses President George W. Bush as "Governor Bush" to succinctly express his view that Bush became president by improper means. This is a clear case of purposive rudeness. Some people might argue that if the mistake is accidental, then it shouldn't be counted as rude. But if you failed to use someone's title accidentally and discovered your mistake later, you would probably worry that you had caused offense and would apologize if given the opportunity. Moreover, in apologizing, you probably would not say, "I wasn't being rude," but, rather, "I didn't

mean to be rude." These normal responses indicate that the classification implied by my definition fits fairly well, on this point, with our normal way of thinking.

18. John Henry Newman, *The Idea of a University Defined and Illustrated* (London: Longmans, Green, 1902), Discourse 8, p. 208.

19. In *Choosing Civility*, P. M. Forni says that he "simply cannot conceive of any circumstance in our own daily lives when it would be appropriate or advantageous to be rude or boorish." (P. M. Forni, *Choosing Civility* [New York: St. Martin's Griffin, 2002], p. 157.) I agree that boorishness in everyday life is almost always objectionable, and on that score I applaud Forni's defense of civility. But he makes his task easier by tending to focus on nonproblematic examples. And by rudeness or incivility, he seems to have in mind something more like boorish behavior. My definition of rudeness may in fact capture at least some conduct he would deem acceptable.

20. Sarah Buss examines in detail an interesting example of this sort that occurs in George Eliot's *Middlemarch* when Dorothea decides to violate social convention and ask Dr. Lydgate directly to tell her the truth regarding the circumstances that led to his being suspected of a crime. Her primary motive is to help Lydgate, whom she believes to be innocent. See Sarah Buss, "Appearing Respectful: The Moral Significance of Manners," *Ethics* 109 (July 1999): 795–826.

21. Some people might argue that rudeness is justifiable when it is the natural expression of overwhelmingly strong feelings with which we can sympathize. For instance, I might hurl invective at the person who has just double-crossed me. But either I am making a choice here or not. If not, then the stream of insults is like a cry of pain, a natural response that requires an explanation rather than a justification. If I am making a choice, then the strong feelings that give rise to my action are not, strictly speaking, overwhelming.

22. A scene in Michael Cimino's film *The Deer Hunter* illustrates perfectly this function of mock rudeness. After a brief stop on a drive into the mountains, Mike (played by Robert De Niro) drives off before John, one of his fellow hunters, has got back into the car. John shouts and curses, and eventually Mike reverses the car back almost

to where he is standing. John walks up to the car, but just as he is about to get in, Mike drives off again. This happens several times. The scene underscores both John's place in the group hierarchy and Mike's intense will to power.

23. Interestingly, Hollywood's representation of the academy tends to remain frozen in the 1950s. Professors in the movies routinely address students as Mr. or Miss. Today this is about as common as the bow ties that Hollywood professors typically wear. Representations of culture generally lag behind changes that have taken place on the ground. One reason for this is that to be readily intelligible they have to make use of clichés and stereotypes that were established in the past.

24. The stickler for titles may say that the proper way for a student to deal with the uncertainty is to ask a professor at the outset how he or she prefers to be addressed. This would indeed be a simple solution, but it is hardly fair to expect it. For one thing, a student may well feel shy or awkward about making this sort of inquiry, which, after all, involves an admission of ignorance. For another, in most cases the professor will not have followed this procedure with every student; so why should one assume that students are under such an obligation?

25. On this point, see Kasson, *Rudeness and Civility*.

26. Mark Caldwell makes a similar point in *A Short History of Rudeness: Manners, Morals, and Misbehavior in Modern America* (New York: Picador, 1999), p. 92.

Chapter 2. The Ethics of Gossiping

1. The term "talk" here covers all forms of verbal communication.

2. In the same way, if a torturer were to say to his victim, "I think another turn of the screw will refresh your memory," this statement has the general form of a report about the torturer's own thoughts; and within that is embedded a prediction; but it is perfectly clear that the illocutionary force of these words is to threaten the victim, and this is how they should be understood and evaluated.

3. The first three exclusions laid down here—lies, breaches of confidences, and disregarding of claims—roughly correspond to the three categories of morally reprehensible gossip identified by Sissela Bok in chapter 7 of her *Secrets: On the Ethics of Concealment and Revelation* (New York: Pantheon, 1982). Reprinted in *Ethics for Everyday*, ed. David Benatar (New York: McGraw-Hill, 2002), pp. 104–16.

4. I am indebted to Samantha Dannick for this observation.

5. Hard-line utilitarians may object to my procedure from a different angle, arguing that utilitarian considerations should be introduced prior to the earlier questions about lies, rights, and claims. In response I would point out (i) the order I follow in this section is intended to reflect as closely as possible conventional thinking; (ii) the order is compatible with rule-utilitarianism (which advocates following moral rules that have proved to be generally beneficial); and (iii) the order in which the "narrowing down" criteria are applied does not alter the domain of controversial gossip that we are left with at the end.

6. There are exceptions to this principle: for instance, some people condemn voluntary euthanasia. But it is precisely because the act in such cases is not contrary to the wishes of the person it directly affects that opinion is swinging toward deeming voluntary euthanasia acceptable. In the case of con men who defend what they do on the grounds that they do as their victims wish, we usually argue that what they do is wrong because it would be contrary to their victim's "informed wishes."

7. Obviously, when I say these actions would be acknowledged by the subjects themselves to be "justifiable according to accepted conventions," it is only the *expressing* of the opinions, not the opinions themselves, that is in question.

8. For a vivid discussion of issues in this area raised by the Internet, see Daniel J. Solove, *The Future of Reputation: Gossip, Rumor, and Privacy on the Internet* (New Haven: Yale University Press, 2007).

9. Hesiod, *Work and Days* 761.

10. See Solove, *The Future of Reputation*, p. 37.

11. For a detailed discussion of how pejorative attitudes toward gossip find expression in the English literary tradition, see Patricia Meyer Spacks, *Gossip* (New York: Knopf, 1985).

12. Leviticus 19:16.

13. Joseph Telushkin, *Jewish Wisdom* (New York: Morrow, 1994), p. 65.

14. See Immanuel Kant, *Foundations of the Metaphysics of Morals*, trans. Lewis White Beck, 2nd ed. (New York: Macmillan, 1990), pp. 38–41.

15. *Richard II*, 1.1.177–79. An opposing view of reputation is offered by Iago: 'Reputation is an idle and most false imposition: oft got without merit, and lost without deserving (*Othello*, 2.3.260–62).

16. The argument I offer here is a familiar one within the mainstream liberal tradition. Thus Joel Feinberg, in *Harm to Others* (Oxford: Oxford University Press, 1984), distinguishes two senses of "harm": (a) a setback to a person's interests; and (b) a violation of a person's rights. We have already established that the kind of talk we are here considering does not involve a violation of anyone's rights. And for it to be a setback to someone's interests it must, surely, involve something more than simply an alteration in the way that person is viewed by others.

17. Someone might object here that if I believe that one person's opinion of another is, in itself, neither good nor bad, then I have no reason to condemn someone who maliciously spreads false rumors about a person who has died. But to spread false rumors maliciously is to lie, and lying that is not well-intentioned was ruled out at the beginning of our analysis.

18. We should note, though, that a saintly person's inability to fit comfortably into a social world could be due less to his or her inadequacies than to the moral deficiencies of the social world in question. Indeed, some of our greatest moral heroes are precisely individuals who refused to fit into societies they viewed as having serious moral failings. I am indebted to an anonymous reviewer from Princeton University Press for this observation.

19. The expression "detrimental to the reputation" should be understood in the broadest sense. Information can damage a person's reputation in someone else's eyes without necessarily reflecting on that person's abilities or moral character. For example, in this broad sense, my reputation may diminish in your eyes if you learn that one of my parents had a history of mental illness.

20. The cathartic function of gossip is apparent from the reported practice of the West African Ashanti. They severely punished malicious gossiping, in some cases by the cutting off of the gossip's lips or even by death, but to provide a release for the buildup of hostile emotions, they held regular ceremonies where these feelings could be publicly vented. See Ralph Rosnow and Gary Fine, *Rumor and Gossip: The Social Psychology of Hearsay* (New York: Elsevier, 1976), pp. 91–92.

21. Psychologist Robin Dunbar speculates that language itself evolved as a substitute for grooming, a practice that, among other things, enables individuals to achieve a better understanding of other members of their group. If this is so, other people, and particularly their potentially dangerous and antisocial qualities, would indeed be the oldest topic of conversation. See Robin Dunbar, *Grooming, Gossip, and the Evolution of Language* (Cambridge, MA: Harvard University Press, 1996).

22. See David Hume, *An Enquiry Concerning the Principles of Morals* (Indianapolis: Hackett, 1983).

23. Babylonian Talmud, Bava Bathra 164b. Cited in Telushkin, *Jewish Wisdom*, p. 67.

24. See Robert Goodman and Aaron Ben-Ze'ev, eds., *Good Gossip* (Lawrence: University Press of Kansas, 1994). Most of the positive aspects of gossip discussed here are mentioned by more than one of the contributors to this anthology. For a good overview of anthropological research on gossip, see Pamela Stewart and Andrew Strathen, *Witchcraft, Sorcery, Rumors and Gossip* (Cambridge: Cambridge University Pres, 2004), chap. 2.

25. For a sophisticated defense of the importance of gossip to our understanding of social reality, see Claire Birchall, *Knowledge Goes Pop: From Conspiracy Theory to Gossip* (New York: Berg, 2006), chap. 4.

26. I take it for granted here that it would be a good thing to bring about a more equitable distribution of power, both in particular contexts, such as the workplace, and in society as a whole. However, it could also be argued that in our political culture, as with individuals, gossip provides a relatively harmless outlet for envy and resentment that, if not discharged, might lead people to challenge the existing

system more vigorously. Talking about the rich may be a substitute for eating them! Celebrity gossip also serves to divert people's attention away from more politically weighty issues.

27. Of course, this phenomenon is hardly new. W. H. Auden called attention to it and (somewhat hypocritically) condemned it over fifty years ago: "Idle curiosity is an ineradicable vice of the human mind. All of us like to discover the secrets of our neighbors, particularly the ugly ones. This has always been so, and, probably, always will be. What is relatively new, however—it is scarcely to be found before the latter half of the eighteenth century—is a blurring of the boundaries between the desire for truth and idle curiosity, until today it has been so thoroughly erased that we can indulge in the latter without the slightest pangs of conscience. A great deal of what today passes for scholarly research is an activity no different from that of reading someone's private correspondence when he is out of the room, and it doesn't really make it morally any better if he is out of the room because he is in his grave." W. H. Auden, "Shakespeare's Sonnets," in *Forwards and Afterwords* (New York: Vintage Books, 1943), p. 80..

Chapter 3. On Snobbery: Is It Sinful to Feel Superior?

1. Remark made by John Roberts on CNN's *The Situation Room*, June 28, 2006.

2. In case anyone thinks that such attitudes are confined to off-the-record opinions of private individuals, this is from the instructions to people applying for a British passport from outside the UK: the applicant must have the application form countersigned by "a British citizen, other British national or Commonwealth citizen who is a Member of Parliament, Justice of the Peace, Minister of Religion, Bank Officer, Established Civil Servant, or professionally qualified person, e.g. Lawyer, Engineer, Doctor, School Teacher, Police Officer *or a person of similar standing*" (italics added). Notes for Form C1, "Application for United Kingdom Passport for applicants 16 and over," issued by the UK Passport Office.

3. For a more detailed and theoretical account of when we are justified in ascribing to people beliefs they deny holding, see Emrys Westacott, "Relativism, Truth, and Implicit Commitments," *International Studies in Philosophy* 32, no. 2 (Spring 2000): 95–126.

4. Even when the Red Sox fan bets on the Yankees to create a no-lose situation—so whatever the result, she can be happy about something—it reveals that her profession of faith in the Sox lacks confidence.

5. Other explanations of my conduct are, of course, possible. I may worry that he would notice that the silver is stolen property, or that he may resent my owning it, or that it would damage my image as a champion of thrift. In each case, though, my action is explained by the attribution to me of a certain belief. The most reasonable attribution offers the most plausible explanation. Which this is depends on the entire context.

6. W. M. Thackeray, *The Book of Snobs* (Winnetka, CA: Norilana Books, 2008), p. 113.

7. Even in sports, modesty is usually expected. When Muhammad Ali first began proclaiming himself "the greatest," he provoked a good deal of animosity. Most champions, even the undisputed ones like Roger Federer, avoid any suggestion of hubris.

8. Comedian Stephen Colbert's self-aggrandizement is funny precisely because he violates the normal conventions that dictate a modest demeanor.

9. "[T]o call someone a snob is a very vague description but a very clear insult." Attributed to George Santayana. Cited in Joseph Epstein, *Snobbery: The American Version* (Boston: Houghton Mifflin, 2002), p. 13.

10. My approach here is slightly different from that adopted in the chapters on gossip and rudeness. In the case of gossip, I put aside the normal meaning of the term and stipulate for the purpose of discussion a definition that is morally neutral. In the case of rudeness, I construct a definition that is intended to accord with common usage, and proceed to argue that rudeness—in spite of the negative charge the word carries—is sometimes acceptable. Here (and below) I do something similar; but instead of saying that snobbery is sometimes

acceptable, I prefer to use "snobbery" to designate a certain sort of objectionable assumption concerning superiority while co-opting the term "elitism" to denote holding beliefs about superiority that are reasonable and so should not be called snobbish.

11. One example of a form of snobbery that my definition may not quite capture is that shown by, say, the butler of a distinguished house toward an untitled businessman. The butler doesn't consider himself *personally* superior to the other, but he nevertheless looks down on him because the businessman's social status is lower than that of the butler's master. Even here, though, the butler's demeanor stems from his association with the higher class/group he serves, and this association is a valued attribute that he possesses and the businessman lacks. (I am grateful to an anonymous reviewer from Princeton University Press for this example.)

12. In the Derbyshire dialect, "tha" (thou) means "you," "dunt" means "do not," and "nowt" (pronounced "note") means "nothing."

13. *Noticing* something about another person—say, that she is Jewish, or sexy, or expensively dressed—is an interesting activity from a moral point of view. It is not really an action one chooses to perform; it is much more like a trait that one has. But whereas some traits, like not having charitable feelings, can be actively modified or at least countered through one's behavior, noticing certain things is something we usually cannot help or do much about. I may wish I were the kind of person who didn't notice so immediately a person's race, or age, or physique. I may think that in this respect I fall short of a moral ideal. But it is hard to see what I can do about it.

14. If Kim thinks that her partner Pat is having an affair, Pat may accuse her of being untrusting—a moral failing. If Pat shows how all the circumstances that led to Kim's suspicions have an innocent explanation, Kim may well accept these explanations and feel ashamed. But if it turns out that Pat is indeed having an affair—albeit one about which Kim had no suspicions—then Kim (and all of us) are likely to no longer see her lack of trust as a moral failing. This is paradoxical, but it shows how the truth or falsity of our beliefs can have moral significance.

15. For further discussion of stereotypes, see below and also chapter 4.

16. Philosophers distinguish among various kinds of certainty. For instance, there is absolute or metaphysical certainty, the kind that Descartes sought and believed he had found when he realized he could not doubt his own existence. There is logical certainty, exemplified by the truths of mathematics. Scientific laws such as the principle of inertia exemplify another level of certainty. And there are countless beliefs that we consider certain for all practical purposes: e.g., if you cut a man's head off, he will die.

17. Making inferences about people from the way they speak is normal practice everywhere. In *River Town*, an account of his time spent in China, Peter Hassler, who is not even a native Chinese speaker, remarks in passing, when describing an argument with a local man, "[F]rom his accent I knew he wasn't educated." (Peter Hessler, *River Town: Two Years on the Yangtse* [New York: HarperCollins, 2001], p. 382.) Nor is this practice less possible or less practiced in America than elsewhere. As Paul Fussell notes, when ordinary people are interviewed by sociologists, "they indicate that speech is the main way they estimate a stranger's social class when they first encounter him." (Paul Fussell, *Class* [New York, Touchstone, 1983], p. 153.)

18. In his well-known study, *The Nature of Prejudice*, Gordon Allport distinguishes between "a generalized judgment based on a certain probability that an object of the class will possess a given attribute," and a stereotype, which he defines as "an exaggerated belief associated with a category." (Gordon Allport, *The Nature of Prejudice* [New York: Doubleday, 1958], pp. 185–87.) It seems to me, though, that nowadays the term "stereotype" is commonly used to mean just a composite of presuppositions about a class of people; exaggeration of some qualities may be present but is not necessary.

19. For a good example of this, see E. D. Hirsch, *Cultural Literacy* (New York: Vintage Books, 1988).

20. We might note in passing that a particularly nasty kind of snobbery involves deliberately discomforting someone by *not* explaining something. For instance, I use a Latin expression without translating it. My assumption that you will know what it means may appear gen-

erous; but its ulterior purpose could be to make you feel inadequate and ill-equipped to move in the sort of circles where a knowledge of Latin is presupposed.

21. In one of Monty Python's funniest sketches, a sensitive young man with a refined way of speaking tries to talk to his family about the pleasures of coal mining. His father is outraged, and in a heavy Yorkshire accent describes his life as a playwright and berates his son for turning his back on culture. The scene does not associate ways of speaking with levels of intelligence. But the humor lies entirely in the incongruity between the form and the content of what is being said—an incongruity we recognize because of our own preconceptions.

22. The notion of multiple intelligences was made popular by Howard Gardner in his *Frames of Mind: The Theory of Multiple Intelligences* (New York: Basic Books, 1983).

23. Shakespeare, *Hamlet*, 3.2.11–12. Elsewhere Hamlet, recalling how a play that he and other good judges judged excellent "pleased not the million," describes it as "caviare to the general" (2.2.433). Of course, Shakespeare is here presumably teasing the audience while perhaps venting his own frustrations. His own lower-class characters are often full of life and wit. The gravedigger in act 5 holds his own so well in a bantering session with Hamlet that the latter remarks how his age is one in which "the toe of the peasant comes so near the heel of the courtier he galls his kibe" (5.1.134–36).

24. It is fascinating to consider how, with the advent of modernity, this idea of a link between social height and inner depth has been continuously criticized (e.g., by writers from Chaucer to Richard Russo) and yet remains with us.

25. An interesting theoretical issue is whether we should describe a medieval lord who looked down on the peasantry as a snob. The obvious answer is yes, but things are not so simple. Even if we apply the definition of snobbery arrived at earlier, the answer is not clear. Everything hinges on whether the aristocrat's belief in his superiority is justifiable. But that has to be decided by reference to moral norms that are historically and culturally relative. From our egalitar-

ian perspective, the medieval norms are mistaken, so the aristocrat is a snob. But from a medieval point of view—which the peasants of that period would generally share—medieval norms are correct, in which case aristocratic attitudes are unobjectionable.

Similar problems arise when we consider applying contemporary concepts such as "gay" or "sexist" or "science" to times and places where these terms were not used or carried a sense quite different from the one we give them today. The danger in applying them anachronistically is that we create a misleading impression, as we would, for instance, if we called a citizen of classical Athens who had a fifteen-year-old boyfriend a "child molester."

26. For some classic studies in the decoding of cultural phenomena, see Pierre Bourdieu, *Distinction: A Social Critique of the Judgement of Taste*, trans. Richard Nice (London: Routledge, 1984); Roland Barthes, *Mythologies*, trans. Annette Lavers (London: Paladin, 1972); and Jean Baudrillard, *For a Political Economy of the Sign*, trans. Charles Levin (St. Louis: Telos Press, 1981).

27. Cited in William Osborne, "The Special Characteristics of the Vienna Philharmonic's Racial Ideology," http://www.osborne-conant.org/posts/special.htm.

28. Matthew 7:1.

29. This point is obscured somewhat by our tendency to use the term "offensive" as a catchall for any belief, attitude, or behavior we find objectionable. But although the view that the Jews are Satan's agents is offensive, I do not think many Jews will *feel offended* by someone spouting such nonsense, just as we are not offended by the rantings of a lunatic. The kind of thing that would really *offend* us is if a friend—whose good opinion we value—wrongly suspected us of immoral conduct.

30. The distinction I draw is somewhat along the lines suggested by Joseph Epstein, when he writes, "the elitist desires the best; the snob wants other people to think he has, or is associated with, the best" (Epstein, *Snobbery*, p. 27).

31. For instance, Mick Jagger and Paul McCartney have both been knighted. Billy Joel has received four honorary doctorates. Ella

Fitzgerald was awarded the presidential medal of freedom. Empirical studies by sociologists confirm this trend, showing that today the higher social strata are identified not so much with specific "highbrow" musical preferences as with more eclectic tastes in general. See Philippe Coulangeon, "Social Stratification of Musical Tastes: Questioning the Cultural Legitimacy Model," *Revue française de sociologie* 46, Supplement (2005): 123–54.

32. See Jung Chang, *Wild Swans: Three Daughters of China* (New York: Simon and Schuster, 1991).

33. "[T]he heaviest lottery players—the 20% of players who contribute 82% of lottery revenue—disproportionately are low-income, minority men who have less than a college education." Christopher Solomon, "Why Poor People Win the Lottery," *MSN Money*, http://articles.moneycentral.msn.com/RetirementandWills/RetireEarly/WhyPoorPeopleWinTheLottery.aspx.

Chapter 4. "That's not funny—that's sick!"

1. Quoted by Avner Ziv, *Personality and Sense of Humor* (New York: Springer), p. 4. The idea that laughter originated as a roar of triumph is defended by Albert Rapp, *The Origins of Wit and Humor* (New York: E. P. Dutton, 1951).

2. See V. Ramachandran, "The Neurology and Evolution of Humor, Laughter, and Smiling: The False Alarm Theory," *Medical Hypotheses* 51, no. 4 (October 1998): 351–54.

3. See Robert Provine, *Laughter: A Scientific Investigation* (New York: Viking, 2000), pp. 75–97.

4. See Konrad Lorenz, *On Aggression*, trans. Marjorie Kerr Wilson (New York: Harcourt, Brace and World, 1966), pp. 293–97.

5. For a comprehensive account of the evolution of laughter that includes a review of recent research, see Matthew Gervais and David Sloan Wilson, "The Evolution and Functions of Laughter and Humor: A Synthetic Approach," *Quarterly Review of Biology*. 80, no. 4 (December 2005): 395–430.

6. For a critical review of all three theories, see John Morreall, *Taking Laughter Seriously* (Albany: SUNY Press, 1983). We might note here the distinction between laughter and humor. Laughter is a physiological phenomenon that can have causes that are not in themselves humorous. Humor covers a range of discourse and behavior from making a face to using an inappropriate word. Not all humor produces laughter, even when successful. Although many theorists have tended to focus on jokes, jokes are by no means the primary cause of laughter (see Provine, *Laughter*, pp. 40–43). They are, however, useful objects of study when humor is under discussion since they are self-contained and can be described briefly.

7. For a detailed account of the history of the superiority theory, see Quentin Skinner, "Hobbes and the Classical Theory of Laughter," in *Leviathan after 350 Years*, ed. Tom Sorell and Luc Foisneau (Oxford: Clarendon Press, 2004), pp. 139–66.

8. One of the most interesting criticisms of the superiority theory was advanced by Robert Solomon, who argues that often laughter expresses a sense of inferiority as we recognize ourselves in the mishaps and follies of the clown. See Robert C. Solomon, "Are the Three Stooges Funny? Soitainly! (or When Is It OK to Laugh?" in *Ethics and Values in the Information Age*, ed. Joel Rudinow and Anthony Graybosch (Belmont, CA: Wadsworth, 2002).

9. "[W]omen's humor generally lacks the aggressive and hostile quality of men's humor. The use of humor to compete with or to belittle others, thereby enhancing a person's own status, or to humiliate others either psychologically or physically, seems generally absent among women." Nancy A. Walker and Zita Dresner, "Women's Humor in America," in *What's So Funny? Humor in American Culture*, ed. Nancy A. Walker (Wilmington: Scholarly Resources, 1998), p. 172.

10. See Sigmund Freud, *Jokes and Their Relation to the Unconscious*, trans. James Strachey (New York: Penguin, 1976), pp. 220–30.

11. See Max Eastman, *Enjoyment of Laughter* (New York: Halycon House, 1936).

12. See Henri Bergson, *Laughter: An Essay on the Meaning of the Comic*, trans. Cloudesley Brereton and Fred Rothwell (New York: Macmillan, 1914).

13. Morreall, *Taking Laughter Seriously*, p. 89.

14. Proverbs 17:22.

15. See David Biello, "Laughter Proves Good Medicine for the Heart," *Scientific American*, January 18, 2006. For a critique of some of the research that supposedly demonstrates the therapeutic benefits of humor, see Provine, *Laughter*, pp. 189–207.

16. Bergson, *Laughter*, p. 6. Both Ted Cohen and Simon Critchley also stress the socializing and the community-strengthening benefits of humor. See Ted Cohen, *Jokes: Philosophical Thoughts on Joking Matters* (Chicago: University of Chicago Press, 2001), and Simon Critchley, *On Humour* (London: Routledge, 2002).

17. See Ronald de Sousa, *The Rationality of Emotion* (Cambridge, MA: MIT Press, 1987). "As an avenue to knowledge, laughter . . . has the advantage of always seeking fresh perspectives. One can be frozen in pomposity; but only angels can be frozen in laughter" (p. 297).

18. George Orwell, "Funny, but Not Vulgar," in *The Collected Letters, Essays, and Journalism of George Orwell*, ed. Sonia Orwell and Ian Angus (London: Secker & Warburg, 1968), p. 284.

19. Louis D. Rubin Jr., "The Great American Joke," in *What's So Funny? Humor in American Culture*, ed. Nancy A. Walker (Wilmington: Scholarly Resources, 1998), p. 115.

20. See Critchley, *On Humour*, pp. 55–56.

21. See Peter Berger, *Redeeming Laughter* (New York: Walter de Gruyter, 1997), chap. 3.

22. See Critchley, *On Humour*, pp. 27–28.

23. Jokes about Chelsea Clinton did appear, but those who related them—like John McCain on one occasion—attracted moral criticism.

24. It should be noted that I am using the terms "ideology" and "ideological" in a nonpejorative way. "Ideology" here simply means a body of beliefs—factual, theoretical, and normative—that is gener-

ally shared by a specific group of people such as a religious order, a political party, a class, or an entire society.

25. Obviously, there is still plenty of discrimination and prejudice in modernized societies. My point here is that hardly any contemporary politicians, jurists, or political theorists in these societies support discrimination or denial of basic rights on the grounds of race or sex. In many countries, gays are still denied certain important rights, most obviously the right to marry the person they choose. But progress is occurring here as the political establishment is finding it increasingly difficult to justify antiegalitarian policies.

26. See Merrie Bergmann, "How Many Feminists Does It Take to Make a Joke? Sexist Humor and What's Wrong with It," *Hypatia* 1, no. 1 (Spring 1986): 76.

27. This point is made by Mac E. Barrick. "The Helen Keller joke has fulfilled an important social function. Like a classical drama it has the cathartic effect of erasing the pity normally felt toward the disabled, so the joke-teller and his listener now accept these on equal terms." Mac E. Barrick, "The Helen Keller Joke Cycle," *Journal of American Folklore* 93, no. 370 (October–December 1980): 449.

28. Kathryn M. Ryan and Jeanne Kanjorski, "The Enjoyment of Sexist Humor, Rape Attitudes, and Relationship Aggression in College Students," *Sex Roles: A Journal of Research* 38, nos. 9–10 (May 1998): 743–56.

29. Of course, it is quite common for people to couch aesthetic criticism in moral terms, as in: "Look at those pink polyester pants! There ought to be a law!" But such comments are jokes, the joke residing in the disproportion between the offense (poor aesthetic taste) and its classification as a sin or a crime deserving of appropriate punishment.

30. A possible objection to the view stated here is that it rests on a preference for a certain sort of humor, the kind associated with men rather than with women (see Walker and Dresner, "Women's Humor in America"). But I am inclined to think that this distinction was more apparent in the past than it is today.

31. For a sample of humor expressing extreme racial hatred, see Elliott Oring, *Engaging Humor* (Urbana: University of Illinois Press,

2003), chap. 4, "The Humor of Hate." After examining a series of racist cartoons in *WAR*, a publication of the White Aryan Resistance, Oring observes: "To laugh at the cartoons is to imagine—rightly or wrongly—other laughers like oneself. Since the readers of *WAR* constitute no organized group—indeed the leadership seems largely composed of marginal, lonely, and isolated individuals—it is likely that such a sense of community is desperately needed" (pp. 56–57).

32. For a nuanced discussion of the relation between racist stereotypes and racist humor, see Michael Philips, "Racist Acts and Racist Humor," *Canadian Journal of Philosophy* 14, no. 1 (March 1984). Reprinted in *Ethics for Everyday*, ed. David Benatar (New York: McGraw-Hill, 2002), pp. 3–20.

33. See Cohen, *Jokes*, p. 3. Laurence Goldstein also calls attention to the odd way that employing a stereotype can make a joke funnier. "To describe someone's face as looking like a bag of nails is funny, but it's funnier when the person so described is one's mother-in-law." Laurence Goldstein, "Humor and Harm," *Sorites* 3 (November 1995): 27–42.

34. Ted Cohen remarks that to understand a Polish joke one does not have to believe that Poles are stupid; rather, one has to understand what a Polish joke is (see Cohen, *Jokes*, p. 21). In other words, one must recognize the genre.

35. Citied by Joseph Boskin and Joseph Dorinson, "Ethnic Humor: Subversion and Survival," in *What's So Funny? Humor in American Culture*, ed. Nancy A. Walker (Wilmington: Scholarly Resources, 1998), p. 219.

36. Alan Dundes sympathizes with those who find Polish jokes demeaning (see Alan Dundes, "Polish Pope Jokes," *Journal of American Folklore* 92, no. 364 [April–June 1979]: 219–22), although he notes that "ethnic humor is more of a symptom than a cause of ethnic stereotyping and ethnic prejudice."

37. Lydia Fish, "Is the Pope Polish? Notes on the Polack Joke in Transition," *Journal of American Folklore.* 93, no. 370 (October–December 1980): 452.

38. Oring, *Engaging Humor*, p. 65.

39. Ibid., p. 66.

40. As Merrie Bergmann points out in a discussion of sexist humor, a prejudiced belief can be incorporated into a joke without its making the joke objectionable. Bergmann cites the example of a cartoon in which a woman is shown engaged in the following series of reflections. "If all women secretly want to be raped, you're not a real woman if you don't want to be raped. But since you always get what you really want, if I haven't been raped, maybe I secretly don't want to be a woman. [The woman sits up.] I've got to find a shrink to help me get raped." (The cartoon is by Ellen Levine in *Pulling Our Own Strings*, ed. Gloria Kaufman and Kay Blakely [Bloomington: Indiana University Press, 1982], p. 105.) As Bergmann observes, the sexist belief that women secretly want to be raped plays a role in the joke but is not assumed by the humorist; indeed, the moral of the joke is that this belief is ridiculous. See Bergmann, "How Many Feminists?" p. 74.

41. See David Benatar, "Prejudice in Jest: When Racial and Gender Humor Harms," *Public Affairs Quarterly*. 13, no. 2 (April 1999). Reprinted in *Ethics for Everyday*, ed. David Benatar (New York: McGraw-Hill, 2002), pp. 40–51.

42. Goldstein, "Humor and Harm," p. 31.

43. See Friedrich Nietzsche, *On the Genealogy of Morals*, 2.16, in *Basic Writings of Nietzsche*, trans. and ed. Walter Kaufmann (New York: Modern Library, 1968), pp. 520–21.

44. Freud, *Jokes and Their Relation to the Unconscious*, p. 147.

45. See Alan Dundes's *Cracking Jokes: Studies of Sick Humor Cycles and Stereotypes* (Berkeley: Ten Speed Press, 1987).

46. David Hume, *An Enquiry Concerning the Principles of Morals* (Indianapolis: Hackett, 1983), p. 74.

47. "Though not an action, amusement is often under our control, and we can justifiably be held responsible for what we can control." Morreall, *Taking Laughter Seriously*, p. 111.

48. Berger, *Redeeming Laughter*, p. 78.

49. Greiner's observation is cited by Berger, *Redeeming Laughter*, p. 80.

Chapter 5. Why Should I Respect Your Stupid Opinion?

1. Thomas Jefferson, Letter to John Adams, April 11, 1823, *The Adams-Jefferson Letters*, vol.2 (Chapel Hill: University of North Carolina Press, 1959), p. 595. It should be noted that in this same letter Jefferson argues in defense of the idea that the world is the product of intelligent design.

2. Thomas Jefferson, Letter to Alexander Smyth, January 17, 1825, *The Writings of Thomas Jefferson*, vol. 16 (Washington, DC: Thomas Jefferson Memorial Association,1905), pp. 100–101.

3. John Adams, Letter to John Taylor, *The Works of John Adams*, vol. 6 (Boston: Little and Brown, 1851), p. 479.

4. Voltaire, letter to Frederick the Great, quoted in the *Encyclopedia of Unbelief* (Buffalo: Prometheus Books, 1985), p. 715.

5. Sigmund Freud, *The Future of an Illusion*, trans. and ed. James Strachey (New York: Norton, 1961), p. 68.

6. Bertrand Russell, "Has Religion Made Useful Contributions to Civilization?" in *Russell on Religion: Selections from the Writings of Bertrand Russell* (London: Routledge, 1999), p. 169.

7. Arthur C. Clarke, "Presidents, Experts, and Asteroids," *Science* 280, no. 5369 (June 5, 1988): 1532–33.

8. Richard Dawkins, "Has the World Changed?" *Guardian,* October 11, 2001.

9. The distinction drawn here roughly corresponds to the distinction Stephen Darwall draws between "recognition respect" and "appraisal respect." See Stephen Darwall, "Two Kinds of Respect," *Ethics.* 88, no. 1 (October 1977): 36–49.

10. See Immanuel Kant, *Foundations of the Metaphysics of Morals*, trans. Lewis White Beck, 2nd ed. (New York: Macmillan, 1990).

11. As a social contract theorist, Kant views the criminal as having already implicitly acquiesced in a system of laws that apply to all. The bank robber's arrest and punishment is thus, at a deeper level, in accordance with his rational will.

12. This point was well illustrated during the controversy over the way the U.S. military and intelligence services under George W. Bush

treated prisoners it designated "enemy combatants." The Bush administration did not like to admit it condoned practices like waterboarding; but even after it became public knowledge that such interrogation techniques had been used, the administration still denied that they constituted "torture."

13. For instance, in 1993 a tenured physics teacher in a Bronx high school, with an unblemished record of over thirty years' teaching, was fired on account of views he had expressed in the North American Man/Boy Love Association Bulletin. The dismissal was upheld by the federal appeals court. In 2005 the National Organization for Woman called for the resignation of Larry Summers, then president of Harvard University, after he gave a talk in which he hypothesized that one reason for the underrepresentation of women in science and engineering at top research institutions might be a difference in "intrinsic aptitude" between men and women.

14. I am indebted to Ben Howard for this observation.

15. This criticism of the principle that people are entitled to have their beliefs respected is made by Peter Jones. (See Peter Jones, "Respecting Beliefs and Rebuking Rushdie," *British Journal of Political Science* 20, no. 4 [October 1990]: 415–37.) Jones distinguishes between a "strong" principle of respect for beliefs, which protects beliefs from substantive criticism, and a "weak" principle, which protects them from disparaging attacks that depart from the "decencies of controversy." He suggests, and rejects, the analogy between beliefs and property when critiquing the strong principle. In my view, though, his criticism applies equally well to both strong and weak versions.

16. Of course, this is not always true. Fans may forgive their idol his unsavory failings—his arrogance, his abusive behavior, his stupid extravagance—for the sake of what he can do as an athlete, actor, or musician. And we can all occasionally become so immersed in some pursuit that we start to prioritize these more specific abilities.

17. Kenneth Wilkinson, *Chinese Language, Life, and Culture* (Chicago: McGraw-Hill, 2002), p. 212.

18. See Karl Popper, *Objective Knowledge: An Evolutionary Approach* (Oxford: Clarendon Press, 1972).

19. See Willard Van Orman Quine and J. S. Ullion, *The Web of Belief* (New York: Random House, 1978).

20. This is one of the points to emerge from Thomas Kuhn's studies in the history of science. See Thomas S. Kuhn, *The Structure of Scientific Revolutions*, 2nd ed. (Chicago: University of Chicago Press, 1970).

21. See Richard Rorty, *Objectivity, Relativism, and Truth, Philosophical Papers*, vol. 1 (Cambridge: Cambridge University Press, 1991).

22. Credo of the Biblical Astronomer, http://www.geocentricity.com/ bibastron/credo.html.

23. The view of truth assumed here is essentially similar to that defended by various contemporary philosophers including Thomas Kuhn, Peter Winch, Richard Rorty, and Michel Foucault.

24. In E. E. Evans-Pritchard's famous study of the Azande, one of the things he clearly found puzzling about the Azande way of thinking was their lack of interest in the theoretical contradictions implied by some of their basic assumptions. See E. E. Evans-Pritchard, *Witchcraft, Oracles, and Magic among the Azande*, abridged with an introduction by Eva Gillies (Oxford: Clarendon Press, 1976).

25. Hilary Putnam, "Why Reason Can't Be Naturalized," in *Realism and Reason, Philosophical Papers*, vol. 3 (Cambridge: Cambridge University Press, 1983), p. 234.

26. See *From Max Weber: Essays in Sociology*, trans. Hans H. Gerth and C. Wright Mills (New York: Oxford University Press, 1958). Weber took the idea from Friedrich Schiller, who talks about the "de-divinization" of the world in his *On the Aesthetic Education of Man*. Nietzsche's proclamation of the death of God is obviously prompted in part by the same insight.

27. According to Netflix, the top-grossing movies of 2009 were *Avatar*; *Transformers: Revenge of the Fallen*; *Harry Potter and the Half-Blood Prince*; *The Twilight Saga: New Moon*; *Up*; *The Hangover*; *Star Trek*; *The Blind Side*; *Alvin and the Chipmunks: The Squeakquel*; and *Monsters vs. Aliens*. Of these, only two, *The Hangover* and *The Blind Side*, are realistic representations of the contemporary world. All the others take us into realms (the supernatural, the distant future, cartoonland) where what is impossible in our world can occur.

28. See, for instance, Karen Armstrong, *The Case for God* (New York: Knopf, 2009).

29. This point is made forcefully by Peter Jones, who argues that to defend religion by deflecting attention away from questions about the truth of beliefs "is to treat the continuance of those beliefs as of greater moment than their truth. It is to hold that it matter less that people should live lives grounded in falsehoods than that their existing beliefs, and the way of life grounded in them, should be undisturbed. . . . [T]hose who seek to 'protect' beliefs so that they become, in effect, exhibits frozen in a social museum run the risk of reducing them to mere objects of curiosity" (Jones, "Respecting Beliefs and Rebuking Rushdie," p. 429).

30. See Friedrich Nietzsche, *The Gay Science*, trans. Walter Kaufmann (New York: Vintage Books, 1974), p. 76.

31. For a well-documented defense of this point of view, see Gregg Easterbrook, *The Progress Paradox: How Life Gets Better While People Feel Worse* (New York: Random House, 2003).

32. This is a salient theme in the work of the Frankfurt School. See, for instance, Jürgen Habermas, *Toward a Rational Society*, trans. Jeremy Shapiro (Boston: Beacon Press, 1970). The position I defend here regarding the nature and desirability of a more rational society owes much to Habermas's writings.

33. See Bobby Henderson, *The Gospel of the Flying Spaghetti Monster* (New York: Villard Books, 2006); Sam Harris, *The End of Faith: Religion, Terror, and the Future of Reason* (New York: Norton, 2005); Richard Dawkins, *The God Delusion* (Boston: Houghton Mifflin, 2008); Christopher Hitchens, *God Is Not Great* (New York: Twelve Books, 2007).

34. See, for instance, the *Pew Forum on Religion & Public Life*: "The relationship between religion and politics is particularly strong with respect to political ideology and views on social issues such as abortion and homosexuality, with the more religiously committed adherents across several religious traditions expressing more conservative political views" (http://pewresearch.org/pubs/876/religion-america-part-two).

Index

Index

Index